THE CLOGHER VALLEY RAILWAY

UNIFORM WITH THIS BOOK

Graham S. Hudson	*The Aberford Railway and the History of the Garforth Colleries*
John Thomas	*The Callander & Oban Railway*
Rex Christiansen and R. W. Miller	*The Cambrian Railways Volume 1: 1852-1888, Volume 2: 1889-1968*
N. S. C. Macmillan	*The Campbeltown & Machrihanish Light Railway*
Patrick J. Flanagan	*The Cavan & Leitrim Railway*
Edward M. Patterson	*The Clogher Valley Railway*
H. A. Vallance	*The Great North of Scotland Railway*
H. A. Vallance	*The Highland Railway*
Edward M. Patterson	*A History of the Narrow-gauge Railways of North East Ireland*
	Part One: The Ballycastle Railway
	Part Two: The Ballymena Lines
Edward M. Patterson	*A History of the Narrow-gauge Railways of North West Ireland*
	Part One: The County Donegal Railways (second edition)
	Part Two: The Londonderry & Lough Swilly Railway
H. W. Paar	*A History of the Railways of the Forest of Dean*
	Part One: The Severn & Wye Railway
	Part Two: The Great Western Railway in Dean
John Marshall	*The Lancashire & Yorkshire Railway Volumes 1, 2 & 3*
David L. Smith	*The Little Railways of South West Scotland*
R. A. Williams	*The London & South Western Railway Volume 1*
G. A. Brown J. D. C. A. Prideaux and H. G. Radcliffe	*The Lynton & Barnstaple Railway*
Colin G. Maggs	*The Midland & South Western Junction Railway*
John Thomas	*The North British Railway Volume 1*
Rex Christiansen and R. W. Miller	*The North Staffordshire Railway*
G. Whittle	*The Railways of Consett and North West Durham*
W. J. K. Davies	*The Ravenglass & Eskdale Railway*
A. D. Farr	*The Royal Deeside Line*
Robin Atthill and O. S. Nock	*The Somerset & Dorset Railway*
Ralph Cartwright and R. T. Russell	*The Welshpool & Llanfair Light Railway*
John Thomas	*The West Highland Railway*

Engines No 2 and No 3 hauling the Fair-Day special through Fivemiletown
(*from a painting by Victor Welch*)

THE CLOGHER VALLEY RAILWAY

by
EDWARD M. PATTERSON
DSc, MRIA, FRSE

DAVID & CHARLES : NEWTON ABBOT

ISBN 0 7153 5604 6

Set in eleven point Pilgrim
and printed in Great Britain
by Bristol Typesetting Company Limited
for David and Charles (Publishers) Limited
South Devon House Newton Abbot Devon

Contents

List of Illustrations

PLATES

IN THE TEXT

CHAPTER I

The Regional Setting

THE VALLEY

The village of Clogher stands a short way within the margin of County Tyrone, where that county plunges its southern boundary between Fermanagh and Monaghan. It is in the heart of the country, fifty-five miles from the western seaboard of Ireland at Sligo, and about the same distance from the east coast at the city of Belfast. To the north of Clogher the outpost hills of the Sperrin Mountains reach towards the waters of Lough Erne, while to the south brown moorlands rise towards Slieve Beagh.

Though built on a hill, the village of Clogher is set in a valley, not a narrow defile but a broad open feature that in Scotland would be called a strath. Here the upper reaches of the River Blackwater gather a myriad of small streams, and grow to form the main river of the region. From Clogher that river flows north-east towards the village of Augher, then lazily turns south-east and meanders for a dozen miles with Tyrone on the left bank and Monaghan on the right. On the way towards Lough Neagh it passes in turn the small towns of Aughnacloy, Caledon, and Tynan. The valley courses through a warm country of small rounded hills, farms, and wooded estate lands, where the regimentation of the factory floor is scarcely known.

Seven miles to the west of Clogher is Fivemiletown and, just beyond its houses, the broad valley brings the traveller into County Fermanagh. The streams now course to the west, to join the Colebrooke River which in its turn feeds Upper Lough Erne. The villages of Colebrooke and Brookeborough are there, names reminding us of the Brooke family that settled there in Cromwell's time. The scenery changes subtly; the village of Maguiresbridge has other family connections, and lies among whale-backed clay hills or drumlins, a veritable swarm of which undulate towards water level and build the numberless islands and the complex shorelines of the Upper Lough.

Geologically the Clogher Valley reminds us of the Midland Valley of Scotland, older rocks forming the hilly country to north and south and the tiny coalfield of Dungannon a miniature of the Ayrshire field.

CLOGHER

The name is Irish and means *the stony place*. It is a common name, and is owned by no less than sixty townlands throughout Ireland, and forms a part of many others. Thus Aughnacloy was *Achadh-na-cloiche*, the field of the stones. Though our Tyrone Clogher thus bears a familiar name, the village has the distinction of great ecclesiastical celebrity, and it still possesses a cathedral, albeit a tiny one.

Pre-Christian colonists must have been numerous in south Tyrone, and evidence of their former presence in the form of stone and bronze artifacts has been turned up in many a field and sandpit. The elevated gravel mounds and tablelands provided these early settlers with living sites that were more congenial than the thickly forested valley bottoms. Megalithic sites are numerous.

The monastic see of Clogher dates from the end of the fifth century, and its diocesan see from 1128. J. J. Marshall in various writings, and W. R. Hutchinson in *Tyrone Precinct* give a picturesque story of the area, dominated until the end of the fifteenth century by the powerful family of O'Neill. English antipathy to the Celtic way of life caused the flight of the Earls of Tyrone and Tirconnell in September 1607. The event afforded to the English Government and its greedy officials in Ireland, a welcome chance to confiscate Irish property. Six counties were declared forfeited to the English Crown, and a scheme of Plantation was formulated between 1608 and 1620. The 'escheated' lands were largely given to selected English and Scottish settlers, who undertook to build fortified houses which were to be places of refuge in times of trouble from the dispossessed Irish.

Under the new regime, Tyrone was to include five 'precincts', one of which was called Clogher, with an area of 12,500 acres. Five corporate towns were planned in the county, one of them Clogher, the others at Dungannon, Omagh, Loughinshollin, and Mountjoy. Clogher became a borough in 1629 and was probably unique in that the Corporation consisted of the Dean and Chapter of the Cathedral. Its members of parliament were named by the bishops. The borough was disfranchised by the Irish Act of Union in 1800, and £15,000 granted by way of compensation. Thereafter Clogher's importance lessened.

THE DISTRICT ROUND ABOUT

Brookeborough, over in Fermanagh, used to be known as Aghalun, and is mentioned thus in a patent from Queen Anne for the holding of fairs. *Achadh lon* means the field of the blackbirds, and tradition held that Lady Maguire, the wife of Lord Enniskillen who was executed in 1604, was fond of these birds. The village probably originated from the huts that were built around the Maguire's castle. The Brooke family took over these lands after the Cromwellian plantation.

In December 1610 an estate of 2,000 acres was granted to one Sir Thomas Ridgeway in a district named Largie, where the village of Aughnacloy came to be built. In 1641 rebellion broke out, the English plantations were destroyed, and during the ensuing state of anarchy the manor of Largie fell into the hands of William Moore, by rather devious and doubtful means. His grandson Acheson Moore was to be one of the characters of Aughnacloy, in the course of a far-travelled and chequered career becoming attached to the Jacobite cause. Acheson Moore's demesne was at Ravella, just west of the village, and he laid out his boggy acres there in ditches based on the shape of a Scottish thistle, complete with leaves. The bulb of the flower was a ditch a mile in circumference, with clumps of trees for down. The 'Castle' of Acheson Moore is long gone and ploughed over, but his fanciful ditches remain as a monument to his eccentricity.

Lewis's *Topographical Dictionary* tells us of the district in the years preceding the Great Famine, and in 1837 the population of Clogher was 523. In the same publication Augher is credited with 726 persons and Aughnacloy with 1,742 folk living in '365 houses the greater number are thatched'. Though Ballygawley town has 972 persons it had the distinction of being one of the industrial centres of the district, with 'an extensive brewery and a large distillery of malt whiskey'. While in Lewis's day the populations of Tynan (243), Caledon (1079), Fivemiletown (758), Brookeborough (480), and Maguiresbridge (848) placed them all in the category of villages, they nevertheless were active community centres in a well farmed district, and fairs or markets were held in them at regular intervals. Caledon, beside the wall of the Earl of Caledon's great deer park, owed its employment to a large flour mill. Tynan, though a small place, had its history centred around the church, the signs of its former glory seen in four stone High Crosses ornately carved.

In 1838 James Fraser in his *Guide through Ireland* credited Ballygawley with linen weaving and with 'what is unusual in this part of the country, a considerable quantity of gloves are manufactured which are in good demand'. In Aughnacloy, the largest of the places that the Clogher Valley Railway was to serve half a century later, he found 'one long street with several lanes branching off it . . . the town contains a Church, RC Chapel, Presbyterian and Methodist Meeting Houses'.

Today, all the villages have shrunk in size and in importance, and have only a half to two-thirds of their population of the mid-nineteenth century. The shrinkage was not a precipitate process, and it was not apparently checked or affected by the coming of the railway. The more likely cause is the enormous growth of Belfast during the nineteenth century, a centripetal influence that still exists. The division of the country fifty years ago into Northern Ireland and the Free State, with the border and the River Blackwater coincident for many miles, had a further adverse effect on the industry and trade of the district. Of Ballygawley's large distillery there is now neither sight nor smell, and in Caledon, the great six-storeyed mill lies ruinous, its walls and its great beam engine alike soon to be demolished to make way for a trunk road.

THE RAILWAY FRAMEWORK

The Clogher Valley Tramway—it started as a tramway but later was renamed a railway—linked two main lines that belonged to the Great Northern Railway, disappearing into the country from Tynan & Caledon station on the Belfast—Clones line at the one end, and at the other reappearing at Maguiresbridge on the Clones—Enniskillen road. The tramway was in fact surrounded by a roughly rectangular frame of Great Northern, and to see the Clogher Valley Tramway in its historical perspective, we must look first at the formation of the adjacent parts of the Great Northern's system.

The early 1860s witnessed the completion of that rectangle of railways, at the corners of which stood the towns of Portadown, Clones, Enniskillen and Omagh. The circuit of the rectangle measured 129 miles.

The first company to build into the rectangle was the Londonderry & Enniskillen. Born of London finance interests, it had been opened in uneasy stages between Londonderry city, Omagh, and Enniskillen in the years 1847 to 1854. Though the company was enterprising, it was never prosperous, and its finances were tottering when the London board decided to lease the line to the Dundalk & Enniskillen Railway. This took effect from New Year's Day 1860. In July 1862, the D & ER, realising that it was working from the east to the north coast of Ireland, rechristened itself the Irish North Western Railway.

On the opposite side of the rectangle was the Ulster Railway which had reached Portadown from Belfast in 1842 on the broad gauge of 6ft 2in. Five years and a Royal Commission later, the Ulster regauged to 5ft 3in, by which time it was already building the rectangle towards the cathedral city of Armagh. Its trains reached Armagh on 1 March 1848. For a time, the Ulster consolidated its position and then on 15 June 1855 obtained an Act to extend from Armagh to Monaghan. William Dargan built that section, 16½ miles in length, for £100,000, and it was opened for traffic on 25 May 1858. Clones was still twelve miles away from the Ulster's railhead, but was entered by the Ulster Railway trains in March 1863.

Clones, a bustling little market and manufacturing town, had already attracted railway construction. The Dundalk & Enniskillen Railway, of which we have already heard, had opened its line piecemeal from the east coast port of Dundalk as far as Clones over the years 1849 to 1858. It then thrust on towards Enniskillen, justifying its title, and on the way passing the village of Maguiresbridge.

On the north, along the fourth side of the rectangle, the Portadown & Dungannon Railway had linked those two towns in April 1858, and had arranged that the Ulster company should work the line. The P & DR widened its interests, became the Portadown, Dungannon & Omagh Junction Railway and was into Omagh by September 1861. The Ulster worked the entire stretch from Dungannon, and logically the two concerns amalgamated in 1876, the PD & OJR disappearing in the process.

By 1863 then, with the rectangle complete, the Ulster and the Irish North ran their trains around it. Within the rectangle enclosing 1,250 square miles of Irish countryside, there were no large towns, no villages even with populations above 2,000, and a considerable area of hilly ground more than 600 feet above sea level. Yet there were many small and comparatively prosperous farms, a number of villages, and several large estates whose owners were prepared to invest some capital in a railway which would be likely to benefit their property. There was a multiplicity of country markets and fairs which could be expected to contribute livestock traffic. There was a complete absence of mineral exploitation, and by cross-channel standards it was scarcely encouraging country for railway operation. Although by the start of the 1880s, no railways had penetrated it, there had been a large number of abortive schemes over the 35 years that had passed since the Railway Mania. Their story deserves a chapter to itself.

CHAPTER 2

The Non-Starters

1845 : THE EARLY BIRDS

The earliest schemes for rail transport through the Clogher Valley date from the year of the Railway Mania. There were two of them, both active during 1845. It was during this year that, according to Mr G. R. Mahon, no fewer than 121 schemes were proposed for Ireland, either by new companies or as extensions to the lines of existing companies.

The first was associated with Sir John Macneill, knighted in 1844 for his part in engineering the Dublin & Drogheda Railway. His activity in the Clogher district was in connection with a proposed Great North Junction Railway. It was to run from Gortmore townland, near Omagh, to Tully townland near Monaghan, at its north end springing from the then proposed Londonderry & Enniskillen Railway, and at its southern end joining with the proposed Irish North Midland Railway and the Newry & Enniskillen Railway. On its way, it was planned to pass via Clogher, Aughnacloy, and Emyvale. A formal map for submission to Parliament was prepared over Macneill's signature—a copy is in the Public Record Office in Belfast—but the scheme was not followed up and the plans and other necessary documents were never deposited at Westminster. Its notice in the *Dublin Gazette* of November 1845 was signed by Messrs Sutton, Ewens, Ommanney, and Prudence, parliamentary agents, and by Messrs J. O. Woodhouse and by Andrew and Courtenay Newton, solicitors. In the same issue of the *Gazette*, it was immediately preceded

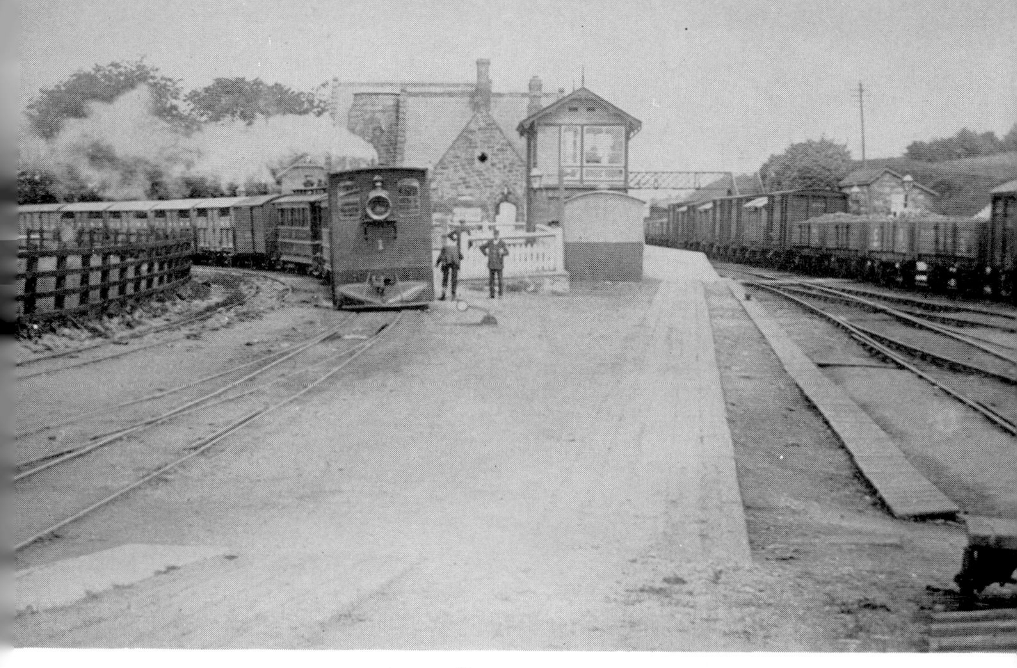

Page 17

TYNAN TO CALEDON

(Above) *Tynan about 1910.* Caledon *and train arriving at the CV platform. A Great Northern train is standing at the up platform*; (below) *Caledon.* Blackwater *brings her train slowly along the street, on the way to Tynan*

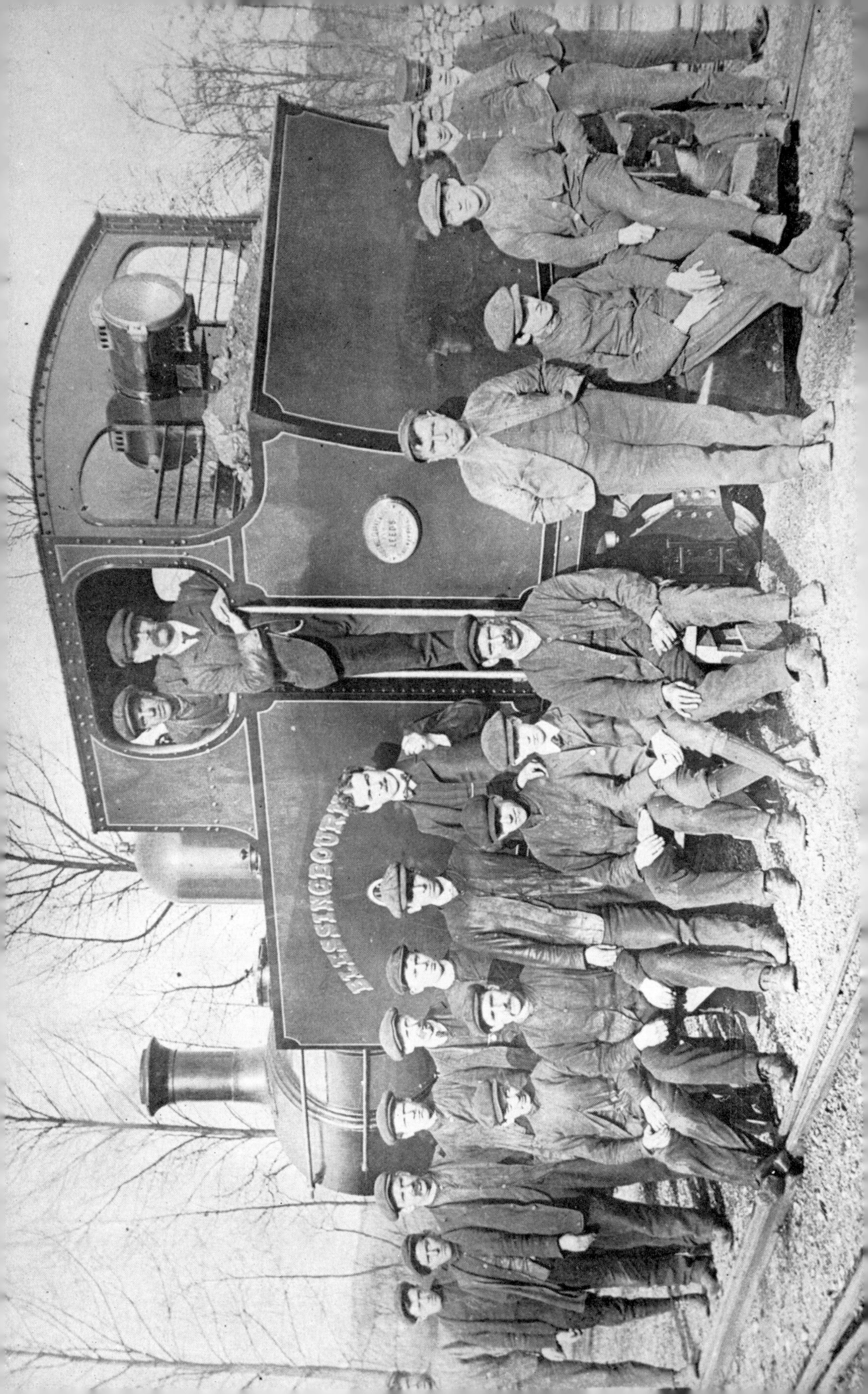

by the notice of an alternative scheme, the Omagh, Dungannon, Armagh & Belfast Junction Railway; this had the same authors, but differed in linking the L & ER at Omagh with the Ulster Railway at Portadown, and in not passing through the Clogher Valley country.

Sir John Rennie was consulting engineer to the second scheme, that of the Newry, Armagh & Londonderry Junction Railway. This was of English origin and was to link Omagh with Armagh, towards which the Ulster were driving from Portadown. On its way south from Fintona, it would have gone near Clogher and Augher, thence close to the Blackwater River and the Tyrone/Monaghan boundary. Aughnacloy was to be passed along its western and northern sides, after which the line was to strike across country past Crilly and Caledon on its way towards Armagh. The notice in the *Dublin Gazette* was signed by Messrs Frazer and Todd and by John Cumming, solicitors. The proposed capital was £400,000, with borrowings of £94,732. A petition was presented to Parliament on 6 February 1846, presumably to allow the bill to be introduced late. The bill was given a first reading in the House of Lords on 16 February, on 10 March it was given the second reading and was committed. It was reported with amendments on 3 April, but on 7 May 1846 it was withdrawn with leave of the House, and there were no further proceedings on it.

1853: THE FINTONA AND ARMAGH RAILWAY

This scheme emerged during 1853. By then, the Londonderry & Enniskillen Railway had been built from its northern terminus as far south as the village of Fintona, and was in the

---

AUGHNACLOY WORKSHOP STAFF IN 1912

On footplate: *Joe Irwin, fireman, W. J. Thompson, driver.* Standing: *John Cuddy, Michael McFadden, Robby Boyle, James Friel, Archy Given, Dick Bennett, Joe Patton, Edward O'Donnell, John Conn (stationmaster), Teddy Camp, Willie Armstrong, Ferris Martin, Charles Meenan, Thomas Owens.* Seated: *Patrick McFadden, William Rea, John Owens, Totty Armstrong, Mick Cullinan* process of getting up steam and capital to complete its course to Enniskillen. The *Dublin Gazette* of November 1853 contained a formal notice stating that the line was to run from Armagh to Fintona by way of Tynan, Aughnacloy, and Clogher. Armagh was then the terminus of the Ulster Railway, and the latter's future course to Tynan would have been taken, then the Clogher Valley's line to Aughnacloy. Thereafter the Blackwater valley would have determined the course to Clogher. There was also to be a branch from Tynan to Monaghan, a section that would have encountered no engineering difficulties for the Ulster Canal had been laid through the low ground there since 1835. The canal was incapable of offering competition. The Ulster Railway was however, proposing to extend to Monaghan and Clones, and the F & A promoters would, in the event of the UR proceeding, only make their line from Tynan to Fintona. No application for parliamentary authority is to be found at Westminster, and withdrawal was probably conditioned by the Portadown & Dungannon company's extension to Omagh.

1861: A DUNGANNON—AUGHNACLOY BRANCH

By this year the P & D had completed their line to Omagh, and had for four years past been restyled the PD & OJR. They were securely placed, and with traffic feeding from both ends, they could afford to look about them. They obtained an Act on 12 June 1861 to make a branch from Dungannon to Aughnacloy. It would have had a length of twelve miles, and have cost £75,000. G. W. Hemans was the engineer to the project. It was planned to run north west from Dungannon to the village of Castlecaulfield. It would then pass between Clonaneese Presbyterian Church and Killeshill Parish Church, where there was to be a station, skirt the village of Carnteel and reach Aughnacloy from the north. The scheme was partly underwritten by the London finance house of Overend, Gurney & Co. and their failure in 1866 resulted in its abandonment.

1872: A NARROW–GAUGE SCHEME, AND A CLOGHER CROSSROADS

Hugh de Fellenberg Montgomery, of Blessingbourne, Fivemiletown, later to be the second chairman of the Clogher Valley, was in 1872, one of the promoters of the Armagh, Tyrone & Fermanagh Railway. James Barton surveyed its proposed course, which would have corresponded closely with that of the Clogher Valley Tramway. In its conception it was contemporaneous with the Ballymena, Cushendall & Red Bay Railway, and like it, the gauge would have been the narrow one of 3ft 0in. There is reference to the Armagh, Tyrone & Fermanagh Railway in the minutes of evidence to the 1922 Railway Commission in Northern Ireland, when H. S. Sloan, then the manager of the Clogher Valley Railway, stated that it was to have run from Armagh to Maguiresbridge.* It seems possible that Sloan was in error in naming Armagh city as the starting point, for that place was adequately served in 1872 by the Ulster Railway. It seems more likely that Tynan would have been the eastern terminus. Owing to lack of financial support the scheme never got further than the discussion stage.

Also active during 1872 was a revival of the old Fintona—Armagh line, together with a Sligo—Cookstown scheme, the latter a grandiose precursor of the Sligo, Leitrim & Northern Counties Railway. The two railways would have crossed in the neighbourhood of Clogher.

1883: RIVAL TRAMWAY SCHEMES

Triggered off by the impending Tramways Act, a committee was formed during the early part of 1883 to build roadside tramways in Counties Tyrone and Fermanagh. The chairman was J. Ellison Macartney, MP, DL, JP of Clogher Park, Thomas S. Porter was the secretary. James Barton and John Lanyon

* Maguiresbridge was invariably written as one word in CVR documents, but as two words in the 1901 Census Index. Ordnance Survey maps used both forms.

were engaged as consulting engineers and at a public meeting held in Omagh on 22 September 1883 they reported on the feasibility of constructing a roadside tramway from Maguiresbridge by way of Fivemiletown, Clogher, and Ballygawley, and from there either to Dungannon or to Tynan. The report and subsequent discussion fragmented the committee into two opposing factions: the chairman favouring the route to Tynan, and the opposition under the leadership of Hunt W. Chambre of Dungannon, favouring a line through that town and terminating in the village of Moy. Barton and Lanyon aligned themselves respectively with the Tynan and the Dungannon parties.

During October 1883 the Dungannon—Moy faction broke away, and formed a separate undertaking under the name of the Tyrone Steam Tramways Company Ltd. It proposed to build a line starting 'at a point in line with front of Mr James Sloane's house on Moy Hill in the village of Moy'. From there it was to follow the public road to the south-west side of the town of Dungannon. It then left the roadside for a distance of a mile to avoid a long curve around a hill. The road was rejoined beside Eskragh Lough, whence a secondary road was followed to Castlecaulfield. The main Dungannon—Ballygawley road was rejoined at Parkanaur demesne, Ballygawley reached, and the mail coach road followed to Aughnacloy. For statutory purposes the Moy—Dungannon, Dungannon—Ballygawley, and Ballygawley—Aughnacloy sections were termed Tramways 1, 2, and 3, and had a combined length of 22 miles. In addition plans were made for six short branches The first of these, termed Tramway No 1A, was an extension from the Moy terminus to Lord Charlemont's Harbour on the Blackwater River which was a navigation between Lough Neagh and the Ulster Canal. Tramway No 4 led to the Moygashel Mills, two miles south-east of Dungannon, and No 5 to a working quarry in Lord Ranfurly's Park. Tramway No 6 was to the Dungannon Gas Works, No 7 to Hale and Martin's Mill in Dungannon, and No 8 to the Dungannon Corn Market. All these branches were merely short industrial sidings. The system was to be worked 'by steam or horse power, or electricity or other mechanical power, upon a gauge of not less than 3 feet'. Permission was sought to improve the harbour at Moy, and to make arrangements with the Ulster Canal Company, which joned the Blackwater near Benburb, a village six miles above Moy. Public notice was given of intention to apply for an Order in Council, under the 1883 Tramways Act. The procedures were followed, but the scheme failed to get approval from that predecessor of the County Council, the Tyrone Grand Jury. The Tyrone Steam Tramways Company Ltd was finally wound up, a notice to that effect appearing in the *Dublin Gazette* of 29 March 1887.

The rival scheme, backed by Ellison Macartney and his supporters, went forward with more success and matured as the roadside tramway of which the history forms the subject of succeeding chapters of this book. The Clogher Valley Tramway Company was incorporated in December 1883 and proceeded to obtain statutory powers to build its line.

CHAPTER 3

Acts, Action and Opening

THE STATE ASSISTS

Many years before the initiation of the Clogher Valley Tramway scheme, the government had began to assist the development of rail transport in Ireland. The famine years of 1846–9, when the potato crop repeatedly failed and starvation and disease caused the death of millions throughout Ireland, focused cross-channel eyes on the almost entire dependence of the country's economy on agriculture. It was clear that some industrialisation was necessary to arrest depopulation. An Act of Parliament in 1860 gave powers for the construction of roadside tramways, but it had little practical effect, because only animal power was to be used for traction. An Amendment Act in 1861 merely made trivial alterations in the procedures of application.

Not until 1871 were roadside tramways permitted to employ mechanical power, but as speed was statutorily restricted to 6 miles per hour along an open road, and to 3 miles per hour in urban areas, the Act did not encourage promoters. There was, however, the offer of a baronial guarantee of the interest on all or part of the invested capital (the 'Barony' being a subdivision of a County, and the 'guarantee' a charge on the ratepayers living in the barony).

THE 1883 ACT

It was not for a further twelve years that more practical

stimulus was offered, by the passing of the Tramways and Public Companies (Ireland) Act of 1883 (46 & 47 Vict., c.43). This was an important step forward in the matter of financial help, and for the first time State assistance was offered as a guarantee to the baronies. However, the Government were most careful that their generosity was not abused, and the statutory procedures to be followed by applicants were both cumbrous and expensive.

Initially the promoters had to form themselves into a company under the Limited Liability Acts. They then published certain notices, and deposited plans, sections, and lists of the owners of property affected with the secretary to any Grand Jury concerned. They had also to satisfy the County Surveyor about the effect the tramway might have on the county roads, and had to obtain a report from an engineer nominated by the Board of Works that the scheme was feasible from an engineering aspect. These preliminary requirements satisfied, the case came before the Grand Jury, or Juries if the line was to be in more than one county. If opposition was offered at this stage, the Grand Jury heard both sides through counsel.

If these hurdles were cleared, a presentment was made and submitted to the Lord Lieutenant in Council 'that such baronies or parts of baronies as the Grand Jury may specify be chargeable with the payment of dividends at such rate, not exceeding five per centum per annum, as the Grand Jury may determine on so much of the share capital of the Company as is for the time being paid-up capital as defined by this Act.'

Should the promoters be unable to complete or work the undertaking, the presentment provided for that to be done at the expense of the district. If the promoters' faults continued beyond a certain period, the undertaking would become the property of the Grand Jury. It is hard to imagine what practical steps such a body could have taken, when saddled with a tramway whose owners could not work it.

That was not all. The next stage consisted in the submission to the Irish Privy Council of a Draft Order in Council. If

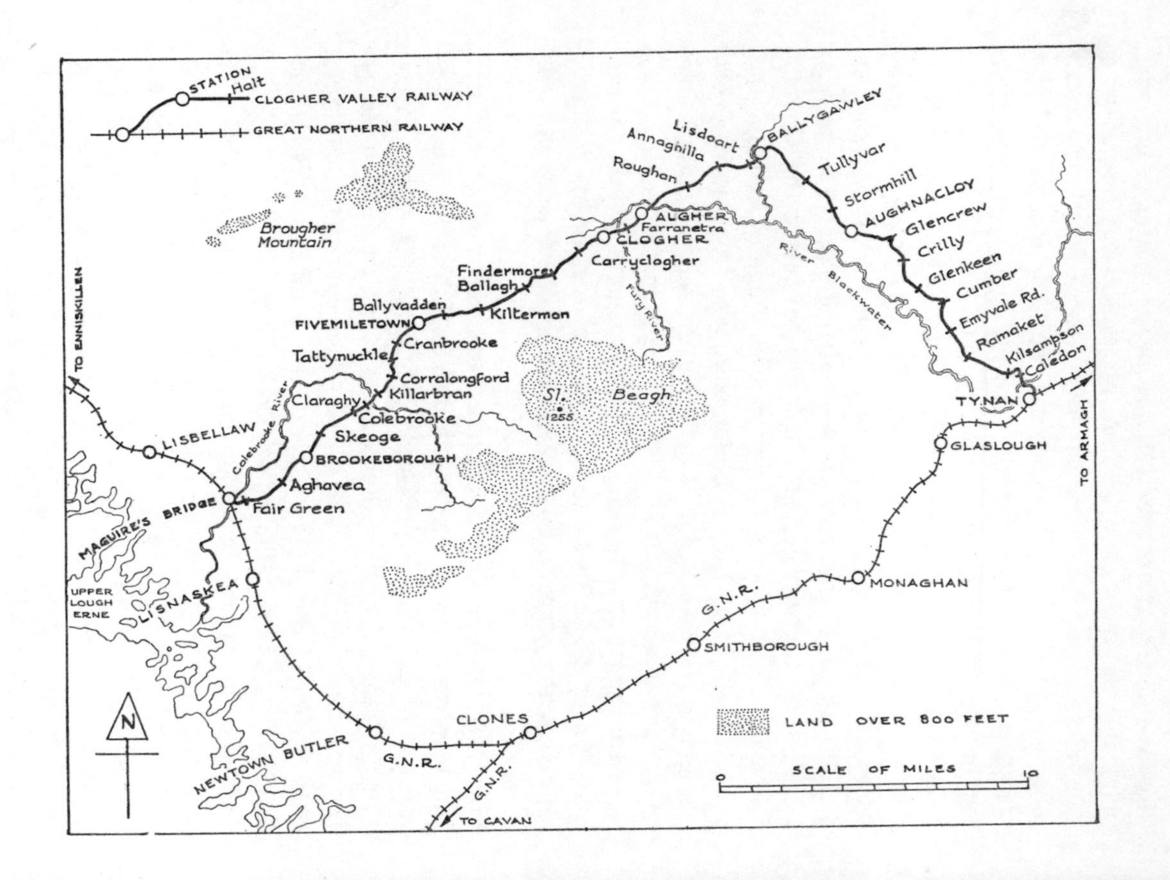
STATION
Halt
CLOGHER VALLEY RAILWAY
GREAT NORTHERN RAILWAY
Brougher Mountain
TO ENNISKILLEN
LISBELLAW
MAGUIRE'S BRIDGE
UPPER LOUGH ERNE
LISNASKEA
NEWTOWN BUTLER
G.N.R.
CLONES
G.N.R.
TO CAVAN
SMITHBOROUGH
G.N.R.
MONAGHAN
GLASLOUGH
TYNAN
TO ARMAGH
Lisdoart
Annaghilla
BALLYGAWLEY
Roughan
Tullyvar
Stormhill
AUGHNACLOY
Glencrew
Crilly
Glenkeen
Cumber
Emyvale Rd.
Ramaket
Kilsampson
Caledon
AUGHER
Farranetra
CLOGHER
Carryclogher
Findermore
Ballagh
Kiltermon
Ballyvadden
FIVEMILETOWN
Cranbrooke
Tattynuckle
Corralongford
Killarbran
Claraghy
Colebrooke
Skeoge
BROOKEBOROUGH
Aghavea
Fair Green
River Blackwater
Fury River
Colebrooke River
Sl. Beagh
1255
LAND OVER 800 FEET
SCALE OF MILES
0
10
N

everything was correct, the case was considered by a committee of the Privy Council, and promoters and objectors represented by counsel as before. The draft Order could be rejected if there were any defects in the formalities. Before an Order in Council could be granted, the Commissioners of Public Works had to furnish the Lord Lieutenant with an estimate of the amount of paid-up capital which was necessary. After they had heard the case, if the Order was unopposed, the committee might finally give it their approval subject to Treasury sanction, or reject it. If the Order was opposed, but granted by committee, the promoters were required to set about getting confirmation by Act of Parliament. Such a procedure faced the Cork, Coachford, & Blarney Light Railway in 1886.

The local guarantee ran from the payment of each instalment of the capital, whereas it was not until the line was open and working that direct pecuniary responsibility of the State began. Under the latter, the Treasury should repay to the barony one half of the amount which it might have paid under the guarantee on account of any half-year's working, provided that:

(a) the line was maintained in working order and carried traffic
(b) no more than 2 per cent on the capital was so paid
(c) the State liability in respect of these guarantees did not exceed £40,000 per annum.

The 1883 Act permitted some relaxations in the existing tramway laws, and where the rails were more than thirty feet away from the centre of the road, there was no restriction on the speed of the locomotives. Along the road, the speed was not supposed to exceed twelve miles per hour.

THE GAUGE DECIDED

During the autumn of 1883, the Clogher Valley promoters adopted a gauge of 3 feet, being the most economical and therefore likely to gain statutory approval. Provisional arrangements were made with the Great Northern Railway company that their stations at Maguiresbridge and at Tynan ('Tynan and Caledon' in the GN timetables) would be suitably altered and made available for the reception of the narrow gauge line. Indeed the prior existence of these Great Northern stations meant that the Clogher Valley had no need to spend money in building their own termini, for at both places the broad gauge facilities were adequate for the combined working. Thus at Tynan the Great Northern had a splendidly constructed goods store, more than ample for their own traffic, and arrangements were made for the tramway to take a siding into one of the halves of the store.

LEGAL FORMALITIES

In December 1883 the Clogher Valley Tramway Company was incorporated and the legal wheels began to turn. In February 1884 a promotion leaflet was issued, headed *Statement of Probable Cost of Construction, Traffic &c and Benefits accruing therefrom*. Such documents were intended to open the purses of investors, and were characteristically enthusiastic. The Clogher Valley one was no exception. It anticipated Henry Forbes' policy of half a century later on the Donegal, forecasting that:

> Most probably special trains would run on fair and market days to take up persons with baskets, small parcels etc. at *any* place on the road, so that instead of driving a cart the whole way into market, anyone wishing to do so, has only to get down to the tram line, and wait until a car comes up, which would pick him up, and carry him in, under cover, at a very low rate.

Numerous sidings for farm traffic were promised and 'merchants in towns could have rails laid, to run waggons right into their yards'. The document ended optimistically: 'It is, therefore, most unlikely that the working expenses would amount to

50 per cent of the receipts, which is the proportion on most well managed railways.'

At the Spring Assizes of 1884 the approval of the two Grand Juries of Tyrone and Fermanagh was asked for and obtained, though not before the county surveyors had reported on the Clogher Valley's application to their respective Grand Juries. Frederick Willson, responsible for the Fermanagh portion, was concerned with the possibility of interference with the roads under his care:

> The construction of the line on a raised platform on one side of the road, will considerably interfere with, and increase the difficulty of the surface drainage of the road at that side. Proper provision should be made for that drainage. There is nothing to show what provision will be made. . . .
> The tramway will reduce the traffic on the roads, but will increase the danger of accidents to passengers and horses, both along the road and at the crossings, specially at night, and on market and fair days, there being no protection provided to keep passengers from getting on the line; and horses traversing country roads will not become so soon accustomed to passing tramcars as in towns. A source of danger also arises from the line not being fully fenced in and protected by gates at crossings, from cattle getting in on the line at cross-roads, and also from vehicles driving on cross-roads probably not having sufficient warning of the approach of tramcars. I think it is right to point out these dangers, although the Tramway Act does not seem to contemplate them as objections, for they not only increase the risk to life and limb, but also from the effect such accidents may have on the expenses of the Company, and in this way may effect the amount of guarantee which may have to be paid. I believe it would be well to have the line fully fenced in, but in any case wherever the Tramway is laid at a lower level than the surface of the road it should be completely and securely fenced in from the road.

Willson continued to sound the dangers, and to warn his Grand Jury in fourteen further paragraphs.

Fermanagh was divided into eight baronies, two of which, Tyrkennedy and Magherastephana, were to guarantee one-sixth of the capital. Tyrone likewise contained eight baronies, of which Clogher and Lower Dungannon guaranteed the remainder of the capital. It is noteworthy that Tyrkennedy was asked to bear a share of the responsibilities, though the tramway did not enter it; however, its south-eastern boundary lay not far from the Fivemiletown—Maguiresbridge section and it was argued that it would benefit from having the tramway and should therefore be prepared to bear charges, should they arise. County Armagh, with only a mile of line, was exempted.

IN DUBLIN CASTLE

The remainder of the formalities were taken on Saturday 17 May 1884 and on the following Monday, when the Judicial Committee of the Privy Council of Ireland met in the Council Chamber of Dublin Castle to consider the application.

Evidence was taken from various experts, and it was emphasised that the company had been entirely promoted by local gentlemen, the inference being that no outside financiers were connected with the scheme. In the Memorandum of Association were J. Ellison Macartney, MP, DL, JP, Hugh de Fellenberg Montgomery, DL, JP. Additional promoters were Thomas S. Porter, James Pringle, merchant and farmer of Anna House, Aughnacloy, Frederick Wrench, land agent, Brookeborough, David Graham, merchant, Fivemiletown, John S. Girvan, hotelkeeper, Ballygawley, Ormsby Vandaleur, JP, Caledon, and Frank Brooke, land agent, Brookeborough.

Opposition to the scheme was offered by the representative of Killeshill parish, preferring that of the Tyrone Steam Tramway, which was to have gone through the parish between Ballygawley and Dungannon, whereas the Clogher Valley scheme ignored it. Evidence was given that if the income of the tramway was £6 10s (£6·50) per mile per week, it would cover expenses, and to back that it was stated that the Cavan—Clones line had begun at £6 11s (£6·55) and was now bringing in £11 10s (£11·50) per mile per week. The Sligo, Leitrim

& Northern Counties line was said to have an income of £5 10s (£5·50), and the Enniskillen to Omagh line £16 per mile per week.

Macartney told the Committee of his previous association with five unsuccessful schemes, and to emphasise the point, spoke of how the great William Dargan had said to him, when on a visit, that if there was any agricultural district in Ireland that would pay for a railway, it would be the Clogher Valley.

Support was given by T. A. Dickson, member of parliament for Dungannon, saying that Aughnacloy market had suffered since other railways had come to serve the surrounding towns. Henry Plews, the traffic manager of the Great Northern, confirmed this and spoke of the 'formerly important pork and flax market' at Aughnacloy, adding that its spinning mill, once employing two hundred persons, had failed and was lying idle because of high freight costs. Plews, whose experience made him a most valuable witness, thought that the tramway was 'much needed'. He spoke of trials that had been made with a steam traction engine between Lisnaskea and Fivemiletown, but which had to be given up owing to the bad state of the roads. From his own company, he evidenced the earnings of the Ballybay—Cootehill branch, earning £9 7s 6d (£9·37½) per mile per week. Maguiresbridge station had, he said, booked out no less that 10,973 passengers during the previous year, and there were therefore twice that number of persons using the station, though it did not yet handle goods traffic. Lisnaskea 2½ miles away, and with goods accommodation, handled 9,200 tons during 1883. The only public transport in that area, according to Plews, was the mailcar, which held four persons and which plied between Fivemiletown and Lisnaskea.

Thomas Dixon, the railway contractor, foresaw no difficulty in construction and reckoned that 'two clear summers' would be sufficient to do the earthworks, prepare the roadway, and lay the line.

For the committee, Rt Hon Baron Dowse commented

sympathetically 'A Man has only to travel through that country, and see its present state, to sigh for any sort of a gauge—broad or narrow.'

Authorisation took almost another three months, then on 7 August 1884 the Order in Council gave the Clogher Valley Tramway Company the green light.

During the autumn of 1884 two necessary appointments were made. In Clogher Courthouse on Tuesday 21 October, the newly appointed directors confirmed the appointment of David James Stewart as the company secretary. Stewart came to them from the West Lancashire Railway, and was granted £30 towards the expenses of the removal of his furniture to Ireland. Then on 15 December, with land purchase in prospect, John Wilson* of Dungannon was appointed to the position of valuer 'at a remuneration of 3 guineas per diem and car hire'. Wilson won his appointment in the face of competition from H. S. M. Barton, H. Babington, A. J. Alcorn, and James Armstrong.

Shortly after Wilson's appointment, Stewart issued the usual formal notice to the public, warning that the line of the tramway had been marked:

> *Clogher Valley Tramway Company, Limited.*
>
> Notice is hereby given to all persons interested, that no one can be permitted to interfere in any way with the 'lockspit' marking the centre line of the Clogher Valley Tramway, nor to plough or break up any lands nearer than *five yards* on *each side of said lockspit*. Any person infringing this rule is rendered by Law liable to a PENALTY OF FORTY SHILLINGS for each offence, which will be rigidly enforced.

* Successive generations of this family had an association with the profession of land surveying and valuation. The father of John Wilson (1825-94) the Clogher Valley valuer, was Andrew Wilson (1781-1850) of Allen townland near Dungannon. A great-great-grandfather of the author, Andrew Wilson was a land agent and surveyor. A son of John Wilson, and a grandson, were later to be on the staff of the Irish Land Commission. In 1883 the name of John Wilson was bestowed on the author's father, J. W. Patterson.

CONTRACTORS ON THE GROUND

The board of directors met on St Patrick's Day 1885 and invited tenders for construction of the tramway. In April the contract was awarded to Messrs McCrea and McFarland of Belfast, whose tender was the lowest, £23,000 for the Tynan—Fivemiletown section and £9,000 for the part from Fivemiletown to Maguiresbridge. On the plans these two parts were termed Tramway No 1 and Tramway No 2. The second best tender was that of John Gault of Ballymena at £37,000, while Collen offered to build for £43,000.

Basil McCrea and John McFarland, who had started as partners in a carting business in Belfast and Londonderry, subsequently entered civil engineering work and had seven years of railway building experience behind them by 1885. They had constructed various waterworks and sewage schemes in the north of Ireland and had built the Banbridge Extension Railway, the Limavady & Dungiven Railway, the Letterkenny Railway, and the Whitewell Tramway. John McFarland was already taking an active interest in the narrow gauge Londonderry & Lough Swilly Railway, of which he was later to be the chairman. The firm were well qualified to tackle the building of the Clogher Valley Tramway. Moreover, two years before, they had bought a secondhand 3ft gauge engine called *Barnesmore* off the West Donegal contract and had motive power for ballasting. They had several young engineers on their staff, and one of them, J. Y. F. Cooke, was placed on the CV contract as the senior resident engineer. Under him he had two junior engineers named Hutton and Palmer.

The ceremony of turning the first sod was performed at Aughnacloy on Monday 1 June 1885 by Mrs Macartney, the wife of the chairman. She was to have been assisted by Mrs Montgomery of Blessingbourne, wife of the vice-chairman but on the day Mrs Montgomery was indisposed. The traditional barrow and spade were presented by the contractors, and are preserved at Blessingbourne, delightful examples of craftsmanship in black bog oak and silver.

On the day the ground was ceremonially broken, the directors gathered in Clogher Courthouse to decide where the company's headquarters were to be sited. A central rather than a terminal position was obviously desirable, but behind the scenes there was lobbying, and local patriotism and favouritism competed with common sense. Hugh Montgomery proposed and Pomeroy seconded that the headquarters should be at Fivemiletown. Alexander put up a counter-proposal for Aughnacloy, which found a seconder in T. S. Porter. A third proposal by Girvan for Ballygawley failed to get a seconder. Montgomery lived at Fivemiletown, Girvan owned the Ballygawley Hotel though, from a practical aspect, any of the three places would have been suitable. The matter was put to the vote, when six were for Aughnacloy and four were for Fivemiletown.

By early November 1885, the company engineer James Barton reported in optimism:

> Messrs. McCrea and McFarland have made considerable progress at the Fermanagh end of the line and some progress at the Caledon end, about one half of the excavations for the line have been executed, about 9000 lineal yards of fencing has been done. The bridge over the Colebrooke River at Maguiresbridge has been erected, and that over the same river at Colebrooke is well advanced, and that over a stream near Caledon and about one half of the culverts necessary have been put in. The laying of the permanent way has commenced.

MIRE AND MONEY

Meanwhile the contractors worked through increasingly wet weather, bringing up materials over the Great Northern to Tynan and Maguiresbridge and having periodic battles with the Bartons, father and son, over the matter of payment for work done. It was no novelty for Basil McCrea, for a running fight had raged between him and James Barton during the

Page 35

AUGHNACLOY WORKSHOPS AND SHED

(Above) *Carriage & wagon shop on left, locomotive shed and machine shop on right, sawmill in lean-to. About 1920. G. F. Akerlind and daughter beyond turntable*; (centre) *Rebuilt Castlederg engine, and a Sharp, Stewart, in the locomotive shed, 24 June 1937*; (below) *The machine shop. Rebuilding in progress on the Castlederg engine, during 1935*

Page 36

AUGHNACLOY STATION

(Above) *Double-headed pig train ready to leave for Tynan, 29 June 1937*; (below) *Looking towards Tynan. Sand-pit, sand drying shed, water tank, and windmill on left. Coaling gantry spanning tracks. Narrow-gauge bogie line from coal stack to loading point, on right*

building of the Limavady & Dungiven line. On 7 January 1886 McCrea received a cheque from the Clogher Valley for £1,867 16s 5d (£1,867·82) and wrote in indignation to his partner 'Cooke thinks it is too little and I agree with him.'

By mid-January 1886 the partners were considering the best way of bringing ballast engines on to the work. *Barnesmore* was to be taken to Tynan, while another engine was to go to the Maguiresbridge end. The Great Northern's charge for conveying *Barnesmore* to Tynan annoyed McCrea: it was a distance of 104 miles, a special train, and the GN wanted to levy 4s (20p) a mile, so he wrote to McFarland on 16 January '4/- a mile is an outrageous charge . . . this is downright robbery'. When a second ballast engine was needed, the use of one of the engines originating from the Glenariff Railway in Antrim was proposed. This was one of a pair of Stephenson 2–4–0 tanks which McCrea and McFarland had bought second-hand in March 1885, and conveyed by sea to Londonderry, where they were used on the Londonderry & Lough Swilly Railway on a hire basis.* J. Y. F. Cooke advised against the idea fearing that Barton would not allow it on the new road over which he had set a weight limit of 24 tons, which the Glenariff engine exceeded by 2½ tons. Eventually a Black, Hawthorn 0–6–2 tank, named *J. T. Macky* and weighing 24 tons, was obtained on hire from the Lough Swilly company.

That the contractors had found an efficient and economical resident engineer in J. Y. F. Cooke, can be judged by a letter which he wrote to John McFarland in the middle of that first wet winter:

Clogher Valley Tramway Works,
Aughnacloy.
January 30th 1886

Dear Mr. McFarland.

I have given an order to F. Loughran, local smith, for 30 single gates at 28/- delivered on site per

* see E. M. Patterson *The Lough Swilly Railway* p. 145 and *The Ballymena Lines* pp. 24-7, 126-7.

C

sample approved by Mr. Barton. There are 130 gates in the contract as amended : if you wish to buy of Dick, Kerr & Coy your order must be below 100. I enclose a list of scantlings which Mr. Barton has accepted, possibly you may get a reduction on a/c of these. I think you might wait and see how the 30 ordered here turn out, and if satisfactory doubt if you can do better.

Certificate this month £1100 : we have had continuous rain all month : further he has not certified for ½ mile of broken stone ballast which he disapproved of. I am very disappointed at the bad return the contract is making so far. Prices and quantities are very tight and when there are loss on items, as Bridges 2 and 4, Tullyvar Cutting etc., there are no large profits to make up for these. The ballasting at this end will be disadvantageous, but should pay better than anything yet, and on Div. II should pay well. I intend on getting a copy of Certifte. to make a Measure Bill and see how we stand by our own measurements. I think fully £1000 better. The founds of Bridge 3, which began as ballast, have become harder than rock and are very difficult to excavate, powder removing very small quantities. The material is pebbles embedded in a hard red stuff like rock. This found will cost a lot of money. The road is closed from Tynan to Ballast Pit except 100 yards at Peg 200 and at 400 there is a piece of side filling to be done. Coy. only got the land for this a few days ago and we are starting the filling on Monday, I hope the ballasting by engine will commence in a week. I am trying to press it on. We have now rails out to Peg 650. No word of Ball. Pit at other end yet, our loss on a/c for want of it is very large, £500 would not cover it. Diversion M near Fivemiletn. I have started and it will be easy.

We got into a row for using the Coy's rails to work a cutting at Brookeboro. I offered to pay Barton for the sleepers 150 at cost price. I cannot get them to send rails forward from Belfast, it is a great drawback for want of attention they pay to these matters at Belfast. The weather continues Bad.

Faithfully yrs. J. Y. F. Cooke.

Before passing this letter to his partner, John McFarland penned on the back:

Dear McCrea,

This refers to the rails purchased off Collins when I was in Belfast. . . . my experience is that I can get nothing I want at Belfast and am not surprised when others complain they are treated similarly. No business can be carried on successfully this way—you told me Cooke was in no hurry for rails, and am not surprised at this when he came to apply for them and took the permanent way rails. Is there any use sending them now and paying freight?

Basil McCrea replied on 5 February:

Mr. Cooke's letter and your memo returned herewith. . . . I am really pleased at the economic way as regards Plant and Labour in which he is carrying out the works, but certainly when he works from 'hand to mouth' he cannot expect we have all he wants in store, ready to hand him at the lowest price when he asks for it.

Particularly on the western end of the contract, it was difficult to get reliable stonemasons, and from time to time, the Bartons had to make justifiable complaints, and require that parts be made good before they would certify work for payment. After a visit that McCrea made to the Fermanagh end on 16 March 1886 in company with 'old Mr Barton' he stated the position to McFarland:

From near Brookeborough on he condemned the pitching generally, also on Division No. 2 the Masonry was not good, and where it is not to be pulled down he wants it pointed with cement. . . . As to the Pointing, consider we can get an extra for it, as to Masonry condemned, I fear we must pull some of it down. . . . I do not consider him on the whole unfriendly, altho' he did not like much of what he saw at Maguiresbridge end of line. Certainly some of the masonry did not look good.

WILLSON OBJECTS

The County Surveyor for Fermanagh continued to watch over what was happening in his area, and made a lengthy and critical report to his Grand Jury for the Spring Assizes of 1886:

> In some instances it appears that the Company contemplate laying the rails somewhat under the level of the Public Road, which would be most dangerous to the Public, and ought not to be sanctioned. . . .
> The direction of the Public Road joining to the Fivemiletown Road (at Tattynuckle) has been altered by the Company without any authority to do so. The alteration is most objectionable in direction, and unnecessary. . . .

Willson was particularly concerned about the quality of the stonework in the river bridges at Maguiresbridge and Colebrooke, about which Barton had not been too happy when he went over the ground with McCrea. For his part, Willson furnished a detailed criticism:

> . . . . the former of these bridges is objectionable, the Masonry in the pier, abutments, retaining walls and backing of arches, being defectively built, with too small stones, and badly bonded together. The face work of this Bridge is most irregular in every direction. During the execution of the filling over this bridge, the retaining walls bulged from the pressure of the filling. . . . The other Bridges besides these . . . and pipes constructed along the line, are of a rough character, and many of the streams are crossed by flagged pipes, instead of arches, which I think is a defect. . . .

Willson stated in his report that he had frequently called the attention of the Engineer and the Secretary of the Company to the objections. The Grand Jury passed on the criticisms to the CV board, who asked David Stewart to reply in defence of the company's position:

> The Committee appointed by my Directors have gone very fully into this matter, and having personally inspected the Works you complain of as being defective, I am instructed to state that inasmuch as the Company's Engineers have answered them as to the unquestionable stability of the Works, they cannot consent to the pulling down and rebuilding of any portion of the same.

THE BARTONS DEFEND

James Barton, speaking for himself and his son (later to become Sir John Barton), felt it necessary to justify his actions, in view of the open criticism to which his reputation had been exposed by Willson's remarks. So he addressed a letter, dated 4 March 1886, to the Grand Jury of Fermanagh which is of more than ordinary interest:

Mr. Foreman and Gentlemen of the Grand Jury

I have read carefully Mr. Willson's report upon the Clogher Valley Tramway Works, and preliminary to replying in detail to his objections, I desire to place before you the position which, acting for the Tramway Company, I have taken from the beginning to the present day—namely, that I was to design and superintend the works, wholly in the interests of the ratepayers of the Counties and no other. If I design expensive masonry, not required absolutely for the safety and performance of the works, the cost of such expensive masonry would fall upon the ratepayers as increasing the sum upon which they would have to pay 5 per cent interest.

The most economical construction, consistent with safety, is just what experience as a Railway Engineer enables me to adopt, and upon that economical construction depends the amount of the County rates. On the other hand, I have no inducement to cheapen down the works beyond that which experience suggests to me as right. My constructing the line a few thousands cheaper gives no advantage to the Tramway Company proprietors who have their percentage fixed, except in the future when all paid by the County has been recouped them by the earnings of the line over 5 per cent, and then it would be their interest that the works should be unquestionably good.

My experience of the construction of Railways, now extending over nearly 40 years, has gradually led me to abandon all the dressed stone and expensive heavy stone work which I used to use, and which was general in the early days of Railways, and we use plain rough work which is found to bear the strains and weights without much of beauty. The real questions raised by Mr. Willson's report are whether I have acted wisely or not in the kinds of work I have adopted. It may be that Mr. Willson has not Railway experience. I think if he had he would not have raised perhaps any of these questions. I have to do with another County Surveyor for three-fourths of the line—a gentleman who had railway experience—and we have not had the slightest difficulty with him, though the works are under the same specification, and the same contractor is carrying them out, and in the Counties Leitrim and Roscommon I have similar works and no complaints.

Having thus disposed of his critic, Barton proceeded to take up the points which Willson had raised. Eleven times his paragraphs began 'Mr Willson objects . . .' and eleven times he disposed of the objections. He blamed the faults in the river bridge near Maguiresbridge on insufficient work by the contractor and 'not up to specification', and went on to say that the defective work had been removed and rebuilt. Barton was adamant that 'the bridge, so far as completed, is a good and sufficient permanent work.'

Undoubtedly Willson was a most conscientious man who took his responsibilities seriously, but he must have been a perfectionist. Though one must sympathise with his pleas, it is clear that out of the Clogher Valley works, a clash of personalities developed between him and James Barton.

By the summer of 1886, McCrea and McFarland's men were busy along the whole length of the tramway. Basil McCrea went to Ballygawley in June to see where a short diversion of the river had been made to allow bridge abutments to be built. He wrote to McFarland:

Pump at work at Blackwater, 7" Woodfords emptied dam in short time, bottom sandy, no report since yesterday as I passed. I think good work is being done about centre of line: Murphy linking in road about a mile beyond Aughnacloy. Two bridges to be built close to Augher, one begun. Palmer linking in rails within about 1½ miles of F'miletown. About 4 miles of centre of line untouched, but this has only to be formed. Am writing Mr. Barton for £3,500, likely we may get £2,000.

In early November 1886, the Bartons reported to the directors, forecasting that the tramway would be ready for traffic in January or February 1887.

About this time, the Bartons, perhaps still smarting from Willson's criticisms, were in their turn critical of some more of the contractor's stonework, and asked for it to be rebuilt. A formal letter went from the firm to the Bartons on 20 November:

Gentlemen,

In reply to yours of 19th inst. relative to rebuilding dry walls on the line. We are of opinion that we were submitting to a heavy loss in offering to do this work at 4/3 per cube yard (we intended this price to apply to all work actually rebuilt) and we regret you have not seen your way to meet our wishes in this matter. Nothing now remains for us but to carry out your orders in the matter of these walls and claim whatever cost we may be put to from the Company as an extra to the Contract whenever they are finished, or as soon as we can ascertain what this expenditure will amount to. Please arrange with our Mr. Cooke the actual quantity of work you want us to do, and on receiving your definite instructions we will proceed to carry them into effect without delay.

Awaiting an early reply, we are gentlemen,

Yours truly, McCrea and McFarland.

A week later, Basil McCrea returned to the valley works and made a personal inspection of the situation, spoke to his senior engineer Cooke, and to Cooke's assistants. He then spent the night in Aughnacloy, and wrote a lengthy report about the visit to John McFarland:

I went over the Tramway on Wednesday and yesterday for the purpose of finding out when the line will likely be completed, and whether any hands can be dispensed with in order to reduce expenditure which is still high. Met Mr. J. G. Barton at Caledon, had a long discussion on dry walls, resulting in my telling 'You and I will not quarrel about the matter'. . . . leaving Caledon he came with us to where the first high wall was underpinned, he had holes made in it, showing work only 18" instead of 2' and work not well done. After consulting with Mr. Cooke I ordered him to get it properly redone without further delay. . . . Engine *J. T. Macky*—repairs completed, were getting up steam on Wednesday. Fitter to return to Londonderry. . . . I complained heavily about finances etc. Arrived at Fivemiletown about 6.30 pm had a long conversation with Hutton and Palmer, former says measurements on his end are correct but one-third is deducted off amount by Mr. J. G. B., no wonder we are short paid nearly 33⅓% and 10% retentions, nearly 43% kept off us. . . .

. . . walked to Ballast Pit with Palmer yesterday morning. Engine carrying 7 wagons Ballast to commencement of Mr. Porter's fields near gate house, no ballast on from this to where the rails met, over a mile. Does about 8 setts a day, siding into Ballast Pit to be altered if it can be done, half an hour lost off engine and men each rake. . . . Burns and 35 men filling ballast, 7 wagons to the sett or 5 men per wagon, ordered him and Agnew to see that no more than 4 men are kept to each wagon, other hands to be reduced as soon as possible. Work still to do : 5 Mile Town station yard, an extra. Brown and 4 men will finish in three days and ballasting will take nearly one day afterward. . . .

Engine calculated to put out 200 cyds a day or better. Palmer calculates all will be done in 6 weeks or less. Cost about £500 to finish all ready for inspection.

FINANCIAL CRISIS

In March 1886 the finance house of Salter & Son withdrew their offer to purchase £70,000 of stock not taken up by the public, and for some months the position of the company was precarious. The public were not coming forward to invest in what seemed on the face of it to be a gilt-edged concern. This tardiness was not confined to the Clogher Valley Tramway, for the three narrow gauge concerns of the Cavan &

Leitrim, Cook & Muskerry, and West Clare were suffering in a similar fashion. Current political uncertainty was behind it, and, as we have seen, it reacted on the contractors.

From the beginning, the objection had been made to the Grand Juries that the guarantee of 5 per cent was unnecessarily high. In order to get the consent of the Grand Juries to a 5 per cent guarantee, the promoters undertook not only to take tenders for the shares and to issue them at the highest price, but also not to issue shares for larger amounts than were immediately required for construction and equipment, and in this way to save the ratepayer from being taxed on idle money. The philosophy behind it was sound, but it meant in practice that the company was living from hand to mouth.

The tenders received enabled the first instalment of shares to be issued at a premium of five per cent, but by the time the second instalment was wanted Gladstone had introduced the Home Rule Bill of 1886. The Bill was defeated on 7 June, and Parliament was dissolved, and a general election held 'to ascertain the sense of my people upon the important proposal to establish a legislative body in Ireland for the management of Irish as distinguished from Imperial affairs.' Ireland, with the reins loosely in Westminster hands, was in one of its periods of political upheaval and from June to September there was more or less continuous rioting in Belfast. The tension reacted on investment, and the public were less ready than ever to commit their money. The CV directors saw that their line might follow in the steps of the unfortunate Letterkenny Railway of twenty years earlier, and they went to the Board of Works for a loan. But nothing was forthcoming since the Clogher Valley was already mortgaged to the counties under the terms of the 1883 Act. It seemed an impasse, but it was solved quickly by the 1886 Public Works Loans Tramways (Ireland) Act, which authorised the Treasury to lend money on the deposit of guaranteed shares. As a result, the Clogher Valley was able to borrow £44,000.

Even this loan gave rise to difficulties. The Treasury claimed that as holders of guaranteed shares they were entitled to five per cent interest from the CV company. The directors contested this, and maintained that the money was really in the nature of a Board of Works loan, the current rate of interest on which was only four per cent, and that the Treasury had only accepted the shares as security for the loan. The Treasury were very obdurate on the matter, and only after much exercise of ability and influence by the directors was the Treasury persuaded to reduce the loan interest to four per cent, for the benefit of the ratepayers. The loan was subsequently repaid in full.

FOOTING THE BILL

Although McCrea and McFarland were awarded the contract on 20 April 1885 on the basis of their original estimate of £32,000, an adjustment was asked for, and a board minute of 4 May 1885 notes a resolution that Contract 2 (between Fivemiletown and Maguiresbridge) 'be let to McCrea and McFarland for £10,000' their tender being wrong 'by a clerical error'. It was a small matter, amicably settled, but heavier costs were to follow, the 'extras' to which Basil McCrea had referred.

By the end of construction, as a result of additions and alterations made to the tramway during its construction, the bill presented by the firm had swelled by around £10,000. For this majestic increase, the Bartons, as guardians of the Clogher Valley's requirements, must carry the blame, even though after much discussion a reduction by around £3,000 was agreed upon. An increase of around a quarter required explanation, and the Bartons presented their version of the facts on 31 May 1888 in a letter to the directors. Four days later the directors gathered at Aughnacloy, 'unanimously approved of the Engineers Report' and the Secretary was instructed to write to McCrea & McFarland admitting that on that date the company owed them £5,607 17s 1d (£5,607·85) 'plus the interest on retentions as provided for by the Contract'. The total came to £5,927 5s 1d (£5,927·25). A month and some correspondence passed before the board authorised payment. The cheque was signed, and the secretary minuted on 2 July that in the event of McCrea and McFarland 'making a further demand for interest on that sum on account of the delay in payment of same, the Chairman and one other member of the Board were authorised to sign a further cheque for the amount of a month's interest on that sum at the rate of 5 per cent—'such cheque to be forwarded to Messrs. McCrea and McFarland as a final settlement'. Their bill had totalled £40,346 13s 10d (£40,346·69).

As we have seen, completion went slowly during that final winter of 1886–7, but the impending opening was being anticipated. Committees were appointed from among the directors to deal with specialist matters, and on 25 January 1887 a Traffic Committee met to consider timetable arrangements and fares. They recommended to the board that first class fares would be twopence (1p), and third class one penny (½p) per mile, with returns at seven-eighths of the double fare. After three months operation, with more empty seats in the first class than in the thirds, the first class fare was reduced to 1½d per mile.

THE STATIONS

Though the Clogher Valley had the distinction of being without stations at either of its two termini, it made up for that deficiency in the rather splendid style of the stations at other places. Red brick was used in their construction, the work being in the hands of Dixon & Co of Belfast at Aughnacloy, Ballygawley, Clogher, Fivemiletown, Colebrooke, and Brookeborough. Delay in getting the land prevented Augher station being built before the opening day, but its construction by James Harvey of Enniskillen soon followed.

There were four designs of station building. As befitted its status as administrative headquarters, Aughnacloy was the largest, a long, two-storeyed edifice in flemish bond. It was gabled at either end, with slated roof and Tudor chimneys.

The windows were brick arched, and the walls had heavy string courses in moulded brick. From the platform, three semicircular arches led to the booking hall and the metalled entrance yard. Outoffices and lavatory formed a walled extension on the west end of the main building.

The second design of station was used at Clogher and Fivemiletown. This had a two-storey portion for the stationmaster's house, with twin gable ends towards the platform. This was flanked by outoffices and lavatory, single storeyed at one side, and on the other side by the booking hall and offices, with a glazed wooden screen fronting on the platform. The brickwork of the building was generally similar to that at Aughnacloy, with heavy mouldings and arched windows. The chimney stacks were plain, but the pots were ornate, and ornamented barge boards set off the gable ends.

Ballygawley and Brookeborough had the third type of design, a compressed version of the second, in that the stationmaster's house had only a single gable facing the platform, while the flanking offices were as before.

Augher and Colebrooke were simpler places, being entirely one storey, but otherwise conforming in the general construction and style to their larger counterparts.

In the Aughnacloy yard, the workshops and goods store were well constructed, with exterior walls of whinstone rubble masonry, relieved by brick arches around the windows and doors.

THE GATE LODGES

The tramway had nineteen level crossings over the public roads and where these were not at stations, they were protected by gates. Gate lodges were sited alongside. Tenders were asked for in an advertisement, and by posters dated 16 June 1886. The building was done by James Harvey of Enniskillen.

The gate lodges were in most cases built to a uniform architectural style, and since they were better living quarters than many of the thatched cottages of the time, they were homes to be proud of. They had two storeys, and those in Tyrone and Fermanagh were built of dressed whinstone, with ornamental brick facings to the doors and windows. The only gate lodge in County Armagh, that at Lemnagore, was of brick throughout. In some instances a walled yard was built alongside, and held a dry closet. The doorway, facing the line, was protected by a slate-roofed porch. Inside the doorway, a small hallway had doors on the left and right, leading to the kitchen and sitting-room. A steep staircase, 2ft 6in wide, rose in ten steps to a tiny landing, lit by a small square window in the rear wall, and off which there opened two bedrooms. The bedrooms each had a single window set in the gable wall.

As constructed, the bedrooms were literally 'under the slates', with bare rafters exposed. From the start, the reports of the County Surveyors were critical of the want of proper ceilings and of the draughtiness and chill that were the result. A good covering of thatch would have been more snug. Willson repeatedly criticised the gate lodges in his annual statement to the Fermanagh Grand Jury, and after the winter of 1887–8 he wrote:

> The Gatehouses are in much the same state as at last Spring Assizes. . . . generally require door steps, and for the warmth of the buildings, the upper rooms should be ceiled. The yard in front of Brookeborough Lodge should be filled with good gravel, and levelled to prevent the lodgment of water. Works should be executed so that the ground floors of all the gatehouses may be at least six inches above the yard or ground outside, in order to keep the houses dry.

Willson had to reiterate his plea for bedroom ceilings, and eventually after nine years occupation and a petition to the board of directors by some of the gatekeepers, it was agreed that more effective insulation should be provided. This was done by lining the rafters with tongued and grooved boards, the work being spread over several years.

The gate lodge at Derryloman, a townland 3½ miles west of Fivemiletown, was an architectural exception and came in for particular criticism. In July 1887 Willson noticed that 'no gatehouse has been provided at the public road crossing in Derryloman, on the Fivemiletown side of the Colebrooke station.' The company took his point, built one, and then had Willson say in July 1888: 'The wind gets up through the floor . . . and the chimney has settled down somewhat, causing a dip in the ridge.' The Bartons rose in defence and wrote to the Grand Jury: '. . . he draws attention to the house at Derryloman, being situate in a very deep bog, this is built of galvanised iron, and is naturally not so comfortable as a stone structure. We will endeavour as far as possible to stop the circulation of air under the floor, and we will straighten the ridge where necessary'. Willson remained unsatisfied, and later called it 'an uncomfortable structure' but as his criticisms eventually ceased, one presumes that the Barton wizardry must have created some improvement in the tin hut.

THE GATEKEEPERS

The lodges were let at a nominal payment to the gatekeeper of one shilling (5p) a week. Normally this wage was made economically viable by ensuring that the lodge was the home of a family, one or more of whom was in full employment by the company. On 3 January 1887 the Traffic Committee resolved to let as many as possible to the company's porters, while the rest were let free of charge pending the appointment of permanent way men. The tenants were to receive 'a remuneration of 1/– a week for attending to the gates'.

Thus for what was virtually free housing, a responsible member of the family had to look after the gates. In some cases the age of responsibility was synonymous with limited school education, and at the board meeting in September 1887 it was 'reported that certain of the company's gatekeepers can neither read nor write. The Committee recommend that where a man cannot read or write, the wife or other members of the family who can, be made the tenant, be employed as gatekeeper, and be made responsible for the gates.' It made interpretation of the Rule Book and the Working Timetable more certain, but the minute books do not say that the folk in the gate lodges were ever examined to establish their literary competency.

RAILS AND ROLLING STOCK

The board minutes do not record the rolling mill that made the rails. They were of flat-bottomed steel, weighed 45lb to the yard, and were 27ft in length. Probably Welsh, they were shipped to Dundalk, where arrangements were made during June 1885 with Messrs Cooper to have them transhipped from the quay to Barrack Street, where they were put on Great Northern wagons to be taken to Tynan and Maguiresbridge.

The supply of motive power and rolling stock was entrusted to a Rolling Stock Committee, made up of Messrs Macartney, Montgomery, Pomeroy, and Porter. The directors, who had after all no personal expertise in railway administration, were already receiving expert general guidance from the company secretary and general manager, David James Stewart, who had come from the West Lancashire Railway in the autumn of 1884. The directors thought enough of him that when, after his arrival at Aughnacloy, he asked for a grant of £30 towards removal expenses, he was paid it. During October 1885 tenders were received from eight locomotive builders. The committee met on 2 November and, feeling a little inadequate even under Stewart's tutelage, they wisely decided to employ a London consultant, J. Tomlinson, who had been the locomotive engineer of the Taff Vale Railway, to peruse the various tenders and advise them. Unfortunately the minutes do not contain the names of all the eight builders, but on 22 December six of them had apparently been rejected and Tomlinson reported that he had discussed the supply with Mr Scott Russell of the Falcon Engine & Carriage Works, and with Mr Darbyshire of Messrs Sharp, Stewart & Co Ltd. This focused the board's attention on two suitable suppliers, but there was no hurry in coming to a decision, for completion of the line was still sixteen months away.

The company still had no mechanical engineer on its staff, and on 4 January 1886 the Rolling Stock Committee 'resolved to employ a locomotive engineer to go into detailed plans of locomotives and consult with Messrs Barton as to details . . .' A decision on the appointment seems to have been delayed during the whole of the year, and the next mention of the post is found in a minute of 3 January 1887, when James Will-goose was interviewed. He does not appear to have been appointed, for his name is not in the monthly cash payments of wages and salaries. In May, again according to the salary sheet, one R. H. Weatherburn joined the staff, a peculiar appointment that appears to have involved a father-and-son collaboration, since the minutes refer to 'Messrs Weatherburn *junior and senior*' on one occasion. Salary payment varied between £12 10s 0d and £13 12s 6d a month, until Weather-burn's resignation in February 1889.

Nothing was minuted regarding the relative merits of the Falcon and Sharp, Stewart engines, but eventually the order was given to the latter firm, who supplied a family of six identical engines. The choice was sound, for in general they had a history of reliability on the tramway, and three of them survived for the long term of 53 years.

No details can be traced about the history of the ordering of carriages and wagons, but due deliberation will have been given in committee to the balance of anticipated traffic between passenger and goods in the mixed trains that were proposed, and the numbers of coaching and merchandise vehicles needed to cope with the expected traffic. During the spring of 1886 a contract was placed with the Metropolitan Railway Carriage & Wagon Company of Birmingham for 13 carriages, 6 luggage, parcel, and brake vans, and 74 goods vehicles, open and covered. An analysis of the 1888–9 Board of Trade returns for minor Irish railways shows that on most of the lines, a 5:1 ratio existed between the numbers of goods and passenger vehicles and the Clogher Valley fell into

Page 53

TWELFTH OF JULY SPECIALS

(Above) *From the footplate between Ballygawley and Tullyvar. Two engines double head a train of two bogie wagons, nine carriages, seven cattle wagons and a brake van. A third engine banks at the rear*; (below) *Platform view at Aughnacloy*

Page 54

TWO SIDES OF TULLYVAR HILL

(Above) *Tullyvar stone siding. The steam engine and stone crushing plant during construction in 1914;* (below) *Dempsey's Crossing. John McKeown flags the 1.15 pm ex Fivemiletown, August 1937. A strengthened train with six carriages, carrying police for crowd control duty in Belfast during Royal visit*

this class. Notable exceptions to the mode were the Ballymena and Larne Railway, where the heavy iron ore traffic yielded a 17:1 ratio, and the suburban Cork & Muskerry where 2:1 prevailed. Always a law unto itself, the Listowel and Ballybunion Railway had a similar balance to the Cork & Muskerry. Carriages demanded a larger outlay of capital per vehicle, and had a much higher annual maintenance charge than wagons, so that care had to be taken from the outset that no surplus of seats existed at normally busy times such as market and fair days.

ALL IS MADE READY

The early weeks of 1887 were upon the company. There blossomed from the board of directors an Opening Arrangements Committee which, meeting on 5 February, expressed the hope that no less a person than the Lord Lieutenant of Ireland might be persuaded to declare the line open. Having hoped, they resolved to leave the matter in the competent hands of their deputy chairman, Hugh Montgomery. Two days later the directors turned their minds towards more practical matters: the goods stores along the line had earth floors, and it was decided to lay these in concrete at a cost of 3s 6d (17½p) per square yard.

The Traffic Committee met on 19 February and knowing that their permanent way was complete, though signalling and many other matters were far from ready, they decided that it would do nothing but good to all concerned if a limited service of goods trains was run. So Stewart was authorised 'to make such arrangements as he might deem advisable for the carriage of any urgent traffic previous to the opening of the line.' No record is known to survive of when such trains ran, but they must have caused delay to the engineering work for Stewart had hurriedly to issue handbills on 17 March, turned out by 'W. Somers, General Printer, Aughnacloy', apologising to the local traders and saying that 'as a continuous working of goods trains may possibly delay the opening of the line for general traffic NOTICE IS HEREBY GIVEN that on and after TUESDAY next, the 22nd inst., and until the opening of the line, no further goods will be carried.'

On 11 and 12 April came the Board of Trade inspection of the line. During his tour, Major-General C. S. Hutchinson was accompanied by the County Surveyors of Armagh, Tyrone, and Fermanagh, the trio acting on behalf of their Grand Juries. Hutchinson's report, written from 1 Whitehall, London, SW of 13 April, was generally favourable, the only engineering defect which worried him being the river bridge at Colebrooke, of which one of the piers supporting the girders was showing some signs of settlement. He noted with interest, but with reserve, the use of cattle grids where the tramway left the roadside to enter private land. He called them 'gridirons with a ditch below them, such as are largely used in America and India' and was clearly not entirely happy about them. 'They must be regarded only in the light of an experiment subject to removal, if found unsatisfactory' he went on, and seems to have visualised their being replaced by gates and gatelodges. In fact, the grids served the Clogher Valley exceedingly well, and the local farmers made no complaints.

The tramway was almost ready to receive traffic. Two and a half weeks were spent in attending to details arising from the inspection, and some goods trains were again worked. One of them had a spectacular up journey, as told in the *Tyrone Constitution* of 2 May:

BALLYGAWLEY

Burning Accident on the Clogher Valley Tramway.

From Our Correspondent.

On Thursday, the 28th ultimo, about 7 o'clock pm, the engine was returning to this town from Maguiresbridge, having a waggon of tow for Belfast, when in the townland of Roughan, situate half-way from Ballygawley to Augher, the tow caught fire with the result that the waggon and the tow was all consumed. The tow is said to be value for £10. A large crowd was at the Station House when the engine reached it.

Perusal of the Cash Book of the company shows that these pre-opening trains brought in some quite useful revenue. There were no recorded receipts during March 1887, but 'Stations Traffic' during April yielded £70 18s 7d (£70·93). Doubtless everyone concerned had some useful practice.

'FOG SIGNALS WERE EXPLODED IN HONOUR OF THE EVENT'

As it turned out, the Lord Lieutenant was unable to perform the opening ceremony, and his place was taken by the High Sheriff of Tyrone, Major Mervyn Knox-Browne of Aughentaine Castle, near Clogher. The date was fixed as Monday, 2 May, and the *Tyrone Constitution* excelled itself in giving a lengthy and detailed story of the proceedings, prefaced by a description of the history and appearance of the tramway.

The visitors and guests converged on Aughnacloy in special trains from Maguiresbridge and Tynan, 'the engines bedecked with flowers and evergreens' steamed into Aughnacloy station to the sound of exploding fog signals. The actual business of the day came at 12.30pm with the company chairman introducing the principal guest, Major Knox-Browne, whom he asked to address the meeting and declare the line open. The High Sheriff spoke briefly and made certain that the line was correctly opened by the expedient of pouring champagne over locomotive No 1. The guests, directors and officials then retired to the goods shed, to do justice to a luncheon supplied by Thompson and Sons of Belfast. Thus fortified, they proceeded to serious business: the loyal toast was followed by 'Success to the Clogher Valley Tramway', proposed by Major Knox-Browne. The chairman, J. W. Ellison Macartney, replied on behalf of the company and recalled his historic traverse of the district with William Dargan 35 years before. Then, in descending order, eight more toasts were drunk: the company secretary, the engineers, the contractors and the builders of the engines, carriages and stations, the Great Northern Railway, the guaranteeing counties, the guests, the ladies, and the Press. The throng then blinked their breathless way out into the

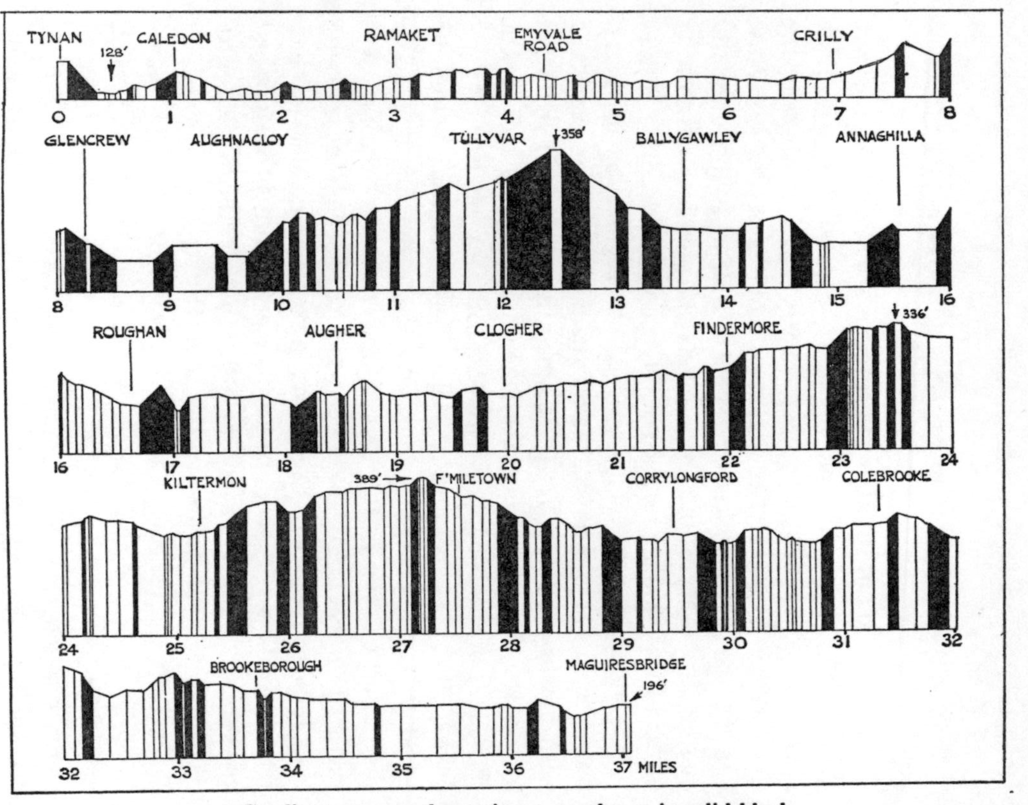

Gradients steeper than 1 in 40 are shown in solid black

afternoon light or, as the *Constitution* reporter preferred it 'the proceedings came to a termination'.

There was time to spare, and the visitors scattered to inspect the station, the workshops, and the array of engines and rolling stock crowding the sidings. To the *Constitution* man the workshops were 'the most commodious in Ireland . . . they more resemble that [sic] which are at a busy English manufacturing town'. By three o'clock the entertainments of the Aughnacloy yard were at their height. The visitors were everywhere, and the newsman saw them as 'a fair representation of the wealth, beauty, and the mercantile community in South Tyrone. It seemed by the bright, smiling faces of the ladies that they thoroughly enjoyed the merry May Day . . . most potent, grave and reverend seignors, grave Puritan Presbyters, vivacious High Church clergymen, and stern-looking Roman Catholic priests, mingled in the conversation freely, smoked cigars and cracked jokes over the tramway. Even bankers were jolly at the happy results of the day. The disciples of *Esculapius* who were present in legion, were making merry . . .'

The jollifications were brought to a close by the departure of the special trains. The down tram left at 3.30pm and pulled out with 'about six carriages attached to the engine' making stops at Clogher and Fivemiletown, before reaching Maguiresbridge, 'in time for the train from Dundalk to Derry'. Secretary Stewart travelled on it, and at Maguiresbridge found time to give the *Constitution* correspondent the news that 'all the most modern inventions will be introduced in every department for the comfort of passengers and the expedition of business, so that if the line does not pay, it will not be the fault of the enterprise of the company.' There was, perhaps, a latent chill in those last clauses. Had the takings from those April goods trains been disappointing? Stewart did not say, but it was a sobering thought that T. S. Porter's forecast of 1883 of working expenses being 50 per cent of receipts seemed to have been forgotten. The tramway was launched and Stewart returned to Aughnacloy to get on with the mundane business of running the concern to the satisfaction of his directors. There were no public trains that day, and in the Cash Book, no receipts.

EXCURSION TUESDAY

On Tuesday 3 May the line was open to the public and Handbills offered 'Cheap Excursion Trains' with tickets 'available over the whole line for the day'. The advertised fares were 4s (20p) for first class travel and 2s 6d (12½p) for third, and there were no reductions for short journeys. First on the move was a train at 10am from Maguiresbridge, another left Tynan at 10.50am. The two crossed at Ballygawley at midday. The up train reached Tynan at 1pm, where the excursionists had to make their own amusements until the return journey began at 3.20pm. That train ran through to the other terminus and tied up for the night there at 6.20pm. Meanwhile the morning train from Tynan had arrived at Maguiresbridge after a journey time of 3 hours 10 minutes and after half an hour at the Great Northern outpost, returned up the valley at 2.30pm. Again the two trains crossed at Ballygawley. The up train was into Tynan at 5.30pm. An hour later, it set off down the tramway, was through Ballygawley at 7.39pm and ended the day at Fivemiletown at 8.42pm. The public had been expected to spend their day cruising up and down the valley as a glorious introduction to rail travel. Their response cannot have been up to the company's expectations, for the station returns for the day only totalled £15 10s 1d (£15·50), representing perhaps the sale of a hundred tickets. It was an income of eighteen (old) pence per train mile per day, or around £2 10s (£2·50) per track mile per week, a figure well down on the optimistic forecasts that were offered in Dublin Castle. Perhaps Excursion Tuesday was not a representative day, but the following day, 4 May, was to give no further comfort for, when the takings were added up, they came to only £14 14s 2d (£14·71).

CHAPTER 4

The Tramway Days 1887-1894

THE COURSE OF THE LINE

With the tramway open, it is appropriate to notice the features along its 37 mile course, though few persons must have had occasion to travel throughout from Tynan to Maguiresbridge on a single journey.

The Great Northern station, named Tynan, Caledon & Middletown and later Tynan & Caledon in their timetables, was on the old Ulster Railway between Armagh and Monaghan. On the west of the line, the original station building was noteworthy for its mock Gothic architecture, giving it a vaguely ecclesiastical appearance. This may have been in deference to the nearby Tynan Abbey, which was not in fact an abbey at all, but a private residence belonging to the Stronge family. Some distance south of the passenger station, the well-proportioned goods store, built of grey limestone, copied the style of the station: at first the Great Northern used both bays, but relinquished one for the narrow gauge line when the tramway was built. Beyond it, the Clogher Valley had its engine shed and cattle pens, nearly a quarter of a mile from the passenger station. This lengthy removal of the tramway's merchandise facilities was necessary to keep the access roads to the Great Northern's passenger and goods stations clear.

At the Tynan terminus, Clogher Valley passengers used Great Northern accommodation, and the narrow gauge trains departed from and arrived at a single curved platform con-

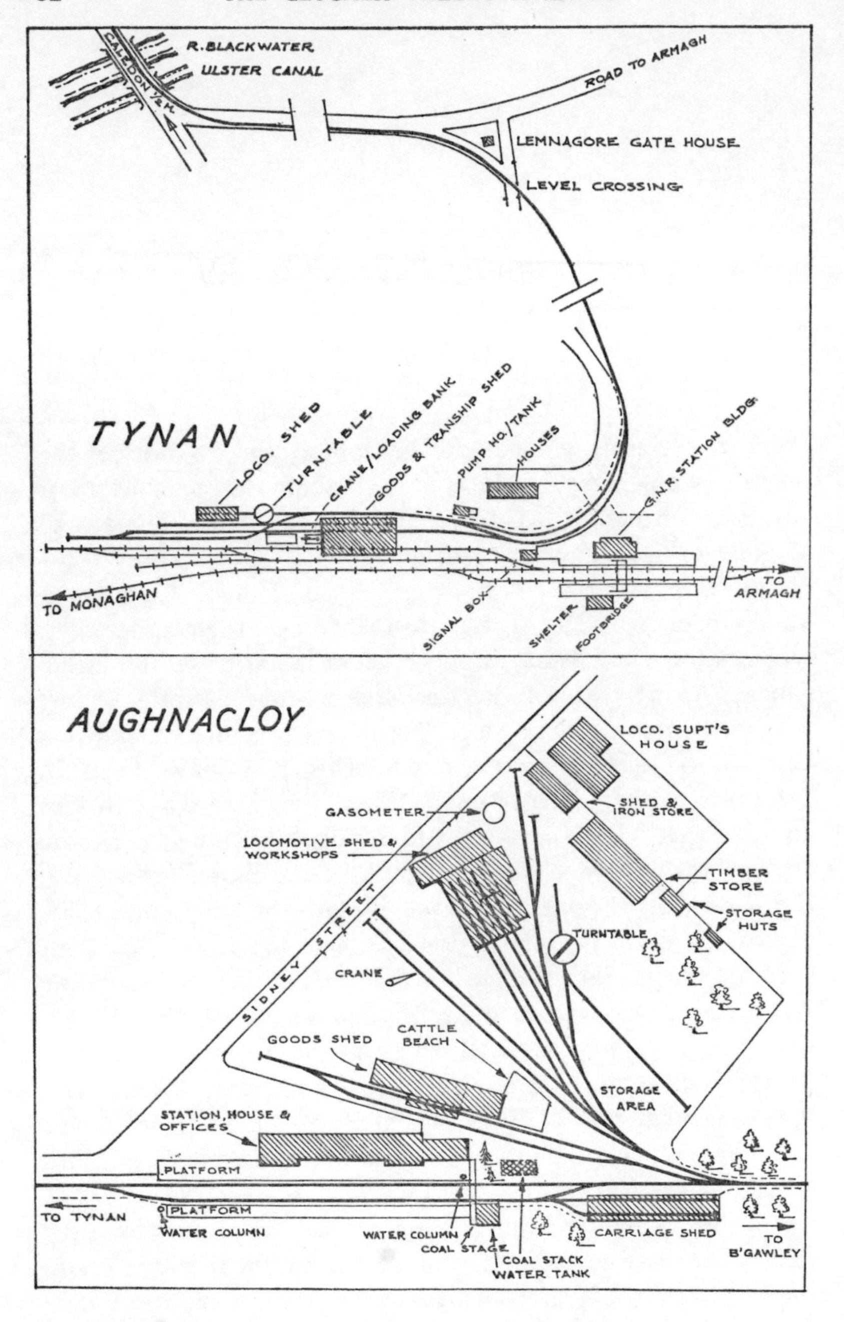
R. BLACKWATER
ULSTER CANAL
CALEDON ½ M.
ROAD TO ARMAGH
LEMNAGORE GATE HOUSE
LEVEL CROSSING
TYNAN
LOCO. SHED
TURNTABLE
CRANE/LOADING BANK
GOODS & TRANSHIP SHED
PUMP HO./TANK
HOUSES
G.N.R. STATION BLDG.
TO MONAGHAN
SIGNAL BOX
SHELTER
FOOTBRIDGE
TO ARMAGH
AUGHNACLOY
LOCO. SUPT'S HOUSE
SHED & IRON STORE
GASOMETER
LOCOMOTIVE SHED & WORKSHOPS
TIMBER STORE
STORAGE HUTS
SIDNEY STREET
TURNTABLE
CRANE
GOODS SHED
CATTLE BEACH
STORAGE AREA
STATION, HOUSE & OFFICES
PLATFORM
PLATFORM
TO TYNAN
WATER COLUMN
WATER COLUMN
COAL STAGE
COAL STACK
WATER TANK
CARRIAGE SHED
TO B'GAWLEY

structed between the back of the Great Northern station, and the private access road.

Over the tramway, the working regulations imposed 'absolute stops' at sixteen places, four of which were for down trains only and one for up trains only. In addition, to further the interests of safety, there were thirteen points at which a 4mph restriction applied, two at 6mph, and two at 10mph. A bell on the engine was used for warning; later a whistle was used.

TYNAN TO AUGHNACLOY

Leaving the Tynan platform, on a left hand curve of 2½ chains radius, the line veered from north-east to north-west, and ran in its own reservation through fields for just over a quarter of a mile, dropping at 1 in 35 towards the valley of the Blackwater River. It then emerged on the public road linking Caledon and Tynan. Here, at Lemnagore Gate Lodge the train had its first statutory stop. Momentarily dodging behind the hedge into a short diversion, the line reappeared alongside the main Armagh to Caledon road, on the other side of which was the Ulster Canal. Rising for a few yards at 1 in 40/69 on a 4½ chain curve to the right, the tram made another 'absolute stop' before crossing from the left to the right side of the main road, and on to the stone arch which carried road and rail over the canal. A 4mph limit was imposed here. A short drop at 1 in 37 carried the line on to the old road bridge spanning the River Blackwater with two 29ft and two 18ft arches. Forty-nine feet of altitude had been lost since leaving Tynan, and the line was at its lowest point, 127·5ft above Ordnance Datum.

On leaving the river bridge, road and tramway rose steeply towards the village of Caledon. Across the road, to the left, passengers saw the lodge and entrance gates and estate wall of Caledon House, seat of the Alexander family, Earls of Caledon. Among the many splendid trees rose a lofty obelisk of white stone, built in commemoration of Du Pre Alexander, second Earl, who died in 1839.

The climb that the tram had to make out of the river valley was a steep one, and slight reverse curves just after the bridge did nothing to help the engine. The gradient was 1 in 31 for 120yd, then came a short level breather, followed by 250yd of collar work at 1 in 31, which lifted the tram to the summit of Caledon's main street, 39ft above the bridge and 370yd past it. On this bank, the engines woke the echoes as the drivers thrashed them to the top. On a few occasions, when they knew that Paddy Brannigan was driving, some of the village lads got black soap from the mill, smeared the rails with it at the steepest part, and retired behind the estate wall to witness the sight and sound of the ensuing struggle. Willie Sheridan of Caledon recalls these incidents, memorable for the barrage of descriptive language directed from the engine cab towards the estate wall, and the lumps of coal hurled by Paddy's fireman. Vigorous sanding usually got the train to the top, but on at least one occasion, when between 20 and 30 wagons of coal formed a massive load, a second engine had to come to the rescue from Aughnacloy.

Entering Caledon the tramway drew towards the crown of the road. There was no station in the village, but an 'absolute stop' was made opposite the Courthouse to control speed on the 1 in 36 descent, and again at the parcels agency opposite the post office, where there was a waiting room. Then came the sharpest curve on the whole line, a right angle turn around a 1½ chain curve, which headed the tram along the road to Aughnacloy. Occasionally the engine left the rails on the curve, and had tc be rerailed by the pinch-bar.

For the next seven miles road and rail were in company, the track being on the left of the roadway on the usual raised reservation, or a few feet from it behind a hedge. A third of a mile out of Caledon, at a junction of the tree-lined roads, came Kilsampson halt, merely a nameboard. There were no long gradients in the first six miles from Tynan, apart from small gables at Wright's Hill, two miles from Tynan, entered at 1 in 38 and left down 1 in 33, and similar slopes at Fitzpatrick's Hill (2·6 miles). Ramaket halt was 3·0 miles from

Tynan at a junction with two minor roads. On this section, the working timetable called for five 'absolute stops' where the line crossed public roads.

For about four miles past Caledon the course of the River Blackwater lay a mile to the south west, and for much of the way it formed the boundary between County Tyrone and County Monaghan. From 1922 this was also the inter-state boundary between Northern Ireland and the Irish Free State. But unlike the Great Northern, neither the Clogher Valley nor its passengers suffered en route from the complications and occasional embarrassments of the border crossings, with their attendant inquisitions by the customs authorities, though Tynan was the NI customs post for Great Northern passengers between Armagh and Clones.

A halt named Curlagh (the timetables spelt it Curlough) was established 4·3 miles from Tynan. As there was promise of merchandise traffic from meal and saw mills at Mullin, on the road leading to the Monaghan village of Emyvale, the tramway company installed a platform, a goods siding and a corrugated iron parcels store here. For thirty-five years Curlagh was moderately busy. Its name was altered to Emyvale Road probably before 1914. The traffic originating from the mills was abruptly ended by The Border, and goods and parcels facilities were withdrawn from 1 August 1922. In the early days at Curlagh there was added excitement for the younger passengers on the tram, the chance of seeing a carriage and pair with liveried driver, bringing or waiting for some of the Monaghan gentry.

Beyond Curlagh, the road and its attendant tramway meandered nearly as much as the Blackwater. The tram turned left to Cumber halt (5·2 miles) on a 5 chain curve, fortunately on the level. Glenkeen halt was a mile beyond Cumber, at the edge of some marshy ground.

At a cross roads and post office, 7·0 miles from Tynan, Crilly halt had the distinction of having a platform, a cattle pen, and a siding. The village of Minterburn lay two miles away to the north. In recent years new road building has taken traffic on a straight course to Aughnacloy, but the old road that the tram followed survives in curves to west and east. On another 5 chain curve, Glencrew halt (8·2 miles) was positioned before a long fall at 1 in 31. A quarter of a mile beyond the halt, at crossing gates, the tramway plunged through the hedge into its own reservation, leaving the road for over two miles. The line entered a boggy valley, and after a few hundred yards up a 1 in 30 grade drew to an 'absolute stop' at a level crossing on the Aughnacloy—Dungannon road. A few yards beyond the gate lodge, Aughnacloy station rose in an imposing frontage of red brickwork, 9·5 miles from Tynan.

The tram ran in beside the down platform. The station façade rose, two-storeyed to the left, behind it the locomotive shed, the workshops, the sawmill, the goods shed, and the yard with its splay of sidings, must have made our grandfathers feel that here indeed was the Dundalk, if not the Doncaster, of County Tyrone. Headed by a twin to the engine which had started from Tynan three-quarters of an hour before, another train would be waiting to cross. Both platforms were busy, the administrative staff peeping with professional interest from behind the curtains of the upper windows, the uniformed porters bustling about, and the steam and sounds of metallic activity coming from the works. Beyond the station the line rose through an avenue of young trees. To the left on its hill the spires, the houses and the whitewashed backyards that ranged along the village street, formed a backcloth to the railway scene, the little village gasworks on the other side of Sidney Street even providing a further touch of industry in the heart of rural Tyrone.

Aughnacloy was a watering place for engines: high over the clump of trees to the right of the line, the stumpy sails of the windpump revolved rapidly, lifting water from the station well to the water tank, on its massive stone-built base at the end of the up platform. There the two lines of rails were spanned by an overhead gantry. On this ran a pair of underslung, wooden hutches which were loaded with coal from a bucket hoist, and which when positioned over the engine bunkers, obligingly dropped a quarter of a ton of fuel into place. The coal bucket was bogied across to the hoist by a few yards of rail from a neat coal stack. The coaling plant was shielded from the sight of passengers by a dignified trio of tall fir trees. The line was now at a height of 170ft OD.

AUGHNACLOY TO BALLYGAWLEY

Leaving Aughnacloy, with a full head of steam, the engine crew faced three miles of climbing, which was to bring the tram to Tullyvar summit. Once past the corrugated-iron carriage shed, the line lifted to the gradient, 1 in 31/34/64, which swept the line smartly out of the hollow and brought it alongside the public road again, at the northern end of the town. Here the old fever hospital stood, built in 1843 and a grim reminder of the Famine days and of the cholera and typhus plagues that followed.

Keeping to the right hand side of the thoroughfare, the line rose 90ft in the next mile and a half. Ahead rose Tullyvar hill, down trains drew to another of the 'absolute stops', and the main road swung across the tramway; the rails kept a straight course, separated by a hedge from a minor road and immediately entered Tullyvar halt (11·7 miles). Here was a crossing keeper's house, a platform, and beyond it a crossing loop. To the left of the line, after 1915, a siding trailed in from stone bins and a rock crushing plant which served a large limestone quarry nearby. This was opened by the County Council for road metal and later came into the private ownership of the Hadden family. Tullyvar halt seems to have been without a shelter hut until early 1909, probably the gate lodge doorway and kitchen offered hospitality before then.

Half a mile past the halt, a minor road made a level crossing; there was an attendant gate lodge, a speed limit of 6mph, and a short 1 in 31 drop, followed by a final grinding rise to the top of the hill, at 1 in 31/80. Here the line was in the deep rock cutting that McCrea and McFarland had found difficult to blast out; there was an awkward left hand 7 chain—5 chain curve, leading into a right-hander of 8 chains over the hump at 358ft OD. There the tram threaded its only overbridge, which took a minor road.

Ahead, an 8 chain curve led downwards, with a 6mph speed check on the 1 in 31 fall towards what everyone called Dempsey's Crossing, but which was officially Tullywinney Gate Lodge. Here the line regained the roadside at 307ft OD. All down trains had a compulsory halt, while the crossing keeper stood in the roadway and controlled traffic with a red flag. The rails crossed to the right of the road, and for the next quarter mile dropped at 1 in 32, 30, 82, eased and fell again at 1 in 30 as it led into a right-angled, 7 chain curve that swept into Ballygawley station. It was a savage climb in the reverse direction, aided only by the non-stop passage of Dempsey's Crossing.

Ballygawley (13·6 miles) had the traditional brick station to the right of the line; the main road was behind it. There was a passing loop, two platforms which were offset, a goods yard, a small carriage shed, the permanent way inspector's office, and workshop. There were cattle pens that were always busy on fair days. In the permanent way shops, the bearded pw inspector Hugh Martin held sway, while his wife looked after a hotel and shop 'in the town'. By the time that the tramway was built, the brewery, the distillery, and the glove-making industry of the early years of the century were fading into history.

BALLYGAWLEY TO FIVEMILETOWN

Once around the Ballygawley curve, the tramway was fairly aimed in the direction of Maguiresbridge and, for the remaining 23 miles, its course was more or less to the south-west.

To the west of the village, the Ballygawley River meandered on its way to meet the Blackwater. Railway construction and later road realignments diverted its course for a short distance, a quarter of a mile beyond the station. Over the centuries the river had filled its valley with gravel, and since gravel formed

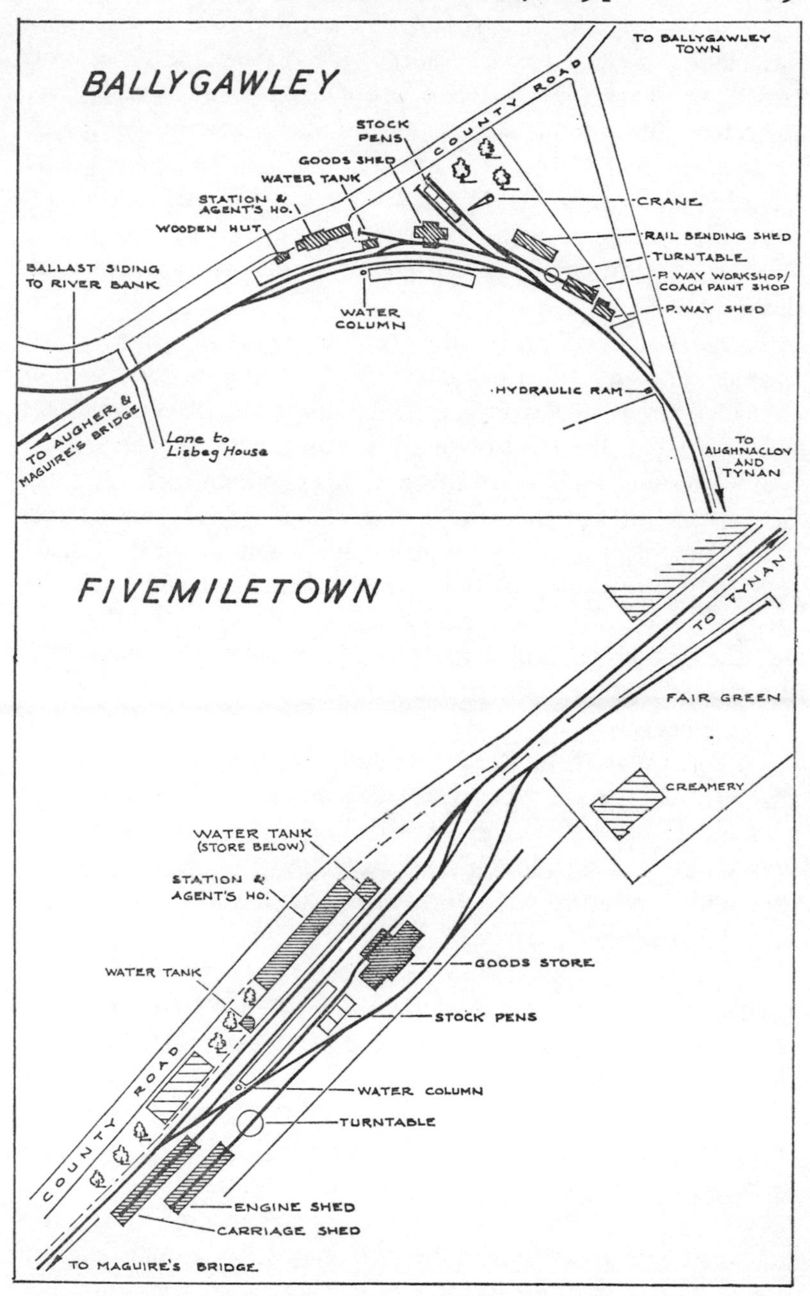
BALLYGAWLEY
TO BALLYGAWLEY TOWN
COUNTY ROAD
STOCK PENS
GOODS SHED
WATER TANK
STATION & AGENT'S HO.
WOODEN HUT
CRANE
RAIL BENDING SHED
TURNTABLE
P. WAY WORKSHOP/ COACH PAINT SHOP
P. WAY SHED
BALLAST SIDING TO RIVER BANK
WATER COLUMN
HYDRAULIC RAM
TO AUGHER & MAGUIRE'S BRIDGE
Lane to Lisbeg House
TO AUGHNACLOY AND TYNAN
FIVEMILETOWN
TO TYNAN
FAIR GREEN
CREAMERY
WATER TANK (STORE BELOW)
STATION & AGENT'S HO.
GOODS STORE
WATER TANK
STOCK PENS
COUNTY ROAD
WATER COLUMN
TURNTABLE
ENGINE SHED
CARRIAGE SHED
TO MAGUIRE'S BRIDGE

the readiest, if not the best ballast, the Clogher Valley at some date laid a siding from the north side of the line down into the river bed. Wagons were propelled down there, gravel shovelled into them, and they were then laboriously hauled up a steep and unrecorded gradient back to the points. The Board of Trade were never asked to approve the siding (though the Tullyvar stone siding got official blessing), but in spite of that omission it served its purpose and on some fair days even did duty as a carriage siding.

From the siding points, the tramway and the county road parted company for three-quarters of a mile, a level section in which the tramway crossed the Ballygawley River by a box girder bridge. The level of the line was 213ft OD. The section was succeeded by a sharp lift at 1 in 31, which took the tram through a cutting and over a wide level crossing at a cross-roads. Beyond the gates and attendant gatehouse was Lisdoart halt, with a wooden platform, and a hut sheltered by laurel bushes (14·4 miles). New roadworks have obliterated the halt, but the gatehouse still stands. Half a mile to the south was the cluster of houses called Lisdoart, with a large flax mill and water wheel.

Fifteen miles from Tynan the line left the roadside, and in this diversion a stopping place was made at Annaghilla level crossing (15·5 miles) where a secondary road went north towards the houses, church, and water mill of Ballynasaggart. Annaghilla received a platform and a shelter hut towards the end of 1911.

The roadside was regained just before Roughan halt (16·7 miles), which had a passing loop and cattle pen. This provided the only crossing place in the 6½ mile stretch between Ballygawley and Clogher.

Apart from a dip into a small stream valley at 1 in 35/37, there was an absence of noteworthy gradients until the tram approached Augher. At a crossroads, the main street was traversed on the level, an unpractical place to protect by gates on account of the width of the roadway, so a compulsory stop was required of both up and down trains. A short distance

BALLYGAWLEY

(Above) *McCann's Crossing, ¼ mile south of station. Castlederg engine, running bunker first, takes a short train towards Aughnacloy*; (below) *Nos 2 and 1 double-head a train about 1910, past the permanent way yard and workshops*

Page 72

AUGHER AND BEYOND

(Above) *No 1 makes a compulsory stop in the street at Augher, shortly after leaving the station, about 1900*; (below) *Ballyvadden ballast pit siding. No 6* Erne *passes with a train for Fivemiletown, 3 May 1938*

beyond the crossroads, the station was sited on the right of the track. A siding ran to the Augher creamery which was adjacent to the station.

After Augher the tramway kept to the right of the roadway. Summer Hill halt, later named Farranetra after the townland, was 19·2 miles out, beside the bridge across the Fury River which gave No 4 engine its name. Here the line was diverted from the road for two miles, to avoid the hill on which the village of Clogher was built. Along the diversion was a succession of gated level crossings over roads converging on the village. Clogher station (20·0 miles) was a two-storey brick building, more than ample for its function. There was a passing loop, and two platforms though only one was in regular use. For merchandise traffic there was a goods store and sidings.

Shortly beyond Clogher, came a halt named Carryclogher (20·9 miles) at a level crossing, while Findermore halt was provided where the tramway regained the roadside. The rails were now on the left side of the carriageway. A 1 in 32 rise for 300yd brought the passengers to Ballagh halt (23·3 miles) sited near a small lough. A short way beyond, came a summit at 336ft OD, which was followed by a long fall at 1 in 226 for nearly half a mile. Kiltermon halt (25·2 miles) was at 295ft OD, situated at a junction of the main and two minor roads, and was followed by a five chain left-hander on a 1 in 64 climb. From there the tram faced 2½ miles of almost unbroken ascent over varying gradients, a long 1 in 38, a brief dip at 1 in 34, and a climb at 1 in 30 past Ballyvadden halt (26·6 miles). This was the nearest halt to Blessingbourne, the home of two of the company chairmen, which stood amongst extensive woods some way to the north.

Still on the left of the roadway, the tram breasted the hill into the long street of Fivemiletown, the rails swung towards the middle of the road, the street rose and the rails with it. Among the houses, the tramway attained its highest point, the summit at 388·5ft OD being 30ft above the Tullyvar crest. Once over the gable, the down grade was 1 in 41 through the street. The Fair Green, market house, and creamery were passed on the left, the rails rose at an imperceptible 1 in 448, and slanted into the station 27·5 miles from Tynan.

Through Fivemiletown, a speed restriction of 4mph was imposed on all trains 'in going into and out of centre of street' according to the working timetable. The street was narrow, the footpaths none too wide, and in the tram's passage there was inevitably some interference with village traffic. Horses particularly had to be controlled to prevent their bolting. Before construction was completed, the far-seeing people of Fivemiletown attempted to have the line diverted as it had been at Clogher, a signed petition was presented to the directors, but the effort was unsuccessful. Once permission had been obtained for the laying of the line through the street, deviation from that route would have meant added expense. The passage of the tram contributed nothing to traffic, for there were no stops en route, and energetic passengers were dissuaded from joining or leaving moving vehicles.

Fivemiletown station stood between the tramway and the village street, its architecture a twin of that of Clogher. The station was the second largest on the system, there was an extensive goods yard, an engine shed, and a siding to the pig market. Some of the trains terminated at or started from here, where the end-on junction came between Tramways Nos 1 and 2, as defined in the Order in Council.

FIVEMILETOWN TO MAGUIRESBRIDGE

Over the remaining 9½ miles to Maguiresbridge the line was mostly in its own right of way, either close to the road, or in cross-country 'diversions' away from the highway. The watershed between the Blackwater and Colebrooke River systems was now a short way to the east, and the tramway was now in the area drained by the headwaters of the westerly flowing Colebrooke River. Generally speaking therefore, as on part of the West Clare Railway as defined by Percy French 'all the way home' was 'downhill'.

For the first one and three-quarter miles the line was on a down-grade, with short stretches of 1 in 32 and 1 in 35, and a quarter mile of 1 in 30 to speed things on their way. Just under half a mile from Fivemiletown station, the line crossed the county boundary between Tyrone and Fermanagh. Passengers looked across the road to the wooded grounds of Corcreevy and Cranbrooke, and Cranbrooke halt was sited 28·4 miles from Tynan. It was hereabouts that the board heard that a tram had killed a cow during July 1887, but immediately repudiated any liability though they decided 'to refund to the owner the amount received by the sale of the skin'.

About half a mile beyond Cranbrooke, a halt was opened in the townland of Tattynuckle after a request by one George Johnston who lived there. The board agreed to his request on 8 April 1890, for a trial period of six months. It seems never to have attained the status of mention in the working timetables, though the public timetables referred to it. It cannot have been remunerative for, on 15 April 1897, the board decided to omit it 'from future timetables'.

Beyond Tattynuckle the line skirted the shore of Corralongford Lough, a three chain right hander being followed by a long five chain curve to the left, and that by four chain right hand bend. On the straight beyond these convolutions was Corralongford halt (29·4 miles), with level crossing gates over a minor road. The line continued alongside the road through the townlands of Tattenaheglish and Tullykenneye, then coming up to Killarbran halt (30·2 miles) in the townland of that name. There was a set of gates here until 1913, when they were replaced by cattle grids.

For 1¼ miles after Killarbran halt, the tramway deviated from the road, and along that stretch crossed the Colebrooke River by a single arch stone bridge. The river flowed from the Slieve Beagh hills to the east, and provided the tramway with gradients of 1 in 32/34 as it crossed the valley. On the deviation was Claraghy halt (31·0 miles). The ground was underlain by thick peat, a secure foundation for the line was difficult to

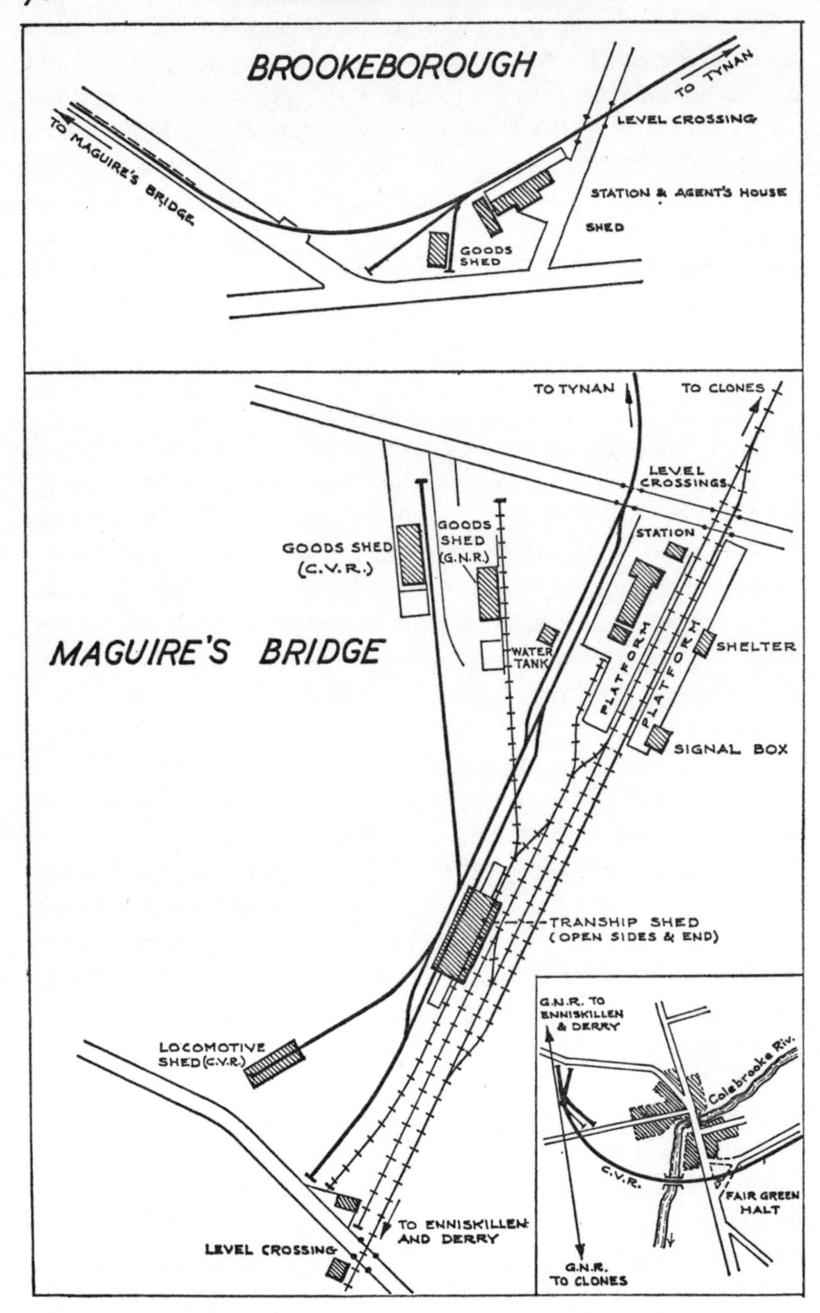
BROOKEBOROUGH
TO TYNAN
LEVEL CROSSING
TO MAGUIRE'S BRIDGE
STATION & AGENT'S HOUSE
SHED
GOODS SHED
TO TYNAN
TO CLONES
LEVEL CROSSINGS
STATION
GOODS SHED (G.N.R.)
GOODS SHED (C.V.R.)
MAGUIRE'S BRIDGE
WATER TANK
PLATFORM
PLATFORM
SHELTER
SIGNAL BOX
TRANSHIP SHED (OPEN SIDES & END)
LOCOMOTIVE SHED (C.V.R.)
TO ENNISKILLEN AND DERRY
LEVEL CROSSING
G.N.R. TO ENNISKILLEN & DERRY
Colebrooke Riv.
C.V.R.
FAIR GREEN HALT
G.N.R. TO CLONES

obtain, and as a result the working timetable provided for a speed restriction of 10mph 'over Colebrooke Bog'.

The tramway rejoined the road in the townland named Derryloman, and it was here that the company built Colebrooke station (31·4 miles), deriving its name from the nearby estate of the Brooke family. It was a Sir Henry Brooke that received the land as a reward for his part in the defence of Donegal in the 1641 Rising during the Cromwellian Plantation. His descendant, Sir Basil Brooke Bt was chairman of the Committee of Management of the Clogher Valley Railway from 1929 until 1941. The Brooke estate was heavily planted with timber, and the woods and deer park covered several square miles of country to the north of the tramway. Colebrooke station was substantially brick-built, with a single platform to the right of the line, and was provided with a siding and a cattle pen. While not a private station, it had some of the attributes of one. Events soon proved that it was making no useful contribution to the revenue of the tramway, and its status was lowered to that of a halt, the board deciding that its care should devolve on the stationmaster at Brookeborough, while the crossing keeper went to live in the station house.

Shortly beyond Colebrooke, the line returned to the roadside, and over the next two miles the public were served by the roadside halts of Stonepark (31·6 miles) and Skeoge (32·8 miles), both situated at junctions with minor roads. Past Skeoge the tram drew to an 'absolute stop' before daring an oblique crossing of the road preliminary to entering a half mile diversion which avoided Brookeborough village, and contained Brookeborough station (33·5 miles). This had a single platform, a station building that matched Ballygawley, and a goods spur. Where the diversion ended was a further compulsory stop, the line crossed to the left of the road, and continued there for three-quarters of a mile.

The companionship of road and tramway ended with a smart five chain curve, where the line veered into the longest of the diversions: a stretch of two and a half miles through fields, with two level crossings over minor roads. At the first crossing was Aghavea halt (34·7 miles). Though it was listed in timetables from 1887, Aghavea had no shelter hut until 1899. Gradients along this section were gentle and there was a welcome absence of sharp curves.

Just over a mile from its western terminus the tramway rejoined the roadside. The village of Maguiresbridge was in sight, the tram came to a compulsory stop at the Fair Green, where there was a halt (36·5 miles) followed by a level crossing. In the early working timetables this halt was named Maguiresbridge (Town) which was logical since it was nearer the metropolis than the actual terminus. The rails were on a 14 chain curve to the right, the Colebrooke River was crossed again by a stone built arch, and on a gentler curve the Clogher Valley tram ran in towards the Great Northern's station, with a level crossing and gates barring the way into the goods yard shared by the two companies. As at Tynan, the Clogher Valley made use of the Great Northern's passenger station facilities, but there were small engine, carriage, and goods sheds, a roofed exchange platform for goods, and a water tank fed by a windmill. The height of the line above sea level was 20ft more than at Tynan, at 196ft OD.

WATER AND LIGHT

The windmills were for many years a lineside characteristic of the Clogher Valley, lofty lattice towers crowned by a multi-bladed wheel that faced the wind, and lifted water from wells or streams and pumped it for storage to the station tanks. The original design of locomotive with condensers needed a prodigal use of water, as the contents of the side tanks heated en route. Thus, at the opening there were six watering points on the 37 miles, five of them fed by windmills. The sixth, at Ballygawley was supplied by two hydraulic rams that drew water from a stream in Buchanan's field, and sent it several hundred yards along a pipe to the station tank.

The Tynan windmill pumped water for a distance of about a quarter of a mile from a deep well near a stream. The well was liable to go dry during a long summer, and when this happened the stream was diverted into the well in an effort to augment the supply at the expense of purity. The tower was very high, and it gave trouble in stormy weather. The minute book records that in February 1905 the windmill had been blown down, and was to be replaced. More than once, high winds blew the wheel and blades off the top of the tower, and they were destroyed in the fall. In 1917 the Irish Railways Executive Committee sanctioned the purchase of a 4hp Crossley oil engine and three-cylinder ram pump to take the place of the windmill. The uncrowned tower remained a feature of the landscape for many years afterwards.

The Aughnacloy windmill was situated over its own well in the spinney at the back of the water tank. The sails were removed during the 1914–18 war and the pump replaced by a double-acting one in the running shed, powered by the works oil engine, and drawing from a deep well below the saw mill.

The Clogher tank was fed by a windmill set on a tower built of pitch-pine. It took water from a well, and later from the Blackwater. In September 1898 a storm destroyed it, and it had to be replaced. In April 1903 a hand-pump was bought at a cost of £5, probably to augment the supply. About 1930, the Clogher windmill was dismantled and its place was taken by a 1½hp Lister petrol engine driving a centrifugal pump, which was housed in a sleeper and felt shed.

Fivemiletown's windmill was out of sight of the station, for it was sited at a lake, whence water was sent nearly a mile to the station tank. Some time during the 1914–18 war, the windmill was taken down, as a local piped supply had become available.

The fifth windmill was at Maguiresbridge, and had a wooden tower. In spite of storm damage on at least two occasions (1899 and 1903 receive mention in the minute books), it remained in use until the line was closed. It drew water from a small well near the river bank. When the river was in flood after heavy rains it washed sand and gravel into the well, and blocked the foot valve and suction pipe. A fitter had then to be dispatched to attend to the matter, since the tank would only hold 5 to 6 days' supply.

The water tanks were of 8,500 gallons capacity, with the exception of that at Ballygawley which was about half the size of the others. The large tanks had radiused corners, and were carried on supporting walls of heavy masonry; the lighter Ballygawley tank was on a brick tower. The space within the walls was utilised for storage, a door and a window were built into the walls. The tower at Aughnacloy had a half loft built inside, and was used to keep oil and cleaning waste.

The premises at Aughnacloy were lit by oil at first, but later by acetylene gas. When a private concern, the Aughnacloy Gas Light Company, built a gasworks in a field across the road from the railway workshops, coal gas was purchased from them, the supply beginning in 1899. Three years later the railway's own pipes were found to be in such bad order that they had to be replaced. The agreement with the local gas company terminated in 1909, and the company again made their own acetylene. Their gasometer was near the Sydney Street wall, alongside the sawmill and locomotive workshops.

Fivemiletown changed from oil to acetylene in 1904, but later took electricity from the local supply, though the old gasometer remained until the final auction. Latterly Ballygawley was electrically lit. Clogher and Brookeborough relied on acetylene, while Augher depended on oil lamps.

THE WORKSHOPS

The Aughnacloy workshops were sited between the passenger station and Sidney Street, on the south side of the triangular plot of ground owned by the company. The main buildings were 131ft in overall length, robustly built of dark grey dressed freestone, the doorways and windows being relieved by brick facings. Two pairs of tracks led into the workshops from the yard sidings, the left-hand pair passed through two arched doorways set in a gable 31ft in width, to enter the carriage and wagon shops, while the right-hand pair of tracks went through a similar gable into the locomotive running shed and repair shops. These two parts of the main workshop block were separated by a stone wall. The slated roof had glass lights, and four tall rectangular flue pipes led smoke from the engine side through the roof. Four engines could be accommodated in the running shed.

Behind the actual workshops a cross wall formed a barrier from the stores, thc locomotive superintendent's office, and the smithy. On the southwest side of the locomotive shops, a lean-to roof, with a pitched extension covered the sawmill and the boiler and engine house, and was roofed with corrugated iron.

A small building to the west of the main workshop block housed the gas plant, and another store. In later years, it was adjacent to the garden of the general manager's house, and his coal store was accommodated in a part of the building.

Being remote from supporting firms, the workshops had to be self-contained. They were roomy, but lacked equipment, so that when Gustav Akerlind took charge in 1889 one of his first requests was for sheer-legs for lifting the engines. In 1909 he persuaded the directors to allow him to buy some machine tools, and obtained a surfacing and screwcutting lathe, a vertical pillar drilling machine, and a power hacksaw.

A steam engine powered the workshops for the first 32 years. In 1919 it was replaced by a new 50hp Crossley anthracite gas engine. Its place was later taken by a semi-diesel oil engine, a second-hand 40hp Blackstone, type FLSI, No 174924. The shops had two iron turning lathes, one about 6 feet between centres, the other about 3 feet. There were also two radial drilling machines, a McDowall planing machine, a Kershaw shaping machine, and a wheel turning lathe. The fitters' shop had two Allday & Onions hearths, one used by the blacksmith, the other by the boilermaker; there were two portable hearths in the carriage shops. The sawmill had a rack and pinion saw bench open to the air, for planing timber out of the log, and also a McDowell circular saw bench with adjustable table and mortising machine attachment. There was also a McDowell planing machine, a wood-boring machine by the same maker, a wood turning machine with a wood bed 6½ feet in length, and a power-driven sandstone.

An American sand-drying plant was bought in 1901, and was housed in a small shed at the end of the tank wall. Sand was filled into a funnel casing, inside which a bell-shaped stove was situated. The dry sand trickled down a half-inch gap, and was screened. The dry sand was used both for the engines, and for the dry toilets at stations.

The permanent way workshop was at Ballygawley from the opening until 1929. It was a wooden building on a concrete floor. Power was supplied by a paraffin oil engine, which drove a circular saw directly. When the saw was not in use, the drive was taken to shafting, which worked a small drilling machine, a boring machine, a power hacksaw, and a rail bending machine. Some distance away from the workshop, and overlooking a stretch of meadow was 'Martin's Hut', a two-storey wooden building on the ground floor of which was a small store; while the top floor reached by a flight of wooden steps at the back, formed Inspector Hugh Martin's office. Maintenance of the permanent way was not the only responsibility, for Martin's aegis extended to the upkeep of all the buildings on the system, with the exception of the Aughnacloy workshops.

THE LINE IS OPEN

The Clogher Valley timetables were based on the times at which the Great Northern trains passed through the two termini. Tynan station witnessed Great Northern connections to Portadown and Belfast in one direction, and Clones and Cavan in the other. Maguiresbridge led to Enniskillen and Londonderry in the down direction, and Clones in the up direction. On the tramway, the two major towns of Aughnacloy and Fivemiletown played important roles in the timetable workings, since each was 9½ miles from the nearest terminal. The terminals were in fact at unimportant villages which made little contribution to the traffic of the system. Nevertheless Tynan and Maguiresbridge needed facilities for stabling motive power in the original conception of tram workings, and for this purpose both had small engine sheds, in addition to those at Aughnacloy and at Fivemiletown. In Clogher Valley parlance, 'down' trams ran from Tynan, 'up' trams from Maguiresbridge. The working timetables after 1890 referred to both up and down *trains* by numbers, thus '*No 2 Up Train*' in 1891 was the 9.55am from Aughnacloy to Tynan.

In the first summer of the tramway, the initial move of the day came from Fivemiletown, at 6.21am, the train calling at all stations and halts to Tynan, where it arrived at 8.55am. A Great Northern train that had left Clones at 8.20am for Belfast, was en route from Glaslough when the Clogher Valley train drew in to Tynan, and was on its way at 9.5am.

Passengers who had made the 8.55am arrival at Tynan, but who were going south, had time to kill, for the first Great Northern train to Monaghan and Clones was the 8.50am ex Belfast, which did not leave Tynan until 10.40am. Their sojourn in Tynan's baronial hall was enlivened by sounds of Clogher Valley activity while the train engine shunted the yard prior to leaving at 10.50am with passengers from the Belfast train. That was the first down train from Tynan; it ran to Aughnacloy, in 49 minutes, and terminated there.

The second train to move in the morning was the 8.7am out of Aughnacloy, which thrashed its way over Tullyvar, and out of hearing towards Fivemiletown. Its peculiar departure time was determined by the 8.6am arrival time of the 6.21am Fivemiletown—Tynan working, and it reached Fivemiletown at 9.47am.

From Maguiresbridge, the first departure was at 9.57am, This Clogher Valley train ran to Aughnacloy, where it arrived seven minutes after an Enniskillen—Clones train had left. at 12.38pm.

The first arrival at Maguiresbridge was at 12.40pm, a train that had left Fivemiletown at 11.44am, probably the same set of stock that had come in there at 9.47am from Aughnacloy This arrival at Maguiresbridge connected comfortably with a Great Northern departure at 12.55pm to Enniskillen and Londonderry, and not unreasonably with a 1.37pm train to Clones. The tram engine worked the yard at Maguiresbridge, and after tying on its carriages and wagons, left again at 1.45pm to make a leisurely voyage to Aughnacloy, taking 2 hours 51 minutes for the 27½ miles.

The 11.39am arrival at Aughnacloy of the first down train from Tynan made a set available for a departure at 12.43pm for Fivemiletown, reached at 2.23pm, half an hour before the 11.45am ex Maguiresbridge came through. Fivemiletown yard was worked, and the train made up the 3.29pm to Maguiresbridge; it got there at 4.25pm, when passengers could cross the platform to a Great Northern train that was due away at 4.37pm, and which had connections to Greenore (due at 7.40pm) and to Dublin (due at 9.35pm). From Greenore a night steamer left for Holyhead at 8.45pm.

In Maguiresbridge the Clogher Valley train rested from 4.25pm until its departure at 6.20pm, nine minutes after a Dundalk—Clones—Enniskillen train had left.

Back at Tynan, the Clogher Valley side of the station slumbered in peace, in spite of the passage of a northbound broad gauge train at 1.11pm. Silence reigned until nearly a quarter to three, when the beat of the 1.56pm from Aughnacloy was heard coming up the bank from Caledon. The Great Northern woke in its turn and the 2.15pm from Clones came through, left at 3.1pm, and was soon followed by the 1.30pm ex Belfast which left for Monaghan at 3.13pm. The tram gathered its patrons from these two long distance trains, tied on any wagons that were ready to go, and set forth at 3.23pm on a working that ended at Aughnacloy at 4.12pm.

Tynan's activity was renewed three hours later, when the 5.11pm ex Aughnacloy arrived at 6pm. This connected with a Belfast—Clones train which had left the northern city at 4.40pm and was timed to be into Clones at 7.20pm. Passengers from the Clogher Valley had to suffer a weary wait of 64 minutes until the 6.10pm ex Clones came in, and they did not see the lights of Belfast until 9pm. They could, if they were so minded, catch a cab to the cross-channel boat, which left at 9.30pm and went to Ardrossan Monday to Friday, and to Glasgow on Saturday.

Tynan's narrow gauge labours ended for the day with a departure at 6.30pm. This was a noteworthy train, for it worked the whole length of the line, getting to Maguiresbridge at 10.5pm. Once there, unsuspecting voyagers need not expect to see the green of a Great Northern engine, for the last Enniskillen train had gone through 40 minutes earlier. In 1887 there was still no carriage shed, so the train engine left the carriages and wagons in the open, took itself off to its own shed, and all was ready to make up the 9.57am train of the following day.

This basic timetable of the summer of 1887 gave a reasonably good service. Though it was not economic to synchronise with all Great Northern departures at the terminals, a fair compromise was arrived at. Aughnacloy folk saw five trains leave in each direction during the course of the day, and the terminal stations had the three arrivals and departures that were characteristic of minor lines.

But that was not all, for there were the fair days to consider, with their mass movements of people and animals. On the second Friday of each month there was Ballygawley Fair, which drew in dealers from outside the region, and a Clogher Valley train left Tynan at 7.0am to join the service 8.7am down from Aughnacloy. No doubt an empty stock working would come out to Tynan to form this 7am special. In the return direction, a fair special left Ballygawley at 6pm, terminating at Aughnacloy at 6.25pm. There was no connection forward to Tynan.

Enniskillen Fair was on the tenth of each month, and anyone attending it had to rise horribly early. An all stations special left Aughnacloy at 4.14am, and arrived at Maguiresbridge at 6.55am. The Great Northern ran a special that left Maguiresbridge at 7.5am.

Tempo is a small village 7 miles west of Fivemiletown and about the same distance north-east of Maguiresbridge, with a population of around 350. A fair was held there on the last Tuesday of the month and it was a sufficiently important market to warrant a special working on the tramway. The same 7am departure from Tynan, that served the Ballygawley Fair, was worked to Fivemiletown. Return traffic that had walked the road from Tempo was catered for by holding back the departure from Fivemiletown of the 1.45pm working from Maguiresbridge, so that it left at 3.20pm rather than 2.56pm. Its arrival at Aughnacloy was correspondingly later.

Clones had an important fair on the last Thursday of the month. It could be reached rather late in the day from Tynan, but a more satisfactory connection was arranged through Maguiresbridge. A special left Aughnacloy at the unearthly hour of 3.47am, and disturbed the sleep of persons down the length of the valley until Maguiresbridge was reached at 6.11am. A regular Great Northern working, the 6.20am from Enniskillen, was timed out of Maguiresbridge at 6.38am.

These fair day specials were, as on the County Donegal and the Lough Swilly lines, and on the Castlederg tramway nearer home, a most important adjunct to the business and social activities of the day and the region. Before the tram service started, cattle and sheep were driven long miles by road to and from the fair greens, while people made their way there on foot, by bicycle, and in farm carts and traps. For those that could afford it, the advent of the Clogher Valley tram made a hard life a little easier.

The summer timetable of 1887 required engines to be shedded at Aughnacloy, Fivemiletown, and Maguiresbridge. For the following winter, some modifications were made. The working timetable issued on 1 September 1887 indicates rationalisation of the service to Maguiresbridge. A morning run was made there, leaving Fivemiletown at 8.48am, and arriving at 9.35am to connect with a train to Clones. In the down direction this was followed by two through workings from Tynan to Maguiresbridge. The first of these left Tynan at 9.45am, and was given 3 hours to cover the length of the tramway; the second left Tynan at 1.51pm and was into Maguiresbridge at 5.31pm. The last down train of the day was the 6.30pm ex Tynan, which finished at Fivemiletown, thereby omitting the late summer entry to Maguiresbridge and obviating the need to shed an engine there.

Up trains were based at Aughnacloy: the first to Tynan left at 7.23am. Two Maguiresbridge—Tynan workings followed, the 9.54am and the 1.45pm, taking 199 and 241 minutes on the through journey, with ample time to shunt the yards at Fivemiletown and Aughnacloy. The train that arrived at Maguiresbridge at 5.31pm spent 44 minutes there, returning up the line at 6.15pm and ending operations for the night at Aughnacloy at 8.20pm.

The special market trains were modified, and gave later starts for those joining them. Enniskillen Fair was served by a train that left Fivemiletown at 4.10am, reached Clogher at 4.45am, and left at 5am to run to Maguiresbridge in 90 minutes.

Fivemiletown also supplied the train that served the Fivemiletown Fair, a working that set out down the line at 6.55am, spent from 7.41am to 7.50am at Maguiresbridge, and then trundled back to Fivemiletown with folk in search of a bargain.

Ballygawley and Aughnacloy Fairs were catered for by early trains between Aughnacloy and Fivemiletown. The former station was left at 7.15am, and the train spent only from 8.41am to 8.50am at Fivemiletown before making the return journey to Aughnacloy.

TRAINS FOR THE TWELFTH

Even in that first summer, the problem of peak requirements by passengers became apparent. The Orangemen held their 'big day'—the 12 July Demonstration, in the park at Caledon estate, and it was a public holiday in every sense of the word for many people in the district: an enormous 'get-together' that allowed friends and relations to meet and eat, to listen to a share of political speechifying and local gossip and to go home to their farms and villages late in the summer evening, full of stories. Before the tram was there, they had walked miles, cycled farther, and journeyed as far again in farm carts and pony traps. Now they could travel in comfort, think less of the weather, and bring the youngest of the family as well. The Clogher Valley Tramway recognised the economic potential of the occasion; they rose to meet the challenge, and realised that their thirteen carriages would be far from sufficient for the demand. But no passengers could be turned away, and the directors considered the situation, advised as to their course of action by D. J. Stewart. Had they referred their problem to the Board of Trade, they might have been sternly dissuaded from using goods vehicles, which was in their minds, in spite of the fact that every vehicle they had was vacuum braked. So they avoided confrontation with authority, hoped that nothing serious would happen, and ordered Stewart to minute 'Cattle trucks if necessary to be fitted up for carrying passengers on 12th July'. There was no accident and no reason why there should have been, for the press of people were far safer locked in the confines of a high-sided truck, than on a verandah-ended coach. The procedure was followed year after year, the cattle wagons were cleaned out and limewashed, and the only disadvantage that the willing passengers suffered was their inability to open the doors themselves. Passenger brake vans and even open wagons were also pressed into service. In this practice the Clogher Valley was by no means alone: the Ballycastle Railway employed open wagons on Lammas Fair Day, and the Donegal Railway put Orangemen into open wagons without incident. The passengers were tolerant of the novelty, and many of them likely recalled that it was only forty years since their grandfathers knew no other form of rail travel.

Page 89

FIVEMILETOWN STREET

(Above) *The diesel railcar pursued by a lorry, at the summit of the railway, 25 June 1937*; (below) *The Castlederg engine on the downgrade to the station, about 1937*

Page 90

FIVEMILETOWN STATION

(Above) Blackwater *at the water tank, with Driver George Leany. About 1939;* (below) *The Castlederg engine takes water. Goods shed on left, carriage shed in distance*

FIREWORK DISPLAY

On the heavy gradients, working for short distances with full regulator and a long cut off was commonplace. The blast lifted the fire, and a torrent of sparks flew from the funnels. Thatched roofs were more common than they are today and at a meeting of the board, held a fortnight after the opening day, Stewart reported 'the firing of premises', listing no less than six persons: J. Kyle, W. Brady, J. Wright, Wm. Maxwell, Wm. Trimble, and R. Trimble. He went on to recite details of the fire that had burned the wagon of tow, and to which the *Tyrone Constitution* had referred before the formal opening. More than one wagon seems to have been damaged, and the minutes mention that a box of bacon was incinerated as well.

Of immediate concern was the burning of the cottages. In four instances settlement was privately effected, but Wright's case was postponed 'to obtain a reduction of claim', and the company rebuilt Robert Trimble's house for him and paid him £15 to cover the loss of his furntiure and to compensate him for the inconvenience he had suffered. The long-term implications were obvious enough. The directors were concerned at the fiery havoc, and immediate steps were taken by the locomotive department to modify the blast pipes. What actually was done is not detailed in the board minutes, but it seems to have been reasonably effective, though a serious fire occurred in March 1889 when sparks set John Stinson's farm house at Milberry on fire. Stinson was justifiably annoyed and claimed compensation, only to find the directors refuse it in June. He pressed his claim until, in January 1890, the board authorised David Stewart to settle for not more than £200. A compromise was reached at £175.

Trials with spark arresters continued for two or three years, and in October 1889, authorisation was given to Akerlind 'to alter style of spark arresters on one engine and place the same inside the smokebox and report on the working of same.' The changes seem to have been successful, for there are no further reports of serious lineside fires. The half-yearly report noted in March 1890 that 'To guard against any further accident, extra precautions have now been taken, the style of Blast Pipe on the Engines having been altered, and the most improved pattern of spark arresters adopted.'

IMPROVEMENTS BY AKERLIND

Passing reference has already been made to Gustav Akerlind as locomotive superintendent. His arrival followed R. H. Weatherburn's resignation in December 1888. Five applications were received for the vacancy, including a letter from a Mr Willgoose. His interest in the post was a continuing one, for he had been interviewed in January 1887, before Weatherburn's appointment. His application must then have been laced with conditions of his own making, for though the board were 'favourably disposed' they offered him the job 'subject to his agreeing to do the work required by the company'. His renewed application on Weatherburn's departure was parried by the directors' wishing to know 'if he will adhere to certain conditions laid down by him on the occasion of his previous application'. There was clearly some incompatibility and, at the board meeting on 7 January 1889, Gustav F. Akerlind became the company's second locomotive superintendent at a salary of £150 a year. A month later the directors turned down his request for interview expenses, but they did not hold it against him, and at the March meeting brought his salary up to £13 a month.

Akerlind was of Swedish extraction and came from the Midland Railway shops at Derby. In appointing him the Clogher Valley company found themselves a conscientious and able engineer, who remained with them for the rest of his working life, and died while still in their service in 1922. A photograph shows him as a tall bowler-hatted, moustached man, a heavy watch-chain across his waistcoat.

When Akerlind came to Aughnacloy, he found that the

six engines were in a neglected and run-down state, even though they had been less than two years in use and he lost no time in reporting on the unsatisfactory condition of the engines. The directors were so concerned at Akerlind's adverse comments that they asked Bowman Malcolm of the Belfast and Northern Counties Railway to give a second opinion. Malcolm could not make the inspection, and the request was passed to J. C. Park, of the Great Northern. Park ran his expert eye over the neglected CV stock, backed Akerlind, and recommended that an additional fitter and a blacksmith should be appointed. For his advice Park was given an honorarium of £20, which was as much as a porter got in a year. His opinion was sought again in March 1893, when he reported that the engines were being maintained satisfactorily.

During the summer of 1889 Akerlind worked hard to bring the engines into good working order. In June Frederick Willson, the Fermanagh county surveyor, made his annual inspection of the line that was in his area, and then looked at the engines and rolling stock before making a characteristically critical report:

> There are six engines . . . of these only three were in working order when I inspected the rolling stock. The other three required extensive repairs. All the engines were more or less defective, and require far more constant attention and repairs. The steep gradients are, no doubt, telling on the engines. I would suggest that four engines should be kept constantly in good working order. . . .
>
> . . . the rolling stock, as a rule, is in pretty fair order, with the exception of some of the tubes of the vacuum brake, both on the carriages, wagons and engines. The outer casing of some of these tubes is worn and in bad order, all want painting and to be kept cleaner.

Akerlind toiled on, improving housekeeping, selling scrap iron that Weatherburn had accumulated, but keeping scrap brass so that he could do his own castings. He attended to the sanding arrangements on the engines, increased their bunker capacity, and replaced the water feed pumps with injectors. In the half-yearly report to the shareholders, made in September 1889 the directors said 'the condition of the Engines and Rolling Stock has greatly improved since the date of the last report.'

His department was still understaffed, and Akerlind asked for more assistance. In June 1890 he was allowed to engage an additional boilermaker, a train and wagon examiner was appointed at a pay of 12s (60p) a week, a 'man to paint wagons' at the same rate of pay, and an apprentice at 5s (25p) a week. Akerlind's own pay rose to £3 10s (£3·50) a week during 1893.

Akerlind could be a strict disciplinarian, but his men thought all the more of him for it. The minute book records that in September 1890 an accident occurred to the engine of the midday down train at Clogher, and that Driver Gallagher was dismissed for having caused it. Then in the following year, while shunting at the ballast pit, a carriage was put off the rails 'due to the carelessness of Relief Driver McLoughlin' who found himself reduced to the rank of fireman as a result.

In the early 1890s the Clogher Valley's coal bill was around £1,000 a year, out of which they were getting about 85,000 train miles. In an effort to reduce the expenditure on engine fuel, Akerlind paid a visit in June 1892 to the Tralee & Dingle Light Railway in County Kerry. That concern operated as a roadside tramway for part of its length, and had five engines, one of which, a Hunslet 2–6–2T No 5, had been fitted with Holden's Patent Liquid Fuel system. Early results with oil firing on the T & D had been encouraging enough to merit the ordering of two additional sets of equipment for other engines, though they were never fitted. When Akerlind returned from Kerry, he submitted a report to his directors. The minutes merely make a formal mention of it, but no further action was taken.

THE CALEDON OFFICE

Before 1816 Caledon was 'but a mean village' according to *Lewis's Topographical Dictionary*, but by the year that gazetteer was published (1837) the writer described it as 'one of the best built towns in the North of Ireland', the houses 'mostly built of stone' and housing a population of 1,079. The improvements were largely the result of the efforts of the Earl of Caledon, who had built extensive flour mills in 1823. The mills, when Lewis wrote, were grinding 9,000 tons of wheat in a year, but at a later date they moved to spinning and weaving woollen cloth.

Caledon presented the tramway company with something of a problem, for though a small place, the mills might be expected to contribute merchandise, parcels, and commuter traffic. The village was situated on a gravel ridge that had been left by the Ice Age, and at the foot of the north-eastern slope of that ridge the mill had been built, beside the Blackwater River that powered it. The main street along which the tram ran, looked down Mill Street, impossibly steep for a siding, and indeed the only access that the tramway could have obtained would have been by a long siding from near the Blackwater Bridge. By the time that the Clogher Valley Tramway came, the mill was established for over half a century and the owners had organised their own carting service to and from the Great Northern station at Tynan. On the way between Caledon and Tynan, the carts passed the warehouses of the Ulster Canal at Lemnagore, further diminishing any inducement for the mill to expend capital on a private siding. So the trams went up and down the middle of Caledon's main street, concerned themselves with the less weighty matters of passengers and parcels, and the mill similarly minded its own business.

There is no record that, for the first three months, any formal arrangements existed to handle Caledon's traffic. Passengers waited on the footpath, or sheltered in a doorway, and joined the tram when it drew to the compulsory stop opposite the Court House. By August 1887 an arrangement had been made with Mr Alexander 'for the use of one of his front rooms as a waiting room and parcel receiving office. Mr. Alexander to look after and deliver all parcels without further payment, at a rental of £10 per year.' Instructions were given by the directors for 'the room to be made habitable', so that it can hardly have been of the drawing-room standard. The arrangement seems to have been short lived for, by the time of the September board, it was noted that 'Mr. Alexander refuses to deliver parcels at Caledon', and the directors withdrew their offer.

The minute books tell a rather fragmentary story of the Caledon waiting room. One was eventually built, across the road from the post office, at some date around 1890. The initiative came from Lord Caledon, and at their meeting on 1 April 1889 the directors proposed to offer him £10 a year as rent 'of waiting room and parcels office as shown on plan of building to be built . . . such sum to include light, fuel and attendance'. Bargaining went on into the summer; in July the company refused to pay the £15 a year asked by the Earl's agent, Major Alexander. Agreement was reached in February 1892, when Lord Caledon offered the lease at £10. It must have been the cheapest station on the tramway. The station agent John McKeown, was paid £8 a year at first, this was raised to £12 in March 1893.

CARTING

The distribution of merchandise and parcels traffic by road into the hinterland could be an additional source of revenue. In the cities, the railway companies contracted the business to specialist firms, but the Clogher Valley attempted to tackle the job itself. The scheme probably started during 1889 at Ballygawley and Clogher. It was extended to Fivemiletown in September 1889, but perhaps by a local carter for on 27 August 1890, the purchase of a horse and lorry to Fivemiletown station was ordered. The acquisition of motive power seems to have been delayed, and at the November board meeting it was noted that the horse was not to cost more than £50, and a wooden stable was to be built to house the animal. Early in 1891 the service was in operation from Fivemiletown, and during the month of March, a modest profit amounting to £1 6s 7d (£1·33) was credited to revenue.

PASSENGERS AND TRAINS IN MOTION

With a system that had so much of its mileage alongside or on the public road, with carriages fitted with end verandahs, and with speed restricted to four miles per hour at thirteen places, there was temptation for passengers to leap on and off when it suited them. The company knew that if an accident occurred, they would have to contest a claim and to protect themselves they discouraged the practice.

Fivemiletown street seems to have been a favourite place for this unauthorised practice, with houses, shops, and pubs only feet from the moving train. In May 1888 the company prosecuted William Richey and William Bryan 'for entering the train in motion', and took proceedings against Edward Orr in November 1889 for alighting under similar circumstances.

WAGES AND HOURS OF WORK

The earlier minute books do not give the reader a complete picture of the terms under which the men were engaged, but it is certain that, even by nineteenth-century standards, the hours were long and the wages were lower than on main railway lines. The limited income of the tramway company would not allow anything else.

As early as June 1887, it was minuted that the wages of drivers, firemen, and guards were to be increased by 2s (10p) a week. More specific information is given in an entry dated 23 April 1888, when drivers' wages were brought up to 5s (25p) per day, and firemen's wages to 3s (15p), while the secretary was authorised 'to make a small allowance in the shape of a further increase of wages to any driver or fireman doing more that 12 hours regular permanent work per diem.' The concept of overtime, let alone overtime pay, had not penetrated to Aughnacloy. A fortnight earlier, the directors had decided to pay the permanent way men at the rate of 2s (10p) a day, and the gangers 2s 6d (12½p). There were eight gangs of four men. Men with houses in charge of a gate were 'to receive 1/– a week for looking after the gate, and to pay 1/– a week rent.'

By 1894 some concessions had been won. On 7 May the board agreed that permanent way men and gangers would be granted permission to stop work at 2pm on Saturdays, and could take three days leave with full pay in a year.

Requests had been made that the company should establish a Sick Fund, but agreement could not be reached, the company claiming that they had no powers for such a scheme. When an accident did occur to an employee, whether or not he received pay when he was off work was at the discretion of the directors: thus in January 1895 the board resolved to pay Ganger Kirkpatrick his wages while he was 'incapacitated due to a tree falling on him.'

Footplatemen were the elite in those days, and they enjoyed large wage differentials over the less exalted mortals who were employed on the ground or in the stations. We have seen how Akerlind could engage a train and wagon examiner for 12s (60p) a week in 1890, and how an apprentice went home after a week's work with the jingle of two half-crowns in his pocket. In contrast, the footplatemen were far better paid, but they petitioned the company for more pay and shorter hours in April 1890. The directors considered the matter, and brought up the driver's pay to 5s 6d (27½p) a day, with overtime paid at time and a quarter *for over 72 hours in the week*! The firemen were still held at their 3s a day. A reduction in hours was asked for in October 1892, but was refused. It may have been a six-day week, but they were long days. The requests were renewed in May 1894, and overtime was granted to both engine drivers and firemen on all time over 60 hours per week.

In that summer of 1894 some relaxation of the wages freeze came in other grades: the stationmasters at Aughnacloy and Fivemiletown had their pay raised to 22s 6d (£1·12½) a week, the Ballygawley man to 21s (£1·05). Guards Smith and Maguire were ahead, with a pay packet of 26s (£1·30). Porter Murphy had to be satisfied with 12s (60p) a week 'this to be the maximum wage for porters'.

SECOND THOUGHTS ON TULLYVAR BANK

The Tullyvar gable between Aughnacloy and Ballygawley, was a sore trial with a heavy train, a matter of thrashing the engine for the best part of half a mile, no matter from what direction it was approached.

During 1893 serious thought was given to circumnavigating Tullyvar. A tunnel was unthinkable, but the hill could have been avoided by a diversion along its south-western flank. This would have started in the townland of Cavankilgreen, a quarter of a mile south of Tullyvar halt, and would have followed a stream valley into the townland of Drumaslaghy, rejoining the original line between Lisdoart and Annaghilla. The diversion would have kept below the 250ft contour and would have shortened the line by 2½ miles, but would have inconvenienced Ballygawley people, with the tramway two miles from the village.

The proposal was discussed by the board on 2 October 1893, and the secretary was asked to get legal opinion of the company's powers, and to determine the cost. On 6 November the board went so far as to resolve to carry the scheme out subject to the consent of the Tyrone Grand Jury. They still had no firm idea of what the work would cost in terms of civil engineering work, or how it would be financed, and when they met on 27 November they wisely decided to do nothing further until a bill of quantities was available. That was the last that was heard of the diversion, for the sound of extension schemes was heard from afar, with the possibility that more powerful engines would eventually work through and take Tullyvar in their stride. So the diversion was laid aside, and the board formed a committee, more in hope than expectation, consisting of the deputy chairman and Messrs Sherrard and McElroy 'to consider how to reduce the gradient at Tullyvar hill'. The only practicable way would have been an enormous cutting, and the company never had the capital to tackle it.

FROM TRAMWAY TO RAILWAY

By 1894 the mileage of narrow gauge *railways* in Ireland was increasing. Tramways were in the minority and the Clogher Valley had as bedfellows the little Castlederg, the West Carbery, and the Cavan, Leitrim & Roscommon companies. There were disadvantages in being nominally a tramway, and to obtain the convenience of through bookings to places on the railway systems in Great Britain and Ireland, and to derive full benefit from the Railway Clearing House system, it was better to be a railway.

The first steps towards the change were taken at the board meeting on 5 February 1894, when it was agreed to obtain Board of Trade sanction to alter the name to the Clogher Valley Railway Company Limited. This was obtained. The Report of Directors for the half-year ending 31 March 1894 introduced the matter to the shareholders in a rather delightful paragraph:

> Your undertaking is really a Railway, and not a Tramway, and the Company find considerable inconvenience in dealing with other Railway Companies and the public in being called a Tramway Company. The Directors have, therefore, decided to advise you to change the name to the 'Clogher Valley Railway Company Limited' and a resolution to that effect will be submitted to the Shareholders at an Extraordinary Meeting, to be held after the Half-yearly Meeting.

The shareholders adopted the change on 11 June 1894, and confirmed it at an Extraordinary Meeting on 2 July. The change in title became effective from 16 July 1894.

PROFIT AND LOSS

The first seven years working showed that the tramway had not been a profit-making concern, and had only been kept moving by help given by the guaranteeing areas and the Treasury:

Year ended 30 Sept	Profit on working £	Loss on working £	Dividends £	Total contribution by guaranteeing areas £
1887	28	—	5854	5826
1888	27	—	6018	5991
1889	—	538	6342	6880
1890	—	786	6339	7125
1891	—	78	6339	6417
1892	222	—	6339	6117
1893	148	—	6208	6060
1894	—	223	6079	6302

The results gave no promise either to the directors or to the ratepayers in the guaranteeing areas that the tramway was ever likely to be a profitable undertaking. The original hopes had dismally failed to materialise. Only the shareholders, certain of their annual harvest of 5 per cent, could be said to be satisfied.

CHAPTER 5

The Extension Schemes

PLANS OF THE EIGHTIES

If there were two narrow-gauge railway companies in Ireland that suffered recurring delusions of grandeur they were the Clogher Valley and the Cavan & Leitrim. Almost from the time they opened, they were anxious to extend, first from their own extremities, then to literally link hands, and later to make a grandiose daisy-chain that would have run a 234 mile narrow-gauge railway from the west to the east coasts. To call these schemes, and bills and Acts of Parliament delusions is perhaps unfair, for they were indeed the responses that one might have expected from the two companies to the succession of statutory financial carrots that the governments of the day were offering to Ireland in a belated attempt to repair the damage done by the Potato Famine.

On the east side of Ireland, the 3 foot gauge Bessbrook & Newry Tramway had opened in October 1885. It was a local line, worked by electricity, and linked the mill town of Bessbrook with the busy port and market town of Newry on Carlingford Lough. When the Bessbrook line opened, the Clogher Valley was under construction, and five months after the CV began to run its trains, the Cavan & Leitrim (then named the Cavan, Leitrim and Roscommon Light Railway and Tramway Limited) opened its main line from Belturbet to Dromod. Belturbet was on a branch of the Great Northern between Clones and Cavan, Dromod was on the Midland, Great

Western's line to Sligo. In May 1888 the Cavan & Leitrim brought its Arigna tramway into use, linking Ballinamore with the little coalfield across the River Shannon. With the separated lines of the Bessbrook (3 miles), the Clogher Valley (37 miles), and the main line of the Cavan & Leitrim (34 miles) working, and all of them narrow gauge, the stage was set for integration.

Plans were already being laid. In November 1888 a deputation from the promoters of a concern called the Ulster & Connaught Light Railway made an approach to the Cavan & Leitrim directors. This fact is known but Dr Flanagan in his history of the Cavan & Leitrim Railway comments that, unfortunately there is no further record of this planned line. It bore a flamboyant title that was to reappear fifteen years later. In the Clogher Valley records there is no reference to the U & CLR, but probably the directors were well aware of it, and ready to be concerned in it, had it developed beyond the embryo stage.

During 1889 joint discussions were held between the directorates of the Clogher Valley and the Cavan & Leitrim about the possibility of joining their two systems. Between the two there was a gap of only 14 miles as the crow flies, but the indented shoreline of Upper Lough Erne made the feasible distance around 22 miles, and there were no adverse gradients. A deputation was sent to the Board of Works, and a joint memorial submitted to the Privy Council praying for a grant under the Light Railways (Ireland) Act of 1889, but the project fell through.

A NEWRY—TYNAN LINK

For nearly five years, ideas of extensions were dormant. Then, on 5 March 1895 and a fortnight before he resigned from his post as secretary and general manager, David Stewart submitted to the Clogher Valley board a proposal for a light railway from Newry to Tynan. The Clogher Valley directors made encouraging sounds and signified their formal approval, for they were not called upon to put their hands in their pockets.

The proposed Newry—Tynan link failed to make further progress until 1899, when the promoters submitted a bill to parliament. This obtained the Royal Assent on 6 August 1900 as the Newry, Keady & Tynan Light Railway Act (63–4 Vict., c.275). The Act named as promoters Thomas Irwin, Arthur McCann, Robert Sands, Samuel Duncan, Alexander Wheelan, Francis Fisher, William F. Redmond, and John Edgar Connor, and gave powers for the construction of three distinct railways. They were:

No 1: Length 28 miles 3 furlongs 4·55 chains, a single line from a junction with the Bessbrook & Newry Tramway to a junction with the Clogher Valley Railway at Tynan. The gauge to be not less than 3 feet, and the estimated cost to be £163,989.

No 2: Length 7 furlongs 7 chains, from the Bessbrook & Newry Tramway at Newry to a junction with the Great Northern Railway (Ireland) at Albert Basin. To be mixed gauge. Estimated cost £8,633–10–0.

No 3: Length 8·6 chains. Short sidings in Newry. Gauge to be not less than 3 feet, and estimated cost £586.

The authorised capital of the company was £150,000, and it was to be used as a light railway, but with no limit as to speed or weight of rolling stock. The local engineer was J. L. Devenish Meares, CE, of Newry.

The railway would have crossed hilly country and would have reached an altitude of 750ft between Keady and Bessbrook. Between these two places it would have been in County Monaghan for about half a mile. Approaching Tynan, the line was planned to fly over the Great Northern on the Armagh side of Tynan station, lose height on an 8½ chain curve, and run in beside the Clogher Valley tramway. No provision was made for through running towards Aughnacloy, to continue on the tramway trains would have had to enter Tynan and reverse.

While the Clogher Valley company were anxious to see the NK & T scheme come to fruition and increase traffic on their own line, they were careful to protect their own interests, since they had no profits of their own to fall back on. During the autumn of 1900 there were protracted negotiations between the two boards of directors. The Clogher Valley had in fact been asked to lease their line to the Newry company, so that it could be worked as a unified concern. While the prospect was appealing, the Clogher Valley wanted a rent to which the Newry men would not agree. A special board meeting on 27 September 1900 resulted in the adoption of a resolution that the Clogher Valley line would be leased to the NK & T as soon as the latter was opened for public traffic. The Clogher Valley board suggested a rent of £500 for the first year, rising by annual increments of £250 to a maximum of £6,500 a year, such rent to be a first charge on the earnings of the joint undertaking.

After protracted argument, the Clogher Valley cut their requirements to £200 for the initial three years, then by an annual increase of £200 until £6,000 was attained. They agreed that the rent was to be a first charge on the earnings from the Clogher Valley section of the united systems, and a second charge on the earnings of the joint line.

A LINK TO THE WEST

With the Newry, Keady & Tynan scheme now formalised, the Clogher Valley directors turned their faces to the west, and disinterred the proposals of 1889. The Cavan & Leitrim board expressed their willingness to help in forwarding a proposed railway between Maguiresbridge and Bawnboy Road, and the Clogher Valley company issued a five page pamphlet with a coloured map, extolling the virtues of the junction scheme. It was pointed out to the reader that the building of the Newry, Keady & Tynan Light Railway would secure to the Clogher Valley 'direct access to a seaport without break of gauge, the want of which has so seriously militated against the success of the undertaking in the past, and emphasise the necessity in the public interest, of filling up the gap between the Cavan and Leitrim and Clogher Valley lines, thus making one continuous line of narrow gauge railway, 138 miles in length, extending from the port of Newry to the mining district of Arigna beyond the River Shannon.'

The pamphlet spoke of the existence of 'an immense tract of country . . . about 300 square miles . . . not served by any railway', and it was claimed that 'the town and trade of Swanlinbar, in particular, would be greatly benefited . . .' Swanlinbar was a village in County Cavan which had little to offer in the way of traffic, though it had a past. At the end of the eighteenth century *The Post Chaise Companion* described Swanlinbar as 'a celebrated spa, the waters of which are excellent for scurvy, nerves, low spirits, and bad appetite.' In 1815 the *Travellers' New Guide* wrote kindly of the place as 'a neat smart village . . . much frequented in the summer season by hypochondriacs, valetudinarians, and patients actually afflicted with scorbutic and cutaneous maladies'. By the middle of the nineteenth century its days as an Irish Cheltenham were over, and by 1900 it held around 300 people, merely a centre of population in a thinly peopled bit of Ireland.

The Clogher Valley's pamphlet gave an approximate cost of £100,000 which would include a bridge over the River Erne, and the supply of rolling stock. It was proposed to ask for a free Treasury grant of £70,000, while the benefited area would be asked to guarantee 4 per cent on the balance, which would amount to £4,000 a year, and would not exceed 4d on the rates. A 'rebate system' was envisaged to provide additional finance, whereby the three companies whose own revenue had increased as a result of the through link, would each make a contribution to the funds of the link line. On the basis of ordinary traffic receipts of £204 per mile per annum, through traffic and rebates contributing £1,512, the gross receipts were forecast at a round £6,000. Working expenses would take £3,700, leaving a net revenue of £2,300. This was claimed to be enough to pay 4 per cent on £75,000 or 2·3

Page 107

COUNTY FERMANAGH

(Above) *Brookeborough station, crossing gates, and siding, looking towards Fivemiletown, 29 June 1937*; (below) *Maguiresbridge. An unidentified Sharp, Stewart engine takes water. The Great Northern station buildings and siding are on the right*

Page 108

LOCOMOTIVES

(Above) Colebrooke *in original form, with condenser*; (centre) Errigal *about 1921, with skirts removed to show steam sander*; (below) Colebrooke *in final form, with high bunker and gravity sanders*

per cent on the whole capital of £100,000. The pamphlet ended by attempting to show that the scheme was feasible without any Treasury help (though it would not have been unwelcome) merely by a 6d levy on a taxable valuation of £68,000.

THE ULSTER & CONNAUGHT LIGHT RAILWAYS

Already a more ambitious scheme was being planned, though not by the Clogher Valley Railway. This was the Ulster & Connaught Light Railways, the bill of which was presented to parliament at the end of 1902. The Act was passed (3 Edw. VII, c.cclxii) in the 1903 session, and sanctioned the 21 mile link from Maguiresbridge to Bawnboy Road on the Cavan & Leitrim Railway. At Bawnboy Road the main line was to face Ballinamore, with a short spur to permit through running to Belturbet. It was proposed to amalgamate the Cavan & Leitrim, the Clogher Valley, the Newry, Keady & Tynan, and the Bessbrook & Newry, and to buy the mining rights of the Arigna coalfield. An extension of the Cavan & Leitrim to the River Shannon at Roosky Lock was also included. This comprehensive scheme stemmed from the activities of the Newry, Keady & Tynan company promoters.

During 1904, the Ulster & Connaught excelled itself by proposing a scheme more ambitious than any that had gone before. As well as the amalgamations already proposed, a further extension was planned. This would have started from Roosky, and would then have gone through Strokestown en route to the important town of Roscommon, which was on the GN & WR line from Athlone to Claremorris and Westport. Crossing that broad-gauge line, the U & C was to strike south-west to the village of Mountbellew in Co. Galway and thence to the market town of Tuam, which was the terminus of a broad-gauge branch line from Athenry. From Tuam, the U & C went west to the village of Shrule. Two branches were schemed to diverge here, one of 8 miles to run north-west to Ballinrobe, and another of 16 miles south to Galway town. From Shrule

CLOGHER VALLEY TRAMWAY.

TRIP OF THE SEASON.

On Monday, 4th August, 1890,

An Excursion Train will leave the undermentioned Stations for Enniskillen, *via* Maguires' Bridge, and thence by Steamer down

LOUGH ERNE

To Castlecaldwell, giving Excursionists an opportunity of viewing the

MAGNIFICENT SCENERY ON THE LOWER LAKE,

Including Devenish Round Tower, Ely Lodge, Rossclaire, Tully Castle, Castle Archdall, The Thousand Islands, and other points of interest.

For the purpose of this Excursion one of the First Class Steamers of the Royal Erne Navy (S.S. Knockninney or S.S. Belturbet) has been chartered to ply between Enniskillen and Castlecaldwell.

As in order to prevent overcrowding only a limited number of Tickets will be issued. Intending passengers are requested to obtain their Tickets not later than Friday, the 1st August.

THE FOLLOWING ARE THE TIMES AND FARES.

			THROUGH EXCURSION FARES.		
			1st Class.	1st Class Tram&Boat & 2nd Class Rail.	3rd Class.
AUGHNACLOY,	Dep.	8-33 a.m.	6s. 0d.	5s. 6d.	5s. 0d.
BALLYGAWLEY,	,,	8-53 ,,	6s. 0d.	5s. 6d.	4s. 9d.
AUGHER,	,,	9-13 ,,	5s. 9d.	5s. 3d.	4s. 6d.
CLOGHER,	,,	9-25 ,,	5s. 6d.	5s. 3d.	4s. 6d.
FIVEMILETOWN,	,,	10-0 ,,	5s. 3d.	5s. 0d.	4s. 3d.
COLEBROOKE,	,,	10-20 ,,	5s. 0d.	4s. 9d.	4s. 0d.
BROOKEBORO',	,,	10-33 ,,	5s. 0d.	4s. 9d.	4s. 0d.
ENNISKILLEN,	Arrive	11-20 ,,			

The Sailing of Steamers will be as under, viz.:—

Enniskillen (Market Quay),	Dep.	11-40 a.m.	Castlecaldwell,	Dep.	3-15 p.m.
Castlecaldwell,	Arrive	2-30 p.m.	Enniskillen,	Arrive,	5-45 ,,

A Special Train will leave Enniskillen at 7-30 p.m., arriving at Brookeboro' 8-0 p.m.; Colebrooke 8-11; Fivemiletown, 8-30; Clogher, 9-5; Augher, 9-14; Ballygawley, 9-34; Aughnacloy, 9-54 p.m.

Children under 12 will be allowed to travel at Half Fares; and a reduction of 10 per cent. will be made on all Tickets purchased by not less than 3 Adults of same family.

Mrs. G. WILLES, of the Imperial Hotel, Enniskillen, has undertaken to provide Dinner and Tea on the arrival of the return Steamer at Enniskillen; but in order to prevent disappointment or delay, parties desirous of obtaining such refreshments should make their wishes known to the Guard of the Clogher Valley Train, when their orders will be conveyed to Mrs. Willes.

By Order.

D. J. STEWART,
General Manager.

HEAD OFFICES, AUGHNACLOY,
21st July, 1890.

[W Somers Printer, Aughnacloy.]

the main U & C line crossed the isthmus between Lough Corrib and Lough Mask, where the village of Cong was sited. It was then to go to Leenane, a hamlet on the coast at Killary Harbour, and then on a south-westerly course to Clifden on the west Galway coast.

The western part of the Roosky—Clifden extension would have opened up a district, practically devoid of railways, which had suffered terribly from the Famine of 1846–9. It is doubtful if rail facilities would have revitalised the hinterland, but it is certain that traffic would have been insufficient to make even a light railway pay. Moreover, though Clifden might be termed the 'capital' of the beautiful and mountainous district of Connemara, it was little more than a village, with around 1,000 people. The Ulster & Connaught plan took little heed of the fact that, since 1895, Clifden had a broad gauge connection to Galway.

For this final effort of the Ulster & Connaught Light Railways no parliamentary powers were ever sought. Had they been approved, and the main line built, it would have spanned Ireland from the west to the east coasts, a length of 234 miles. Over it, the journey time would have been ten to twelve hours: for unbroken night journeys there would probably have been sleeping cars, and restaurant cars for daylight travellers. The main line would have been composed of the following sections:

Greenore–Newry	14	miles	(Dundalk, Newry & Greenore Railway)
Newry–Bessbrook	3	,,	(Bessbrook & Newry Tramway)
Bessbrook–Tynan	25	,,	(Act of 1901)
Tynan–Maguiresbridge	37	,,	(Clogher Valley Railway)
Maguiresbridge–Bawnboy Rd	22	,,	(Act of 1903)
Bawnboy Road–Dromod	23	,,	(Cavan & Leitrim Railway)
Dromod–Roosky	2	,,	(Act of 1903)
Roosky–Clifden	108	,,	(U & CLR proposal)

THROUGH KEADY AGAIN

The main reason for the failure of the Ulster & Connaught's scheme lay in disagreement between the promoters and the Cavan & Leitrim directors. Though the proposals were moribund, interest in them reawakened during 1905 when a further Act was obtained (5 Edw. VII, c.ccvii). The company reverted to its original and less flamboyant title of the Newry, Keady & Tynan Light Railway, and obtained an extension of time to cover construction of the Bessbrook—Tynan section. In the same year, the Clogher Valley directors considered working agreements between themselves and the U & CLR and the NK & TR though neither had ever to be implemented.

Other steps were meanwhile being taken by the main line companies to secure rail access to Keady. The valley from Keady down to Armagh was steep, and the River Callan dropped almost 500ft over eight miles, powering a large number of water mills. Their trade offered inducement to railway promoters intent on making a north-south line. The Midland Great Western had promised support for a Kingscourt, Keady and Armagh Railway and that concern obtained its Act in 1900. The Great Northern, fearing the incursion of the Midland into their Armagh territory, came to terms with the Kingscourt, Keady & Armagh, with the result that the Keady scheme was relegislated in the 1902 session of parliament. Out of the change emerged the Castleblayney, Keady & Armagh Railway company. The Great Northern were empowered to give it massive financial support, and rail connection between Armagh and Keady was opened on 31 May 1909, the remaining Keady—Castleblayney section following in November 1910.

With Keady amply provided with rail access to north and south, there was no hope of success for a narrow-gauge line coursing from west to east. None the less, the CK & A had to acknowledge the existence of the NK & T on paper when its embankment north of Keady station was being built. Accordingly a concrete tunnel was placed through it, with stair access from above, giving space for the narrow-gauge line that would have made Keady a railway crossroads among the hills of south Armagh.

The Newry, Keady & Tynan Railway company was slow to expire, and even as late as 1909 it obtained a final Act of

Parliament (9 Edw. VII, c.140) giving extension of time. By 1910 the scheme was extinct, leaving only the little Keady tunnel as a reminder of a quarter century of planning.

CHAPTER 6

The Railway 1894-1928

MODEST PURCHASES

Elevated in name, though not in prospects, the Clogher Valley Railway made some modest increases in its rolling stock: in December 1894 four new cattle wagons were ordered from the Metropolitan Railway Carriage & Wagon Co, at a cost of £72 15s (£72·75) each. For the carting business, a new horse was required, so the old horse was sold 'to best advantage' at Fivemiletown.

No extravagance was permitted, and when Mary Ann McKay was hit by a train at Goland Level Crossing and killed, the company felt themselves to be free from blame, and the directors contented themselves by asking the landowners there to trim their hedges 'to lessen danger'.

For Fair Day traffic, management continued to find the wagon stock inadequate, and in August 1897 Irwin was authorised to advertise for tenders for 20 more. Again the contract was secured by Metropolitan, and they supplied ten open and ten covered wagons. Three years later, a quadricycle, described in the minutes as 'a light inspection car' was bought at a cost of £21. For the twenty wagons, the necessary capital was found by the sale of 120 5 per cent guaranteed shares; this brought in £1,200, added to which the sale brought in a premium of £581 9s 6d (£581·47½), yielding a total of £1,781 9s 6d, which usefully covered the Metropolitan's bill and left the company with thirty shillings (£1·50) in hand.

THE COUNTY INQUISITIONS

There was neither history nor likelihood of profitability, and the pursuit of economy had to continue. The county surveyors continued their search for faults in their respective counties, a task for which they were paid at the rate of £1 a mile.

In County Fermanagh, with seven miles to cover, Frederick Willson sustained his pressure for perfection, though many of his complaints were of trivia which would have been attended to by the company in the ordinary course of events. To the Summer Assizes in 1895 Willson wrote 35 lines of print, 19 of which were devoted to 'Stations and Gate Houses'. He had apparently spent an interesting hour at Killarbran listening to the tales of woe of the inmates, where 'The gate house . . . requires to have the kitchen either ceiled, or a ceiling of timber put up, and the floor repaired. This house also wants whitening and repairs to the plastering, and glazing of the windows.' At Colebrook his notebook had been in his hand, for 'the concrete to the yard of the dwellinghouse wants repairs, the kitchen and rooms to be whitened; the ridge of the house wants some pointing; the WC at this station is a very rough concern and badly fitted, and the woodwork of this station would be the better of painting.' Of the engines he had little to say other than that they were 'in tolerable working order, but show wear', which was as much as a civil engineer could be expected to say. At Maguiresbridge he thought that the windmill should have a coat of tar.

In Tyrone, John Dickinson had been County Surveyor until 1895, when his place was taken by John W. Leebody. Leebody held office for the lengthy term of 39 years. He usually made his inspection during August, and walked every foot of the line that was in Tyrone. He took two conscientious days over the task, the first day from Caledon to Ballygawley, the second from Ballygawley to the county boundary just west of Fivemiletown. In the early days he was driven by jaunting car from Dungannon to his starting point, and picked up in the evening by the same car at his finishing point, a long day's work with a field notebook loaded with details of defective sleepers, missing spikes or fishbolts, and the state of the ballast and drains. In later years a taxi took the place of the horse-drawn jaunting car.

Prior to 1898, in the days before the County Councils succeeded the Grand Juries, one of John Leebody's reports was ventilated in the House of Commons. A copy normally went to the Board of Works. An Irish Member asked the President of the Board of Trade whether he had seen 'the report on the condition of the Clogher Valley Railway, presented to the Tyrone Grand Jury recently by Mr Leebody, County Surveyor, in which he expressed his regret that the permanent way is in a very unsatisfactory state and that both line and stock appear to be carelessly attended to, especially between Ballygawley and Fivemiletown; whether he is aware that one third of the permanent way men for the past two months have been employed in taking gravel out of a river at Ballygawley which is sold to the Great Northern Railway Company, the remainder being employed at Tynan and Aughnacloy unloading coals, and the line from Tynan to Fivemiletown being often left without a man to look after it; and whether any means will be taken in this case to give better security to the travelling public.' Apart from John Leebody, it was evident that the member of parliament, Mr MacAleese, had evidently been doing some homework. Like so many parliamentary questions, it was a melange of half-truths taken out of context and flavoured with a dash of spite.

MARTIN THE MAN

The company minute books do not mention the formal appointment of a permanent way inspector, and in all probability his engagement was left to the general manager. The first mention of the office is seen on 6 February 1893 when Permanent Way Inspector Martin applied to 'have his house

CLOGHER VALLEY TRAMWAY.

TYNAN HUNT RACES.

ON EASTER MONDAY, 30th MARCH, 1891,

EXCURSION TICKETS

will be issued by the following SPECIAL and ORDINARY Trains to CALEDON, viz. :

STATIONS.		A.M.	A.M.	RETURN FARES. 1st Cl	3rd Cl.
MAGUIRESBRIDGE	dep.		9.54	3/6	2/3
BROOKEBORO'	,,		10.8		
FIVEMILETOWN	,,		10.42	3/0	2/0
CLOGHER	,,	8.57	11.22	2/6	1/8
AUGHER	,,	9.5	11.31		
BALLYGAWLEY	,,	9.25	11.58	2/3	1/6
AUGHNACLOY	,,	9.55	12.24	1/8	1/2

Tickets are not Transferable and are available for Return only on day of issue by the following Trains, viz. :—ORDINARY TRAIN leaving Tynan at 6.30 p.m., RUNNING THROUGH to MAGUIRESBRIDGE, if required ; and SPECIAL TRAIN leaving Tynan at 8.10 p.m., arriving at Aughnacloy at 8.50 p.m., Ballygawley 9.10 p.m., Augher 9.30 p.m., Clogher 9.38 p.m., and Fivemiletown 10.13 p.m.

NO LUGGAGE ALLOWED.

By Order,

D. J. STEWART,
General Manager.

Head Office, Aughnacloy,
28th Feb., 1891.

4077 Printed at the Enniskillen Gas-Power Printing Works.

at Grange partitioned'. The directors agreed to it, but stipulated that the work was not to cost more than thirty shillings. The 'house at Grange' was Martin's own office in Ballygawley yard, beside the permanent way workshops. It was half a mile from the village, in the townland of Grange.

Since there was no civil engineer permanently on the railway, Hugh Martin was directly responsible to the general manager. His post was an important one, he was a 'key man' in modern jargon, and in the minutes it was usually his *salary* that was referred to. On 4 March 1895 the board having decided that permanent way men should work an eleven hour day, resolved that 'Permanent Way Inspector Martin's salary be increased from £7 11s 8d to £8 0s 0d per month'. In April 1902 his 'wages' were 'to be increased to £2 5s 0d per week.'

Hugh Martin and his wife lived in Ballygawley, where they owned a small hotel and drapery shop. Their son, Ferris, entered the Aughnacloy shops as an apprentice fitter in June 1907, and the board, pleased to see a member of the family joining them, waived the customary £25 fee that was one of Akerlind's 'perks'. In February 1912 an old ballast pit at Lisdoart came up for sale; it had been known as Mrs Barratt's pit, and there had been a siding into it: for £10 Inspector Martin became the owner of some real estate.

It was in 1913 that Martin became so incensed with the criticism meted out in John Leebody's report to the Tyrone County Council that he withdrew to his little office in the shady corner of the yard at Ballygawley, and penned the following letter to his general manager:

Memo. from Permanent Way Inspector's Office, Ballygawley. 20 Sept. 1913.

to H. S. Sloan, General Manager, ref. Mr. Leebody's letter re loose fish bolts.

Sir These loose bolts have now been replaced with new ones as they were worn and would not screw up, not that there was any danger with these as 1/32 part of an inch will leave a bolt that you could shake it, and this will not allow a joint to get foul. It is very bad practice to

> have the joints too tight screwed up during the summer months as the rails could not get expanding or contracting. During the warm weather in July, we had to take out four rails and cut 3½″ off each one of them to keep the line from buckling. It is the practice on railways to slacken the fishbolts in summer. If Mr. Leebody had seen some of the railways 30 years ago he would not be talking about a loose fishbolt. On the railway that I learned anything that I know there were no fishbolts, they used only a sheath, something similar to ours, and that company has been as free from accidents as any I know. Providence has been more than good to them.
>
> Yours faithfully,
>
> H. R. Martin.

Hugh Martin's task must never have been easy. On the state of the track depended the safety of the travelling public, and there were very few derailments. Yet he was never given enough men and, as the House of Commons performance showed, his men had to be diverted from systematic maintenance to the periodic unloading of coal for the locomotive department, who themselves had no labour to spare, nor any men as handy with shovels as Martin's gangs. The ballast that the CVR used was always washed gravel, and there was an ample supply of it to be taken from lineside openings in the hummocky moraine country between Ballygawley and Fivemiletown, and also in the banks of the Ballygawley River. There were no mechanical diggers then; Martin's men opened their own ballast pits on a suitable site, laid in a siding, and when it was worked out, they levelled the ground for sale.

The successive critical reports of the County Surveyors must have taxed Martin. It is likely that the appointment in 1913 of J. J. S. Barnhill, AMICE, a professional civil engineering consultant whose office was in Londonderry, must have come as something of a relief, rather than a slight on Martin's own ability. The day that the Clogher Valley directors approved Barnhill's appointment (at £30 a year), they also raised Martin's salary, bringing it up from 45s (£2·25) to 50s (2·50) per week, which was more than they gave Paddy Soraghan their accountant. Barnhill made a quarterly inspection and report, and he and Martin appear to have worked amicably together for sixteen years. On the periodic inspections they went over the length of the line together, seated side by side on the quadricycle, pedalling gently along, Barnhill cherry-cheeked and invariably smoking a pipe. Between them, they kept the permanent way and buildings in remarkably good order on a shoe-string. During 1921, when post-war economies were being made in wages and salaries, Martin had his salary of £260 per year cut back to £208. Soon after that, the strictures increased, and he had to pay off five of his men.

MANAGEMENT

In March 1894, during the negotiations to transform the tramway into a railway, the first secretary and general manager, David J. Stewart, tendered his resignation. He had been appointed to the post of traffic manager on the Dublin, Wicklow & Wexford Railway.

Applications for the vacancy came from Horace S. Sloan, the Clogher Valley's accountant since 1886, from William Irwin, who was secretary and general manager of the Castlederg & Victoria Bridge Tramway, from John Duff of the Sligo, Leitrim & Northern Counties Railway, and from R. A. Parkes, the secretary and general manager of the Tralee & Dingle Light Railway. Interviews were extended to Sloan, Duff, and Irwin, and each was asked whether, though the post had previously been a joint one, they would agree to come either as secretary or as general manager. All three agreed to the proposition. It was decided to bring in Irwin as the new general manager at a salary of £250, and to elevate Sloan to the position of secretary and accountant, and to pay him £225.

Irwin was well-liked by staff and public, and became known

locally for his interest in cattle breeding. He died suddenly in November 1907, as he was hastening to catch the midday train to Tynan, en route to a meeting in Belfast. At the December meeting of the board, Sloan was elected to be Irwin's successor, but in the joint capacity of secretary and general manager, at a salary of £325. At the same time, P. M. Soraghan, who had been clerk in Sloan's office, was made accountant and audit superintendent at £100 a year, and John Bennett, the office clerk, found his salary raised to £40 a year.

When Sloan joined the infant tramway in 1886, he was starting a lifetime association with the concern. When he decided to get married, the directors held him in such esteem that they decided to acknowledge the step formally and on 4 December 1905 asked Akerlind to act as secretary and collector to a joint fund of board members and staff. There was hesitation on somebody's part, for the procedure was repeated at the board meeting on 3 September 1906. Thereafter, events moved to their happy conclusion and after the board meeting on 5 November 1906, Hugh de F. Montgomery, the chairman, made the presentation of an inscribed silver salver to Sloan; having acknowledged the gift, Sloan wrote the facts in the minute book.

Sloan is said to have been a remote and rather austere person, so far as his personal relationships with the employees and passengers were concerned—'not much come or go with him', which was counted a defect by some, in a friendly rural part of Ulster. His management may be said to have been efficient, and though the authors of the Killin Report criticised him for lack of initiative, he would have had to justify adventurous expenditure to a wider audience than his board of directors. He continued as secretary and general manager until 1928, when as the next chapter tells, the day-to-day control of the company was placed under a Committee of Management. Under that regime, he retained his title until 1929, thereafter becoming secretary of the shareholders' committee and 'adviser' to the management.

The difficult situation which met Gustav Akerlind when he came to Aughnacloy in 1889 has been mentioned. Once in Tyrone, he settled down to a long and fruitful working life of 33 years there. Seldom taking a day off work, he was greatly attached to his family and home, and much of his spare time he spent in attending to his garden, over the wall from the workshop yard. He was fond of music and for a number of years he was choir-master and organist in one of the local churches. The design and construction of the McIlwaine Memorial Hall in Aughnacloy owed much to his professional abilities. With the public, he was on the best of terms, and it was not unknown for him to arrange and assist with minor repair jobs at the local scutch mill, lending a fitter to do the brasses and make cylinder joints. With his general manager, Sloan, relationships were less easy, and one may gauge that if there was a fault, it was not Akerlind's. One of his two sons, Frederick, had similar interests to his father and was admitted to the locomotive department as an apprentice in December 1912.

When the post-war economies came during late 1921, Akerlind's salary was reduced from £420 to £350, a loss which on a percentage basis was much heavier that that suffered by Sloan. Not long after that, Gustav Akerlind became unwell, and in April 1922 the directors allowed his son to assist him in the running of the department, paying Frederick £3 10s (£3·50) a week during this period. But poor Akerlind's illness was one that could not be cured, and after much suffering death came in June 1922. On the day of the funeral, Sloan refused to allow the workshop engine to be silenced for more than the single hour during which the men were permitted to pay their respects to their old chief.

The directors convened a committee to appoint a successor, and during August four persons were interviewed for the vacancy. They were, Frederick Akerlind, who had grown up in the Clogher Valley shops, W. H. Holman of the Londonderry & Lough Swilly Railway, and who had been fitter-in-charge there during two inter-regnums, David N. McClure who had started his career on the Caledonian Railway and had some experience in railway engineering work in Spain, and G. H. Pollard, the locomotive superintendent of the Castlederg & Victoria Bridge Tramway. On 8 August 1922, the board appointed McClure to succeed Akerlind at a starting salary of £350.

The first chairman of the board of directors was J. W. Ellison-Macartney, DL, JP of Clogher Park, Clogher. He held office until 1898 and then resigned owing to failing health. The vice-chairman, Hugh de Fellenberg Montgomery, DL, JP, of Blessingbourne, Fivemiletown then assumed the office of chairman, his deputy being David Graham of Cranbrooke, Fivemiletown. Montgomery remained chairman until his death in November 1924. In his place, the directors elected his son, Major-General Hugh Maude de Fellenberg Montgomery, CB, CMG, also of Blessingbourne, who remained the chairman into the days of the Committee of Management. Also on the board for many years was the Earl of Caledon, and a member of the Brooke family. The number of directors was 15, later 13, this apparently unwieldy number being due to the fact that not only were the shareholders represented, but also the county councils.

TRAIN SERVICES

Being generally adequate to the needs of the community, train services of the CVR remained basically similar to those of the CVT, with fair day specials playing an important, if occasional part. In the summer of 1906, for example, the first train was the 5.50am up from Fivemiletown, calculated to waken the village as it climbed up the length of the street. It was in Tynan at 8.5am, where it connected with the Great Northern's 7.35am ex Clones that was in Belfast at 9.50am. A Belfast—Clones—Cavan train left Tynan & Caledon station at 9.28am, the CV train waited until it had gone through, and returned down the line at 9.40am, working through to Maguiresbridge, where it arrived at 12.20pm.

Aughnacloy had dispatched a down train at 7.15am, which made port at Maguiresbridge at 9.30am. This enabled passengers to catch one or other of two Great Northern trains that left in opposite directions at 9.43am. After that frenzy of activity, Maguiresbridge saw off its Clogher Valley train at 9.54am, a working which crossed at Clogher around 11.15am with the 9.40am ex Tynan, and was itself in Tynan at 12.55pm.

The 12.20pm arrival at Maguiresbridge was hardly in time to hear the down 'Bundoran Express' thunder through, it having left Clones at 11.50am, but the Clogher Valley people met the following GN train, 11.58am ex Clones. Southbound passengers had a long wait until the 11.10am all stations ex Derry came in, leaving Maguiresbridge at 1.47pm. Ten minutes after that, the CV train returned up the valley, and took 50 minutes to get to Fivemiletown. There it sat down for 58 minutes, crossed with a down train, and then set off on a journey of 2 hours 25 minutes to Tynan, where it arrived at 6.10pm. It returned from Tynan at 6.51pm, ten minutes after a Clones—Belfast train had gone through, and ended the day at Fivemiletown at 9.3pm.

Tynan had received a down working from Maguiresbridge at 12.55pm. This set down passengers in good time for the 1.16pm for Belfast (the 12.30pm ex Clones). At 1.20pm the Clogher Valley train returned down the valley, crossing the 1.57pm ex Maguiresbridge during the latter's palaver at Fivemiletown. The down train had 18 minutes allowed at Fivemiletown, and arrival at Maguiresbridge was timed for 4.42pm. This connected with the Great Northern's 2.30pm all stations ex Derry, due away at 4.57pm, and in Dundalk exactly two hours later.

After 18 minutes at Maguiresbridge, the CV train left at 5.0pm, to terminate in Aughnacloy at 7.12pm, with only 12 minutes dallying at Fivemiletown on the way. Last movement of the day was at the western end of the valley, by a 5.30pm train out of Fivemiletown: this was due in Maguiresbridge at 6.12pm and out again at 6.25pm. During this period, the

Page 125

LOCOMOTIVES

(Above) *No 7* Blessingbourne *at Aughnacloy, 18 Sept. 1929;* (below) *Atkinson-Walker Steam tractor. Aughnacloy carriage & wagon shop, 18 Sept. 1929. Spray wagon beyond*

Page 126

THE CASTLEDERG ENGINE

(Above) *Arrival at Maguiresbridge, October 1934. The two GN cranes lifting the engine from the bogie well wagon*; (centre) *In C & VB livery by the Aughnacloy turntable, prior to rebuilding*; (below) *At Aughnacloy, 13 May 1937, after rebuilding*

4.25pm Great Northern train ex Dundalk made its call, leaving at 6.15pm for Enniskillen, Omagh, and Derry.

Enniskillen Fair Days continued to attract traffic, and had a 5.55am Fivemiletown—Maguiresbridge train. For Fivemiletown Fair there was a 6.45am working from there to Maguiresbridge, coming back at 7.50am with people off an early Clones—Omagh train. The fairs at Aughnacloy and Ballygawley were served by an 8.50am special from Fivemiletown, which left Ballygawley at 9.58am and arrived at Aughnacloy at 10.16am. To Ballygawley Fair, Tynan sent an 8.45am up train, and to assist returning shoppers a special ran from Ballygawley to Aughnacloy at 1.49pm, and was smartly timed over the 3½ miles in 20 minutes.

The 1910 *Bradshaw* shows an unaltered picture, though no specials were run by then to Enniskillen Fair. The timings appear to have continued unchanged through the 1914–18 War.

In the winter 1921–2 working timetable, there is still the early up train from Fivemiletown to Tynan, now timed to start at 5.40am. The other three up trains were the 9.54am, 1.55pm, and 6.28pm, the first two terminating at Tynan, the third at Aughnacloy. In the down direction were the 7.10am Aughnacloy—Maguiresbridge, the 9.38am and 1.30pm Tynan—Maguiresbridge and the 8.30pm Tynan—Fivemiletown. The latter train ended its work with a 10.45pm arrival in Fivemiletown, distinctly later than any pre-war trains. Its progress down Fivemiletown street in the dark of a winter's night would have been a fit subject for an artist's brush: the great single headlamp moving cautiously between the rows of lighted windows, moving shafts of orange light from the firedoor on the whitewashed walls, a curtain lifted there, a wave from an open doorway to acknowledge the return of a friend from far-off Belfast, and the line of carriages, lit by acetylene lamps, creeping down to the red-brick station at the bottom of the town.

Fair Day requirements in 1921–2 were the 4.40am Tynan—Aughnacloy, on Aughnacloy and Ballygawley days. On the same occasions a run was made from Fivemiletown at 8.50am, to the appropriate town. Out of the Ballygawley Fair was a 1.49pm working to Tynan, and corresponding to it, a train ran from the Aughnacloy Fair at 2.25pm. Both had to be in Tynan for 3.10pm. No special provision was made for either the Enniskillen or Clones Fairs.

SUNDAY SPECIALS

From the outset, the Clogher Valley board resolutely set their faces against the running of trains on Sunday. It was only fifty years since the Belfast Presbytery had administered a verbal rebuke to the Ulster Railway on hearing that the company was proposing to run Sunday trains. At the time one clergyman was reported to have declared to his congregation that he 'would rather join a company for theft and murder than the Ulster Railway Company' and went on to make the claim that the company's business was 'sending souls to the devil at the rate of 6d apiece'. He backed that up by insisting that 'every sound of the Railway Whistle is answered by a shout in Hell.'

Arguments for and against Sunday trains during the nineteenth century have been ventilated elsewhere, and certainly in some parts of England the opposition of the Sabbatarians was shown to be an ill-considered attempt to make a distinction between uncontrollable 'private' travel by the well-to-do in coaches, and controllable 'public' travel by the working classes in trains. In areas of dense population, where the 'dark satanic mills' formed the weekday environment of many, a Sunday excursion by train to coast or country could have done much for the mental and physical health of the factory workers. But the Clogher Valley folk had no such problems and, in truth, probably had little need for rail transport on Sunday, though its lack made visits from their Belfast cousins practically impossible. Certainly a rest day was most needed by the railway staff themselves, to whom a seventy hour week was commonplace.

Beyond the bounds of the Clogher Valley, the Great Northern took a broader view, and in the Catholic south Sunday trains, and cheap Sunday excursions were a normal part of their operations. In July 1902 the Clogher Valley board was approached by Rev McGuire CC of Brookeborough, with a request that a train should be run on Sunday to connect with one of the Great Northern specials that went through Maguiresbridge. But as he probably expected, his request was met with a refusal.

The first break in the ice came in the following year. At the end of April 1903, Rev J. W. Booth, PP of Aughnacloy, asked the board to consider running a special on Sunday 17 May from Ballygawley to Caledon and back 'for the convenience of children and their friends attending a confirmation service'. It was not an *excursion,* such a reasonable request could scarcely be refused, and the directors agreed, but had it minuted that their consent 'be not taken as a precedent for running Sunday excursion trains for any purpose, religious or otherwise.' Father Booth asked again for a Sunday special during February 1904, but was refused.

However, a precedent had been set, and Father Booth requested that the Clogher Valley co-operate with the Great Northern on Sunday 24 July 1904 on the occasion of a consecration service in St Patrick's Cathedral in Armagh. Reluctantly, the Clogher Valley directors agreed, allowing 'only a train from Fivemiletown to Tynan and back. Due consideration to be given to conscientious objection to Sunday work by any officials. Not to be a precedent.'

Further moves towards a relaxation came into the board room on 6 July 1908, when Mr McCann proposed and Mr McLaren seconded that Sunday trains be run fortnightly in the months of July to September to Tynan and to Maguiresbridge to connect with existing Great Northern excursion specials to Warrenpoint and Bundoran. The motion was opposed by Messrs Lendrum and Graham, who had their way.

Father Booth continued his requests from time to time and, as a result, in June 1909, he succeeded in having Sunday trains arranged in connection with a temperance demonstration in Armagh. But not long after that, a refusal was given to the Gaelic League of North West Ulster when they asked for a special train on 8 August. Two years passed, and Father Booth requested a Sunday special to Maguiresbridge in connection with a Great Northern Railway excursion to Bundoran organised by the Roman Catholic Temperance Society. The Clogher Valley directors debated that one, a proposal that the train be run was put by Messrs Betty and McLaren, but when it was put to the vote the motion was lost, and no train was provided. No relaxation in the attitude towards Sunday trains was permitted until the mid-1920s. By 1926 several summer Sunday specials were run to Maguiresbridge to give connection with Great Northern specials to Bundoran. By 1929, the board left the general manager 'to make any arrangements he considered desirable.'

EVENING AVOIDANCE

One evening, a double-headed cattle special had been worked from Ballygawley to Tynan. It had been a busy fair day, and George Leany with Joe Girvan firing to him, uncoupled and went promptly back to Ballygawley to bring up a second cattle train that was waiting there. Meanwhile, the other engine shunted Tynan yard.

The light engine made such good time on the return run from Ballygawley, that at Aughacloy it was decided to let it go on to Tynan with a written pass from the Aughnacloy stationmaster. Tynan was telephoned with news of the second special, and told to hold the shunting engine in the yard. The two engines were then to work empties back to Aughnacloy.

Then at Tynan, someone *forgot*. The staff was handed to John Maguire, who was firing, and William Thompson and he set off down the line with empty cattle wagons behind them. Then at Tynan, consternation, and no way of calling back the cavalcade. They rounded the curve at Lemnagore and, fortunately, caught a glimpse of the smoke from the engine of the second cattle train; by then it must have been creeping down towards the Blackwater River bridge. Brakes on, into reverse gear, and back Thompson and Maguire propelled the half mile into Tynan. It might have been a much nearer thing had they been on the blind curves near Kilsampson. As it was, nobody was any the worse, and the incident was kept very quiet. Unlike the Swilly in the wild west, the Clogher Valley respected the staff and ticket system. On the one and only occasion when James McNeece left a station on a scheduled run without the staff, the matter was reported, and he was fined £1, no small penalty in the days before World War I, when his pay was 37s (£1·85) a week.

COAL SUPPLIES

Apart from their own requirements for locomotive and station coal, the Clogher Valley Railway acted as primary distributors in their area, transhipping it from Great Northern wagons in the sidings at Tynan, and running it as required to various coal merchants at the stations along the line. After some years working, during which coal lay in the open, the railway company built coal sheds at Fivemiletown, Clogher, Ballygawley, and Aughnacloy, simple erections on which they spent £74 of capital in 1896–7. The Clogher shed was moved to Ballygawley in 1909 for use by the permanent way staff.

The provision of locomotive coal was left to the general manager, who reported his decisions at the next board meeting. In general a shipload of coal was bought, unloaded at Newry, railed by the Great Northern to Tynan, shovelled across to Clogher Valley wagons there and railed to Aughnacloy for storage. For instance, in mid-1894 a cargo of Birchgrove Colliery coal was shipped from Swansea, and cost the company 11s (55p) a ton. By 1910, coal costs for the year ending 30 September were £1,239, out of which the company ran 94,636 train miles.

Clogher Valley Tramway.

BANK HOLIDAY!

On SATURDAY, 26th of DECEMBER, 1891,

CHEAP EXCURSION TICKETS

Will be issued by any Train to and from all Stations at

SINGLE FARE

FOR THE DOUBLE JOURNEY.

☞ No Excursion Tickets will, however be issued where the reduced fare amounts to less than 10d.

These Tickets will be available on day of issue only.

BY ORDER,

DAVID J. STEWART,
GENERAL MANAGER.

Head Offices, Aughnacloy, 10th Dec., 1891.

4947—Trimble, Printer, Enniskillen.

The impact of cross-channel labour troubles on supplies was mentioned as early as 1898, and in the half-yearly report dated 7 November, a decrease of £162 in the traffic receipts was blamed on 'the fluctuations of commerce and the Welsh Coal Strike'. A more serious situation arose in 1912, when a miners' strike brought about a shortage of fuel from March, and some trains had to be cancelled. The situation was eased by June, but at the board meeting that month, the manager reported an offer of 600/700 tons of Ebbw Vale coal at £1 per ton, a price which he described as 'exorbitant'. The directors left the matter in Sloan's hands, and he was able to report the purchase of a cargo at 16s 9d (84p) a ton fob Newport.

At the end of the 1914–18 war coal prices rose steeply, and stocks were kept as low as possible to avoid tying up cash. On 6 June 1921 it was reported that the stock represented only two weeks' usage. As a panic measure a bridging supply of American coal was obtained from the Great Northern, and on 1 August some degree of normality returned with a cargo of 247 tons of Welsh coal.

The General Strike of 1926 had a more profound effect than anything that had happened before. In June Sloan was authorised to reduce the train service to eke out the coal stock, and Bundoran excursion trains were cancelled. Prices rose steeply and in August, 100 tons of 'foreign coal' cost the company £2 10s (£2·50) a ton. In October they were glad to get 100 tons of 'patent fuel', probably briquettes, for £3 5s (£3·25) a ton, and by November they were scraping the bottom of the barrel and paid the Great Northern Railway at the rate of £3 10s (£3·50) for 25 tons. Also in November, 18 tons were supplied by John Kelly Ltd, the Belfast importers, at £3 15s (£3·75). Worse was to come. The crisis continued into December, when Sloan reported to his directors that he 'had purchased small lots of loco coal during the month at 60/–, 65/–, 80/–, 90/– and £6 per ton.' Coal was rapidly pricing itself out of the market, and the stage was being set for the introduction of diesel haulage, though on the Clogher Valley that was still eight years away.

WAGES AND WAR

Prior to 1911 there are few references in the minute books to wage increases, and it is safe to assume that in most instances the original rates still held. At the board meeting in October 1911, the directors agreed to certain increases in weekly wages; these affected Miss Bloomer, agent at Caledon, who received a rise to 10s (50p), R. Ferguson, head porter at Fivemiletown (to 15s [75p]), W. Devine and A. MacCollum, booking clerks at Aughnacloy and Clogher (to 13s [65p]). At the same time, certain gatekeepers found their pay increased, though it is not clear whether this was on grounds of personal hardship or of responsibility. A rise to 3s (15p) a week was given to R. Crawford (Carryclogher No 1), Andrew Hackett (Carryclogher No 2), William Noble (Terrew), James Murphy (Ballymagowan), and Robert Boyd (Clogher). Yet Francis Droogan at the difficult Lisdoart crossing only rose to 2s 6d and James Donnelly at Annaghilla to 2s.

On 1 July 1912 there were increases in stationmasters' wages in four out of six instances, the minute book recording:

Aughnacloy to rise from 25/– to 27/6
Ballygawley to remain at 21/–
Augher to remain at 20/–
Clogher to rise from 19/– to 20/–
Fivemiletown to rise from 25/– to 27/6
Brookeborough to rise from 18/– to 20/–

Though Great Britain and Germany went to war on 4 August 1914 and, within a day, the entire railway system of England, Scotland, and Wales was placed under the control of the Railway Executive Committee, there was no similar imposition of control in Ireland. Unified direction did not begin there until over two years later, and during the interim the railways continued to operate under their accustomed management.

Prices began to rise and, in common with other Irish railway workers, the Clogher Valley men began to make requests for higher wages. The first demands came before the directors towards the end of 1915; at the board meeting on 4 October various increases were agreed upon, but on an individual rather than a general basis, and only after application had been made personally. The minute book lists increases agreed upon at that meeting which, apart from mere statistics, are of interest in that they provide a record of the names of staff at that time.

TRAFFIC DEPARTMENT	
F. McLoughlin, clerk, Fivemiletown	to rise from 15/– a week to 16/–
W. Devine, clerk, Aughnacloy	to rise from 15/– a week to 16/–
W. J. Stinson, clerk, Ballygawley	to rise from 10/– a week to 12/–
A. McCollum, clerk, Clogher	to rise from 13/– a week to 15/–
J. Devine, head porter, Aughnacloy	to rise from 15/– a week to 16/–
E. Cassidy, night watchman, Fivemiletown	to remain at 13/– a week
LOCOMOTIVE DEPARTMENT	
P. Brannigan, engine driver	to rise from 37/– a week to 38/–
G. Leany, spare engine driver	to rise from 22/6 a week to 25/–
J. Maguire, fireman	to remain at 20/– a week
J. McKenna, fireman	to remain at 20/– a week
R. Irwin, fireman	to remain at 20/– a week
J. Girvan, fireman	to rise from 15/– a week to 18/–
W. Rea, stationary engineman	to rise from 15/– a week to 18/–
J. Friel, carriage fitter	to rise from 20/– a week to 22/6
J. McFadden, carpenter	to rise from 24/– a week to 26/–
R. Lynn, cleaner	to remain at 14/– a week
J. McAdam, labourer	to remain at 15/– a week
J. Cuddy, labourer	to remain at 13/– a week
H. Irwin, labourer	to remain at 11/– a week
J. Boyle, coal man	to remain at 13/– a week
A. Given, fitter	to rise from 24/– a week to 26/6

At the November board meeting, further applications were considered and decisions made:

R. J. Campbell, p.way carpenter	to rise from 18/– a week to 19/–
C. Meenan, porter, Clogher	at 13/– a week, decision adjourned
W. J. Thompson, engine driver	to remain at 37/– a week
J. McNeece, engine driver	to remain at 37/– a week
J. Maguire, fireman	to remain at 20/– a week
J. McKenna, fireman	to remain at 20/– a week

A month later, three men were reconsidered, and received rises:

J. Cuddy, labourer	to rise from 13/- a week to 14/-
Drivers Thompson & McNeece	to rise from 37/- a week to 38/-

In January 1916, permanent way gangers received a rise in pay of one shilling a week, but increases were refused to James Boyle, the locomotive coal man and to Thomas Smith, a cleaner. Three months passed before further changes were made, and at the April board meeting the pay of Fitter Girvan was brought up to 30s a week, and that of Carpenter P. McFadden to 36s. In May 1916, one shilling a week was granted to R. Gillespie, carpenter and J. Boyle the coal man; while in July Boilermaker Cullinan went from 36s to 38s, though Blacksmith Carberry remained unchanged at 36s.

In 1916, disturbance to main line traffic elsewhere occurred as a result of the uprising that took place during Easter Week, but the effect was localised in the vicinity of Dublin and Wexford. Bodies of the Irish Volunteers took over Westland Row and Harcourt Street stations in Dublin, and the Dublin & South Eastern was the main company to suffer damage. On the Great Northern, the main line was blown up in two places, but traffic was not greatly disrupted. The Clogher Valley was virtually unaffected. Indeed during that troubled spring the only incident had a comic flavour, for on 6 March one Thomas Watson travelled for two miles on the buffer of a wagon of the 3.55pm down train between Fivemiletown and Corralongford. To discourage such light-hearted demonstrations, the company issued a summons against Watson, but agreed to withdraw it upon payment of costs and expenses. In their leniency towards Watson, the company's attitude was consistent with their treatment three years earlier of a Miss Wallace of Clabby, who 'attempted to enter No 1 train in Fivemiletown street in motion'. She was 'cautioned severely by the general manager' but no further proceedings were instituted, surely a contrast to the three court cases in 1888 and 1889.

As the war went on, over the whole of Ireland the men's

wage demands continued, and were dealt with piecemeal. In December 1916 the locomotive men on the Great Southern & Western demanded a permanent increase of 6s a week, or a further War Bonus of 10s. No agreement could be reached. Both management and men were dissatisfied with the existing uncontrolled conditions and government control was requested from both sides. The GS & W locomotive men were in fact due to strike at midnight on 16 December, but that afternoon it was announced that the government had decided to assume control of the Irish lines, and the strike was averted. The Order in Council placing the Irish Railways under unified control was issued on 22 December 1916, and the Irish Railways Executive Committee took up duties on 1 January 1917. Thereafter wage increases were general, initially 7s a week, but followed by an all-round War Bonus of 5s a week from 9 April 1917.

Changes made by the Irish Railways Executive Committee mainly affected the main-line companies, but a coal shortage in early 1918 caused the management to watch their stock position closely, though no restrictions had to be placed on the running of trains. On the main lines, speeds were to be reduced to save coal, but that could scarcely be applied to Clogher Valley movements.

During 1918 the supply position became critical in other ways. New rails, which were badly needed, were not obtainable, and neither were sleepers. The company probably regretted that in October 1912 they had refused a Sligo, Leitrim offer of old rails at £3 5s (£3·25) a ton. One matter which did affect the Clogher Valley profoundly was a general shortage of calcium carbide, used to generate acetylene gas and which was imported. The carriages were acetylene lit, so were the great engine headlamps, and at least two of the stations, and there was a rush to procure oil lamps.

Barnhill continued to press for decent maintenance of his track, and with no new rails to be had, the Clogher Valley turned to the Great Northern for succour. In March 1915 they had bought 120 tons of secondhand rails from that source, but by 1918 the Great Northern could not help, though the Sligo, Leitrim could. By June 1920 the Great Northern had some rails to spare, and 120 tons were purchased at £14 a ton, with in addition 7 tons of fishplates. They were old 55lb rails, and were badly needed to reinforce the shaky Clogher Valley track, where the original 45lb rails were wearing badly on curves.

Neglect had also affected the telephone system and during the summer of 1920 the company approached both the Great Northern Railway and the Post Office authorities with a request that these experts perform a thorough overhaul. Neither was willing, so a contract was made with Gilmour & Co of Belfast, which became effective from 2 August.

Government control over the Irish railways ended on 15 August 1921, and after five years of living in artificial conditions, the companies faced the problem of running their own businesses again. Things were different, and would never be the same again. During control, the cost of working had increased disproportionately to receipts, with the effect that, over Ireland as a whole, expenditure had gone up by 265 per cent and receipts by 95 per cent since 1913. Compensation was to be paid by the government for services rendered. After much argument, the Irish railways received a round £3 million, and out of that kitty the Clogher Valley got £16,732. It might have bought them a couple of new engines. But the grossly inflated wages bill remained, and a complicated and substantial reduction in wages became necessary and was made by all companies during 1921. On the Clogher Valley the wages of 88 men were reduced by a flat rate of 10s from November 1921, two men had cuts of 7s 6d, and one man of 3s 6d, giving a total weekly saving of £44 18s 6d (£44·92½). Reductions were made in the officers' salaries, that of the general manager dropped from £670 to £600, that of the accountant from £365 to £300, and reference has already been made to the reduction from £420 to £350 in the locomotive superintendent's pay. In the following month action was continued to reduce the wages bill. We have seen how Martin lost five pw men, in addition a locomotive apprentice resigned, and one of the Aughnacloy clerks got a month's notice. It was a sorry sequel to victory.

THE TROUBLES AND THE BORDER

Before the control of the IREC had been relaxed, it was apparent that unified British rule over Ireland was coming to an end, and in 1921 the island was partitioned into two separate self-governing units. Of the thirty-two counties, twenty-six formed the Irish Free State, the remaining six formed Northern Ireland, loosely called Ulster. Before and after the division internal tensions and civil disorders rent the country, and inevitably the railways were a favourite target for acts of sabotage. Among other branches, the Great Northern closed the Dundalk—Enniskillen line from 20 September 1920 until early 1921, in the process denying Maguiresbridge any passing traffic.

The Clogher Valley Railway's line lay entirely within the new state of Northern Ireland, and thus did not suffer the problems that faced the Great Northern, whose tracks crossed the political frontier seventeen times. County Monaghan was now within the Free State, and therefore much of the Tynan—Ballygawley section lay only a mile or so from the Border. Because their Monaghan hinterland was virtually denied to traders along the Clogher Valley, the established pattern of business, such as attendance at cattle fairs and the import and export of cattle and sheep, was radically altered.

On the two narrow gauge railways in County Donegal traffic was interfered with by refusals to work trains conveying military or police personnel, and by sabotage of signalling and track, and the pre-partition troubles went on into the succeeding period of civil war. On the Great Northern, and on the Donegal lines, normal working was subject to occasional obstruction until 1923. On the Clogher Valley, apart from a few rifle shots aimed at passing trains, the storm passed by, and the only incident of note took place in the townland of Curlough.

Curlough was a place that seemed insignificant in 1887, but soon showed promise of useful traffic both to and from the Monaghan side of the river. Plans for a siding, goods store, and office were approved by the board in November 1894 and Keenan of Dublin built the corrugated iron store and office for £133. As traffic developed, the place was renamed Emyvale Road, since the village of Emyvale was two miles to the south-west. Partition put an abrupt end to the traffic from Monaghan, and the road was not 'approved' for cross-border car traffic. The deterioration continued a stage further when, in August 1921, the store was broken into, though the burglars only took away a box of ferrets, which cost the company £7 14s (£7·70) in compensation. Then in March 1922 a platoon of 'specials' or auxiliary police, was quartered in the store. It was about then that the only recorded interference with a train took place, when one was illegally held up and searched a short way on the Caledon side of the halt. It was a very trivial incident compared to those in Donegal, but it was ironic that it took place near to where the specials were quartered.

Along the Lorder, customs posts sprang up on railway lines and on certain cross-border roads. Tynan & Caledon was one of the Great Northern stations where passengers were scrutinised by the Northern preventive men. The southern examination was done four miles down the line at Glaslough, or at Monaghan. Passengers off a Clogher Valley train were not allowed to board a northbound Great Northern train until the passengers that arrived on it had been subjected to customs examination. Passengers going south and joining at Tynan were given a cursory look over before the Great Northern train arrived. Maguiresbridge had none of these excitements for on that line, the customs officials were at Newtownbutler and Clones.

THE 1922 COMMISSION

Lengthy evidence was given by H. S. Sloan before the Northern Ireland Railway Commission which was held in May and June 1922. The members of the Commission failed to agree in their findings, and in due course a majority report and a minority report were issued inside one cover. The majority report was signed by the chairman, Mr Justice Brown, and by Major D. G. Shillington, Messrs H. L. Garrett, W. Grant, MP, and W. Jackson, MP. The minority report was issued over the names of Alderman S. Kyle and G. M. Donaldson.

As regards the Clogher Valley Railway, the majority report traced its history and financial position, noted that it had made a yearly loss in working on 20 out of 27 occasions since 1894, and that it had never made a profit since 1912. The maximum loss after 1912 was in 1916, when it rose to £1,479 and the baronies had to contribute £1,645. Of the total liability, a part was refunded by the Treasury.

The majority report considered, as a whole, the merits and demerits of nationalisation, unification, and amalgamation under private management. It was not considered that the directorate of the railways was top-heavy, and regarded the fees that they received, around £5,000 a year, as being 'practically a negligible proportion of the total wages bill'. It was recommended that private management should continue, but that the Clogher Valley should be absorbed into the Great Northern, and the Ballycastle Railway in the north of County Antrim into the Midland (Northern Counties Committee). Other recommendations were made which concerned the consultative machinery between the companies and the railway trades unions, and the matter of parity of pay between Great Britain and Northern Ireland.

The minority report by Kyle and Donaldson laboured the existing low wages of the lower grades of railwaymen, and recommended that all the railways in Northern Ireland should come under public ownership, basing this on the apparently wasteful administration, whereby 1,259 miles of line were under the control of thirteen different managements.

The reports were not acted upon by the Government of Northern Ireland. Only incidentally was one of the proposals of the majority report carried out when, after failure of the Ballycastle Railway Company, it was bought out by the LMS (Northern Counties Committee) in 1924. The Clogher Valley, buttressed by annual contributions from the baronies and the Treasury, continued on its unsteady way, providing a service to the travelling public and in the movement of cattle and goods. However, as the 1920s wore on, the Clogher Valley, in common with all the other railways in the province, came under the increasing menace of road transport. The Government took no action to stem unrestricted and often unfair competition until 1927, when an Act was passed giving the railways power to run motor buses for the conveyance of passengers, and to compete in a field that was already overfull.

STORM CLOUDS AHEAD

The progressive deterioration in finances was causing concern by the middle 1920s, not only to the County Councils and the government, but also to certain members of the directorate. On Tuesday, 8 December 1925, fourteen directors gathered for the board meeting. Before them, they had the financial results for the half year that had ended on 30 September, and they found no pleasure in the sight. When the minutes of the November meeting had been read and confirmed, John Bloomfield moved a lengthy resolution:

> Owing to the very serious consideration of the heavy responsibility of the ratepayers of the contributory areas in the Counties of Tyrone and Fermanagh for the upkeep of the Clogher Valley Railway Company, and with the shadow of a still heavier burden about to fall on them owing to government subsidy being almost exhausted, I beg to move that steps be immediately taken before disaster arrives to provide by the following or other means as may be propounded a Shareholders' Redemption Fund:
>
> No. 1 That all employees get 3 months notice to terminate their appointments.

Page 143

ROLLING STOCK

(Above) *Bogie carriage No 15. Fivemiletown, July 1933*; (centre) *Butter wagon No 36, Fivemiletown, June 1937*; (below) *The spray train.* Fury's *boiler on wagon No 62. Locomotive No 3. Aughnacloy, July 1933*

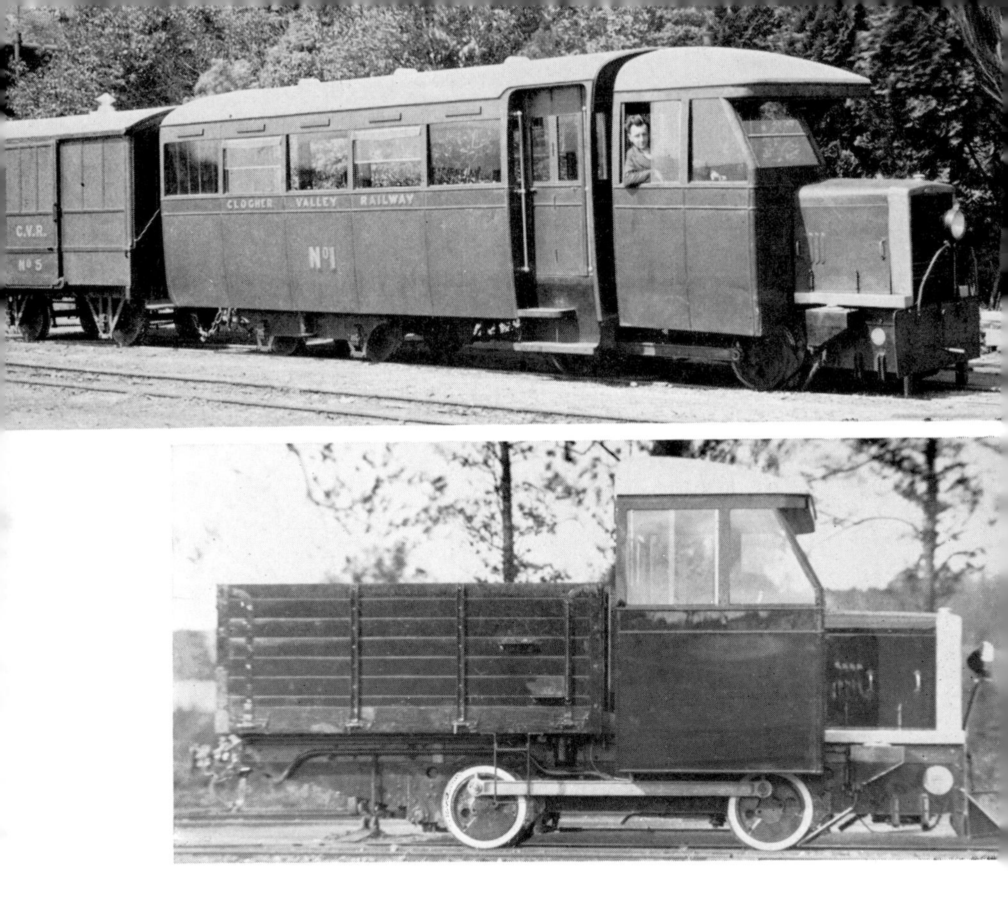

Page 144

THE DIESEL VEHICLES

(Above) *Railcar No 1 with brake van No 5. Fivemiletown, May 1937;* (centre) *'The Unit'. Tractor No 2, Aughnacloy, September 1933. Cab in original state;* (below) *'The Unit', with brake van No 1 and carriage No 15. Fivemiletown, May 1937. Cab cut away, following crossing gate collision; leading cowcatcher removed*

No. 2 That steps be taken in the meantime to realise the entire concern either by disposing of it piecemeal or selling it in one or more lots to some company or individual and that the amount raised be placed to the credit of the above fund.

No. 3 That the Northern Government be approached and asked to capitalise their 2 per cent guarantee and the amount placed to the credit of the above fund.

No. 4 And that owing to the Government's liability under the Local Government Act of 1898 they be demanded to give a large free grant to the above fund.

No. 5 And that the deficit if any be raised by obtaining a loan at a small rate of interest repayable by a small percentage on the rates of the contributory areas in a number of years principal and interest.

No. 6 That a committee of the directors (ratepayers and shareholders) be appointed to approach the County Councils of Tyrone and Fermanagh or a committee of both who would ask the Members of Parliament for the said counties all to meet and consult together and form plans for approaching the Northern Government on the lines indicated above.

Bloomfield's motion found no seconder and it fell to the ground. Had it been accepted, it would have spelled the end of the railway. But it produced a flutter in the dovecots, and the minutes tell of a discussion that followed on the need to reduce expenses. Towards this end, an Economy Committee was formed, of the chairman and Messrs Bloomfield, Johnston, Jackson Stewart, Hadden, McCann, Watson, and the general manager.

Eight weeks later, the Economy Committee gathered, and viewed a revised timetable, drawn up by Sloan to reduce working costs. They then adjourned for a fortnight to chew things over. On 15 February they met again, at Fivemiletown, decided to make no change in the timetable as it stood, but to economise by shutting Colebrooke halt, by 'substituting Claraghy and Stonepark for it', and by stopping trains at every halt in an effort to attract custom. These economies, which were trivial, received more concrete support by the dismissal of the Brookeborough porter, the Colebrooke caretaker, and the Fivemiletown night porter. Sloan reported that he had 'made reductions in the stationmaster's office at Aughnacloy which would reduce expenses, for two years, by 54/3 a week' and said that he was giving his own typist notice from the end of March. It toyed with the problem, but heralded far more stringent cuts that were to be recommended from outside in the following year.

THE 1927 INQUIRY

By 1927 the Government of Northern Ireland decided that the special position of the Railway merited investigation, and set up a three-man committee for that purpose. Its terms of reference were:

> To enquire into the affairs of the Clogher Valley Railway Company Limited, and the administration and working of that undertaking; to report whether, and under what terms and conditions, the railway should continue working, or, in the alternative, what arrangements should be made to close down the railway and to liquidate the Baronial Guarantee; and also to ascertain if and what alternative facilities would be required in the districts concerned.

The committee consisted of Walter Abbott, OBE, for the Ministry of Finance, Arthur H. Coote, JP, for the Tyrone County Council, and Hugh Kirkpatrick for the Fermanagh County Council. In their inquiry they required expert technical advice and, towards that end, Lord Craigavon, the then Prime Minister of Northern Ireland, asked Sir Josiah Stamp, chairman of the London, Midland & Scottish Railway to recommend a suitable person. The task was entrusted to Robert Killin, OBE. With three members of his staff, Killin spent two days on the ground.

Robert Killin had joined the Caledonian Railway in 1882, and by 1897 was night stationmaster at Carlisle. Eleven years later he was promoted to be assistant district superintendent of the Western Division of the Caledonian Railway, and in 1910 he rose to be superintendent of that same division. In 1912 he became assistant superintendent of the line, and in 1916 superintendent of the line. At the grouping, the Caledonian became a part of the LMS, and Killin was eventually put in charge of the Northern Division. He thus had a long and varied experience of railway operating when Stamp asked him to look at the Clogher Valley.

The 37-page report of the Committee of Investigation was put on sale by the Stationery Office in January 1928, and it contained as a lengthy appendix Killin's statement of the facts, and his recommendations. The whole publication has been loosely referred to on occasions as the Killin Report, since that technical contribution made up about a third of its bulk. In view of the fact that Messrs Abbott, Coote, and Kirkpatrick based many of their recommendations on Killin's statements, the latter are of much interest.

The Killin Report

By the time of Killin's study, it was costing about £17 a day to keep the line open. Having considered the history of the line, Killin formulated three considerations:

(i) whether the railway could be made a paying concern
(ii) if it could not be made to pay, should it be continued
(iii) if discontinued, what alternative transport was there for the district.

He found that stations were 'all capacious and well equipped and much bigger than the traffic to be handled warrants'. The permanent way was in need of heavy expenditure to bring it to a satisfactory state, so that passenger trains could be run at speeds to compete with road buses. The engines and rolling stock likewise required massive expenditure. Killin's findings as regards the engines are discussed in detail in Chapter 7 of this book. He considered that by the beginning of 1930 only three engines would be fit for use. When he examined the line, two double-shifted engines were normally in service; on

Fair Days and holidays, the remaining engines, often in poor shape, were turned out to cope as best they could with the additional traffic.

Killin described the carriage bodies as 'very frail', apart from two on which £200 had been spent on a recent overhaul. The freight vehicles were 'in good condition, and have been kept up to a very good standard.'

After very briefly considering if any cheaper method of working the passenger traffic by rail motors or by what he called 'the tramway system of working' was feasible, Killin concluded that the most satisfactory method of operating would be to cease to carry passengers, and work only freight trains.

Killin pointed out that there was already one passenger motor bus running in competition, and that not long before there had been two, one of which failed when the railway brought their fares down. On removal of railway passenger services, he visualised renewed competition between rival bus companies, and a consequential lowering of fares. 'In any case', wrote Killin, 'the railway has very little chance of competing successfully with the motor bus at speeds of up to 25 miles per hour. . . .'

He estimated that by ceasing to run passenger trains, and confining the operations to freight, the annual cost of working the railway would be reduced by about £10,269. This would not put the line on a paying basis, but would effect a great reduction in the amount to be paid by the guarantors.

The freight service envisaged by Killin was to consist of a working by one steam engine stationed at Aughnacloy, between there, Tynan, Fivemiletown and back. Between Fivemiletown and Maguiresbridge the traffic was light, averaging seven wagons per day, and to work it Killin advocated an Atkinson-Walker steam tractor. Comment on Killin's strong preference for this make of steam tractor is contained in Chapter 8, and is difficult to understand. Killin was an operating rather than a locomotive man, and in practical terms, his recommendation was a complete fiasco. Moreover, when

Killin recommended the Atkinson-Walker, the company that marketed it was on the verge of bankruptcy, and a worse choice it is difficult to imagine.

Drastic economies in manpower were possible under Killin's scheme, the numbers of management and men being cut from 116 to 38. At the top, he considered that one person could act as manager, locomotive superintendent, and accountant with the help of one clerk, and at a salary of £350 per year. The seven 'station agents' would be replaced with Grade 2 porters. All of the 18 gatekeepers would be dispensed with, and the gates replaced by cattle grids except in two or three cases where they would be worked by the train crew. An annual saving of £7,118 in salaries and wages would result.

Killin proposed that permanent way upkeep should be altered and 'the French system should be introduced and one ganger appointed for every five miles of the line.' These men would do light repairs. Heavy repairs would be attended to as required, by a flying squad of a sub-ganger and four platelayers who would transport themselves either by freight train or by motor lorry. Between times, the lorry would deliver goods.

Inattention to detail could certainly not be attributed to Killin, when he turned his thoughts to the electric lighting of the stations at Ballygawley and Fivemiletown. These, he discovered, obtained current from an outside generating station at a price of a shilling a unit. At both these stations, the stationmaster's house drew electric light from the same source:

> and while at Fivemiletown the Station Agent pays direct to the Generating Authority at the rate of 1/– a unit for the current used in his house, at Ballygawley the current used is taken from the company's supply and the Agent pays a fixed charge of £2 10s 0d per annum. It is desirable that the occupants of houses should provide their own light, or at least that the supply of current from the company's main should be discontinued unless adequate payment is made by meter.

An overhead charge is conducive to waste, and is not fair to either party.

Of such a statement, the best that one can say is that it was Caledonian parsimony at its most niggling.

More constructive was his suggestion that double transhipment of coal should be ended by the establishment of a dump at Tynan, the shovelling of coal and the transhipment of heavy traffic being done by a 'coalman', who was to be remunerated for his solitary toil at the rate of £103 a year.

Killin finalised his report with a paragraph 'In estimating these savings a fair margin has been allowed, and if there is a wholehearted effort on the part of the staff, these savings will not only be achieved, but be increased. If it is made known to the staff that the railway is on probation for the next few years and their situations depend on successful results, it will no doubt, provide the necessary incentive in this direction'. Thus ended an astringent report, necessary to point the way to economies, but never mentioning the possibility that road competition might develop in freight and livestock conveyance, nor considering in any detail passenger conveyance by light railcars. As regards the latter omission, in all fairness one may say that at the time Henry Forbes had yet to establish success in passenger railcar working on the Donegal line.

The Abbott Committee in action

Apart from Killin's study, formal public meetings were held by Abbott and his colleagues at Aughnacloy, Fivemiletown, and Brookeborough, at which the ratepayers were given full opportunity to voice their sentiments. General resentment was expressed because of the burden which the railway placed on the rates, often on people who never made use of it, and there was a unanimous demand for a reduction or removal of the burden. In the Caledon area the opinion was strongly in favour of closure of the line, an understandable reaction since they were within walking distance of the Great Northern at Tynan, and the railway had never integrated with the mill, which was the main employer of labour. In contrast,

CLOGHER VALLEY TRAMWAY.

BALLYGAWLEY FAIR.

A Special Train will leave Ballygawley for Tynan at 2-20 p.m.

Cattle for shipment by that train must be loaded up not later than 2-0 p.m.

D. J STEWART,
General Manager.

AUGHNACLOY,
9th June, 1892.

W. Somers, Printer, Aughnacloy.

however, the people of Fivemiletown, Augher, and Clogher were said to want to retain the line. Some of the witnesses demanded 'economy and retrenchment, combined with improved and accelerated services' but the Abbott committee commented that they had 'got very few practical suggestions as to the method by which these ideal conditions might be attained'.

The committee received a statement of the company's case from Major-General Montgomery, the chairman, who imputed blame to the Imperial Government for the wage inflation during 1917–22, and stated that his board of directors had found it impossible in the post-war climate to bring expenditure to within reasonable sight of revenue. According to the Abbott report, Major-General Montgomery proposed the introduction of light steam railcars and the removal of the existing 12 miles per hour speed limit, by which two processes he hoped that £2,000 a year might be saved. The report mentions that in these proposals the chairman 'was supported by the evidence of the General Manager and the Locomotive Superintendent, who thought that the introduction of two Sentinel or Clayton steam cars would increase the passenger traffic and enable considerable economies to be effected'. The capital cost of two such cars was estimated at £9,000 by McClure, while he had stated 'that an additional sum of £2,000 would be required for repairing and reconstructing as an articulated unit, two old locomotives whose boilers are now worn out'. These proposals show a flexibility of thought that was greatly different from Killin's reiteration of the merits of the Atkinson-Walker steam tractor. However, the Abbott committee made their opinion of the Clogher Valley management very clear when they wrote of 'a spirit of *laissez-faire* and a lack of imagination and initiative required to meet changing conditions'. The proposals of McClure had come too late, and Sloan and the directors had failed to seize the chance offered for such adventurous changes when money was available out of the lump sum paid by the government on decontrol in 1921.

The Abbott committee accepted Killin's recommendations, differing from them only in trivial details. In their opinion money should not be spent on improving the track so that passenger services could be continued on an accelerated timetable; there were road buses which gave an adequate service, and the retention of freight train workings was all that was needed. The reduction in numbers and status of staff, envisaged by Killin, was approved of with only minor adjustments. The committee hoped that redundant staff would be sympathetically treated, but they had no remit to cover that.

The committee were not too happy about the coal dump at Tynan proposed by Killin. They laboured his points, but arrived at no definite conclusion, and merely hinted that 'an arrangement might be feasible whereby the Great Northern Railway Company would coal the locomotives . . . but failing such . . . we are disposed to fear that the loss of control over the coal would outweigh any advantage from keeping it at Tynan'.

An interesting question of ownership was highlighted by mention of the safeguard contained in Article 42 of the Clogher Valley Tramway Order of 1884. This provided that if the Baronies had paid money to maintain or work the undertaking during a period of three years 'the undertaking and all the property of the Company connected with it, shall become the property of the Grand Juries'—now the County Councils. This contingency had of course arisen even before the turn of the century, and legally the railway belonged to the County Councils. The committee commented that the County Councils had not yet exercised their rights of ownership ' . . . being either unaware of them, or content to allow the Company to continue in possession and control . . .'

Having thus dryly disposed of that legal point, the Abbott committee proceeded to recommend to the Minister of Commerce and the County Councils the fundamental changes which from 1928, were to place the railway under the control of a joint committee of management. This was to be done by the Ministry of Commerce by means of a Statutory Order.

The report ended with a reference to the shareholders. The register showed a total of 470 names and institutions. The market price of the £10 shares, often sold at a premium before the line was opened, was in 1927 fairly stable at about £4 10s (£4·50) to £5. The shareholders were gently warned that, to buy them out and thereby end the annual payment of dividends, neither the government nor the County Councils were under any obligation to repay at par. The committee indicated that £6 a share would be a fair price, since the annual contribution of £6,166 would in 20 years, find the money needed to be borrowed for share repayment at the then current interest of 5½ per cent.

CHAPTER 7

The Last Thirteen Years 1928-1941

NEW TENANTS AT AUGHNACLOY

In due course, the recommendations of the Abbott Committee were implemented by the Ministry of Commerce of the Government of Northern Ireland, and there came on the statute books The Clogher Valley Railway (Committee of Management) Order 1928, whereby a new nucleus of top management was created. The Committee of Management was formed by an amalgam of members appointed by the Tyrone and Fermanagh County Councils, plus two members appointed by the Minister of Commerce, and they took over the running of the railway from the shareholders' directors. The government did not, in the event, buy out the shareholders, who continued to receive the guaranteed dividend as before, their interests becoming a mere formality, to be taken care of by the board of directors, which remained in existence for that purpose alone. Matters of policy and financial decisions were in the hands of the Committee of Management, with day-to-day operations under their control.

The two members of Committee appointed by the Minister of Commerce were Robert Darragh, JP and Henry Forbes, both practical railwaymen. Darragh was an old Belfast & Northern Counties Railway man, Forbes was Secretary and Manager of the County Donegal Railways Joint Committee and had already 18 years experience of managing a narrow-gauge concern.

FIRST MEETING

The early meetings of the Committee of Management, held towards the end of the summer of 1928, rapidly shaped the format of the future operations of the Clogher Valley Railway. The Committee, although appointed as a result of the Abbott investigation, were not bound to accept the recommendations of the report and, as will be seen, their decisions differed from those recommendations in a number of important details.

The first meeting was held in the Board Room at Aughnacloy on Thursday 28 June, and the members faced a 13-point agenda. The minutes of that meeting list the nine members present. They were, in alphabetical order, Mr Hugh Best, Sir Basil Brooke, Bart, Mr Robert Darragh, JP, Mr Henry Forbes, Mr James Higgins, JP, Mr T. C. W. Marshall, JP, Major-General H. Montgomery, CB, CMG, Major A. G. Moutray, and Major William Stewart, JP, while Mr Hill, secretary to the Tyrone County Council, 'also attended'. They had first to find themselves a chairman and, on the motion of Mr Higgins, seconded by Major Stewart, Major-General Hugh Montgomery was unanimously elected to that office, thereby continuing a long family association with the direction of the Clogher Valley Railway. He had been chairman of the board of directors since 1924, and continued to hold that position.

The second matter to which the new Committee attended was the appointment of a secretary and general manager, a formality perhaps, but none the less necessary, since under the new regime the position held by Horace Sloan had ceased to exist. So it was proposed by the chairman, and seconded by Mr Higgins, 'that H. S. Sloan be appointed secretary and general manager'.

A decision had to be taken on a regular time and day of meeting, and it was agreed that it should be at 12.15pm on the first Monday in each month 'unless otherwise arranged at the previous meeting'. The matter of admitting the Press to meetings was discussed at length; hitherto the Press had come to the annual shareholders' meetings, but were never admitted to board meetings. Following the latter practice, it was decided not to admit the Press to meetings of the Committee of Management, but the secretary was given discretionary powers to issue a short report to newsmen.

The obvious fact that the Clogher Valley was entirely surrounded by the lines of the Great Northern Railway came up for discussion. If that prosperous main line company could be persuaded to make the Clogher Valley a narrow-gauge appendage to its system, many of the long-term worries of the Committee would be solved. It was agreed that attempts should be made to arrive at an amalgamation or working agreement with the Great Northern. Towards that end, Sloan had already drafted a letter to the chairman of the board of the GNR(I), it was tabled at Aughnacloy, and on Mr Higgins' motion, Mr Best seconding, it was decided to instruct the secretary to forward it to Dublin.

As part of the urgent economies, agreement had already been reached between the old board of directors and the National Union of Railwaymen on the unpleasant matter of a 10 per cent reduction in wages and salaries, and steps were taken to implement this without delay.

Various minor matters were discussed. Darragh and Forbes, the Ministry representatives, were to receive a fee of £5 for each attendance, an unsuccessful attempt was made to transfer the company's account from the Northern to the Ulster Bank, Sloan was to get a copy of the printed CVR Order and send a copy to each member of Committee, who were also to be issued with annual free passes. Then, with the annual big day not far off 'authority was given to the General Manager to use wagons for the conveyance of passengers on 12th July if found necessary'. Finally Sir Basil Brooke, pointing out that he was the only member of the Fermanagh County Council on the Committee, asked permission of the others that in case he found himself unable to attend any meetings in the future, the Fermanagh County Council might, with the approval of the Ministry, be allowed to appoint a substitute. The Committee of Management agreed to the proposal.

Robert Darragh and Henry Forbes, as practical railwaymen, were strongly placed to shape the future of the Clogher Valley. They were given a remit by the Committee to examine the line and 'to give their opinion as to future working'. Towards that end, the meeting was adjourned for three weeks, while Darragh and Forbes, with the Killin Report in their pockets and a great deal of practical ability in their own heads, thoroughly inspected the railway, and assessed its place in the community.

THREE WEEKS LATER

The 'wagons for the conveyance of passengers' had lain empty for a week when, on Thursday 19 July, the adjourned meeting reconvened. Under Major-General Montgomery as chairman, the full complement of members attended. In the absence of Sir Basil Brooke, the Fermanagh County Council was represented by Mr Hugh J. Stewart of Tempo.

At first, financial matters occupied the members. A letter had been received from the Ministry of Commerce, which pointed out that difficulties might arise through the fact that, under existing legislation, the Committee had no power to borrow money on the security of the rates in the guaranteeing area. The chairman hastened to report that he had received a private letter from the Secretary to the Ministry 'assuring him that he might count on the co-operation of the Ministry in getting over the difficulties, and that the legal snag need not in any way deter the Committee from planning . . .'

A formal 'take over' was necessary and to achieve this, Major Moutray proposed, Mr Higgins seconded and the Committee passed unanimously that they should 'hereby take over the Ownership, Management and Control of the Company's property and the funds of the Undertaking and all transactions and business done since 10th September 1927, the date of the last published accounts of the Undertaking'.

Hopes that the Great Northern Railway might adopt the Clogher Valley were lessened, when the secretary reported that only a formal acknowledgement had come from Dublin. There had, however, been a suggestion that the Clogher Valley might like to run a connection from Tynan with a GN train that was to leave Belfast at 5.35pm during the summer months. The reaction of the members of Committee was unenthusiastic; another working would have had to be added to their schedule, and one that would have hardly promised much traffic.

Much of the time of the meeting was occupied with the submission of a report by Darragh and Forbes, following their inspection of the railway. Forbes read the report to the Committee, discussion followed, and 'it was unanimously agreed that a Passenger service be continued and that on and after 1st September, 1928, 1st class fares be no longer issued. First class carriages to be used, as far as possible, for the conveyance of all passengers.' By their decision, the Committee cast aside that main recommendation of the Killin Report.

In the insistence that passenger traffic should continue, one cannot but detect the enthusiasm and confidence of Henry Forbes. On his Donegal Railways for the previous two years, he had been experimenting with passenger railcar operation. His efforts had been attended with success, and by 1928 Forbes had four petrol-driven railcars at work. Compared to the conventional steam-hauled trains which they had replaced, they were less expensive to run, they were less damaging to the track and, provided that their limited seating accommodation was not unexpectedly overwhelmed, they offered an adequate and economically viable service to a district that was not dissimilar to that of the Clogher Valley.

On the Donegal Railways, only one of Forbes's railcars (No 4) was of new construction. The others were rebuilds. By 1928, the first of the series was twenty-one years of age, while Nos 2 and 3 had come as secondhand acquisitions from the Derwent Valley Light Railway, outside York, and had been regauged from 4ft 8½in. Their detailed story has been told elsewhere.* In their homespun non-standardisation they might be called a motley collection, but this would be unkind, for they performed well on the whole, and they fully justified Forbes's adventurous excursions into the early railcar field. It can fairly be claimed that they showed the way for the Clogher Valley purchase.

Before a railcar could appear on the Clogher Valley, the Committee had to make improvements to the existing steam-hauled train services. It was considered essential that the lighting of the carriages should be improved, and 'that either electric or some other system' should be adopted. McClure was asked to prepare a report for the next meeting. Acceleration of passenger services by running them separately from goods workings was agreed upon in principle. So long as steam traction remained, this was difficult to achieve, but as a first move 'it was decided to experiment with No. 1 Up and No. 4 Down trains' as accelerated services. These were the early morning Fivemiletown—Tynan and the evening Tynan—Fivemiletown trains.

As regards new motive power, a sub-committee consisting of Messrs Darragh and Forbes, with the general manager, the locomotive engineer, and J. J. S. Barnhill 'was appointed to get full information regarding new tractors and to make recommendations to the Committee on the subject as soon as practicable'. Until their report was made and considered, nothing was done about the negotiation of a loan for that purpose.

CHANGES

By 13 August when they met again, the Committee of Management were feeling their feet, and more drastic changes were implemented. It was decided to close the permanent way workshop at Ballygawley, and to transfer the

* *The County Donegal Railways* by the author, published by David & Charles.

equipment from it to Aughnacloy. This was a more complete alteration than that decided the previous month, when it was accepted that new permanent way stocks should be stored at Aughnacloy, and the Ballygawley establishment and stocks allowed to run down. The centralisation of all the engineering activities at Aughnacloy must have seemed logical. But the change went further, for the services of Inspector Hugh Martin, in charge of the permanent way since 1893 or perhaps even earlier, were to be dispensed with from 1 September 1928. A carpenter and a painter were also to be made redundant.

It will be recalled that, since 1913, permanent way upkeep had been under the periodic supervision of J. J. S. Barnhill, who had collaborated with Inspector Martin. With Martin out of the way, the supervision of the permanent way was allocated to D. N. McClure, in addition to his duties as locomotive engineer, and because of his increased responsibility his salary was to be unaffected by the general 10 per cent reduction, and was to remain unchanged at £350 a year. It is noteworthy that, so far as McClure's supervision of civil engineering matters was concerned, he was to be responsible to Barnhill, who remained in his existing capacity.

At the September meeting of the Committee, a note was submitted from Barnhill, which detailed McClure's duties regarding the upkeep of the permanent way, the older man no doubt feeling that it was wise that McClure's terms of reference should be clearly defined from the outset, perhaps because he was by training and experience a mechanical engineer and not a civil engineer. The Committee agreed to Barnhill's proposals, and it was minuted that McClure was responsible 'for the safety of the line', while Barnhill was to be in a consultative capacity. This was confirmed at the Committee meeting held on 1 October 1928, when it was noted that McClure was to supply Barnhill with a copy of his monthly report.

The September meeting also faced a request from their ex-permanent way inspector for superannuation, since apparently no provision had been made over the years for a pension. They agreed to Martin's request, but minuted that it was not to form a precedent, probably fearing an avalanche of demands from others finding themselves similarly displaced. They went on to decide to close the Caledon office from 1 November 1928, disregarding the inevitable protests from local traders.

The attempt to persuade the Great Northern to adopt the Clogher Valley came to nothing, the Dublin-based company's directors 'being unable to entertain the proposal' to absorb the CV system. They did, however, hasten to assure the CV Committee that they would help in any way possible in effecting economies. The Clogher Valley took them up on that one, dispensed with their own checkers at Tynan and Maguiresbridge, and thus eliminated duplication of effort by accepting the GN check of goods at those two places.

As elsewhere, road omnibus competition was making itself felt, and it was decided to fight back by opening more roadside halts. Forbes was doing a similar exercise on the Donegal with some measure of success, and Sloan was asked to list suitable halts. In fact, there was little real need for more stopping places, for there were 34 in the 37 miles and a balance had to be struck between timetable acceleration, and the slowing that would result from a rash of roadside halts, many of which would yield little revenue.

By the autumn of 1928 it was decided to follow Killin's recommendation of an Atkinson-Walker steam tractor, and an order was placed with that firm. Delivery was made in January 1929, but as described in more detail in Chapter 8, the vehicle was a failure from the start. It was as well that, in the contract, Messrs Atkinson-Walker had agreed to take the vehicle back free of cost if it was not satisfactory. During the summer they tried to improve matters by fitting a larger boiler, but achieved nothing. By October the firm was bankrupt.

MCCLURE AT THE TOP

After a connection with the Clogher Valley that had extended over 35 years, Horace Sloan retired from the position of general manager and secretary in January 1929. In his place, without advertisement of the vacancy, the Committee appointed David N. McClure, to be 'general manager and engineer', his salary to be £500 a year, rising by £20 increments to a maximum of £600. The dour Sloan remained in the background as 'adviser'. To the secretaryship came Paddy Soraghan, who combined that office with his position as accountant.

As no less a person than general manager, McClure's subordinate relationship to Barnhill could not easily have continued. But already the latent friction between the two men had flared into undisguised enmity. On 11 January, Barnhill had addressed a letter to Sloan, criticising in systematic detail what he regarded as neglect on the part of McClure to maintain the permanent way in a proper state of repair. The letter was considered to be of sufficient importance to be circulated to all members of the Committee of Management and to be attached to the minutes of the following meeting as an Appendix. It became 'Appendix A', for by then McClure was in power, and vigorously and successfully defended his position in a letter to the Committee dated on the last day of January 1929.

Barnhill wrote to Sloan on 11 January from his own office in Baltic Buildings, Londonderry:

> I have to report that on 9th inst., accompanied by Mr. McClure, I made an inspection of the whole of the Line, and found that the general condition of the Permanent Way had fallen noticeably below the standard at which Mr. Martin was accustomed to maintain it, and I regret to find that no relaying had been done in the quarter. Mr. Martin and I had arranged for relaying at two places which we pointed out to Mr. McClure on site on 25th September.

On the same day we showed Mr. McClure a defective crossing on the main line at Colebrooke and instructed him to replace it with a new crossing intended for it, to be taken from the store at Ballygawley. The defective crossing remains untouched, and on asking Mr. McClure for an explanation on 9th inst., his excuse was that there was no time for it, yet time was found for the larger work, in no way urgent, of removing 45 yds. length of the siding to which the defective crossing gives access.

I regret also to have to report that the diary of Permanent Way inspection, recording the lengths walked over each day, which I asked for in my letter to you of 29th August, and which the Committee at their meeting on October 1st, ordered to be kept by Mr. McClure for inspection, has not been kept, with the result that I had no means of knowing what was being done and no opportunity of giving advice on the steps to be taken to meet the special difficulties of maintenance of particular curves, and so on.

This is perhaps of less consequence as Mr. McClure took the trouble to explain to me on October 1st, in the hearing of Messrs. Darragh and Forbes, that I might give advice but that he need not take it unless he liked, but that that was his funeral.

Now one might have supposed that a young man entering upon a difficult work of which he had no previous experience might welcome advice from those qualified to give it.

I have mentioned the preceding details with one definite purpose only, namely, to have it put upon record that under the system instituted by the Committee on 1st October, I am prevented from exercising reasonable supervision over the maintenance of the Permanent Way, and cannot therefore be charged with any responsibility so long as this system of working continues.

Nominally, I have been relieved of all responsibility for the safety of the Line, but if and when an accident occurs, I shall properly be held very culpable, if as an experienced Engineer I now silently acquiesce in the working of a system, regarding which I was not consulted in the first instance, and which after three months experience, does not, in my opinion, tend to safety.

I take the opportunity of repeating the view I have always

expressed that a 37 mile length of line of the character of the Clogher Valley Railway, demands for its proper supervision the full time of an experienced Inspector of Permanent Way.

Yours faithfully,

J. J. S. Barnhill.

McClure's reply took its place in the minute book as Appendix B, and was addressed, not to Sloan, but to the Committee:

Gentlemen,

Replying to criticisms embodied in the above letter, I must, in the first instance, protest most emphatically at Mr. Barnhill's sweeping statement that the general condition of the Permanent Way had fallen noticeably below the standard at which it was previously kept.

Mr. Barnhill travelled over the line with me on the No. 2 Up regular train from Maguiresbridge to Tynan on the 9th January.

He did not leave the train at any point, or stop at any place for the purpose of examining the track, during the entire run.

From the engine windows, as well as I could, owing to the heavy rain which continually clouded the glasses, I pointed out the more important points which I was attending to, such as, for example:

(1) Curves at 35 miles, where the formation is weak.
(2) Steps taken to rectify and hold curve at 31¾ miles (Colebrooke)
(3) Hollow at 30 miles, which required lifting.
(4) Condition of points in Fivemiletown station and repairs carried out through street.
(5) Steps taken to hold curves at 25¼ miles (Kiltermon).
(6) Re-sleepering and elevation of curve at 22 miles (Findermore).
(7) Curve at 20¾ miles (Carryclogher) re-sleepered.
(8) Curves at Farranetra—19¾ miles.
(9) Repairs to line at Augher (Co. Surveyor's complaint).
(10) Pulling and straightening of line—10¾ to 10¼ miles.
(11) Work carried out in Aughnacloy yard for amalgamation of Depts.

(12) Hedge cutting in Tynan section (Co. Surveyor's complaints).

Mr. Barnhill made no observation to me, good or bad, nor did he point out any special places where he considered things had been behind as regards maintenance.

All he did ask me, were the following questions:

(1) Why I had not carried out any relaying
(2) Why I had not put in the new crossing at Colebrooke siding.
(3) How often I walked the line.

My answers to these three points, which are the only details Mr. Barnhill specifically alludes to in his letter, were, and are here, repeated:

(1) Relaying at curve 31¾ miles (Colebrooke Bridge)
do. do. 29 miles (Loch Curve)

Owing to transfer of Rail-bending machinery from Ballygawley, and re-arrangement of Works at Aughnacloy, for the amalgamation of the two departments, it was impossible to consider any relaying work up to the latter half of November.

By that time, short days, bad weather, and intervention of Christmas, precluded any but the most important work being undertaken.

This most important work, in my opinion, was comprised in the complaints lodged by the County Surveyor, in his report of 15th September last, particularly regarding Fivemiletown street, also the Ballasting of the Line and re-sleepering.

His further complaints re condition of line at Augher, dated October, and notices in November re hedges and trees, had to be attended to.

Complaints were also forthcoming from farmers in the Ballygawley district re drains which were causing flooding of their lands, owing to not having been cleaned for some considerable period.

All the above details were left on my hands through previous neglect to attend to them. Hedges had not been cut for 3 years, drains had not been cleaned for 2 years, and the condition of the line through Fivemiletown street and at Augher, could not by any means be attributed to me. In these circumstances, I pointed out to Mr. Barnhill, my only course was to put the curves, above referred to, in the best condition possible, pending more definite repairs.

I did this by (1) lifting, pulling and packing the curve at 31¾ miles and (2) the Loch Curve has since been put in a better condition, by the expedient of crowing the joints.

Neither of these curves has given the slightest trouble or cause for uneasiness since. The speeds over them are not excessive, and this I have ascertained by careful and repeated checks on a number of trains passing these and other points.

(2) New Crossing at Colebrooke station.

In order to undertake this work, it is necessary to consider the maximum time available between trains, for carrying it out. This time is 2¼ hours, at this point, and a gang of 3 men could not do the work in this time. It is, and has been necessary, to send 2 extra men to assist in carrying it out.

There was no particular hurry about this matter, nor did Mr. Barnhill, when he originally pointed it out to me in September, make any particular insistence on it. I gathered from his remarks, that it should be attended to sometime, but not of any pressing need.

It was a far simpler matter to lift the 45 yards of siding, when the local gang were effecting repairs to the loading beach, a matter raised by traffic requirements, and this did not involve cutting the main line nor the attendance of extra men, who were required elsewhere.

(3) How often I walk the Line?

I told Mr. Barnhill that I invariably walked the whole track between Maguiresbridge and Aughnacloy every fortnight, and the Tynan section, about every three weeks. This does not include frequent runs on the footplate as well. He did not express any opinion to me, so I presumed that his silence signified assent.

Finally Mr. Barnhill complains that he has no means of knowing what has been done, nor what is being done, in maintaining the line. I sent him copies of my three monthly reports to the Committee, and as regards my Diary, I told him that he was at liberty to see my rough notes in my general work diary at any time.

When Mr. Barnhill was with me he never referred to it in any way, nor expressed any desire to see it. Neither did he propose to come over to my office, where he could have got any further particulars, if he had wanted them.

In my letter of 4th January I pointed out that, so far as I was informed, Mr. Martin never kept a Diary, or at least, if he did so, none was forthcoming when I took over the Department.

Mr. Barnhill mentions that it is impossible for him to have a fair concept of the state of maintenance without such information.

I submit that it is equally, if not more important, that such Diaries, if they have been kept at all, should have been handed over to me, more so, when I was assuming the direct handling of the work.

Although I do not like to mention it, I must say that I have not been given much assistance in taking over the Permanent Way. No Maps or Plans of any use were given to me; the Relaying Map, which I presume was kept up to date was taken away. No Survey Instruments, Chains or Gauges were to be seen and, as I said before, no Diaries.

This, Gentlemen, is my answer to the contents of Mr. Barnhill's letter.

Aughnacloy, 31st January 1929 D. N. McClure, Engineer.

Matters proceeded to a swift conclusion: it was clear that further collaboration between Barnhill and McClure was not to be expected, and at the meeting of the Committee of Management on 4 February 1929 it was decided that Barnhill was to be paid his salary to 30 September 1929 *in lieu of notice*.

THE SECOND YEAR

Requests continued for Sunday specials which would connect with the Great Northern's excursion trains from Dublin to Bundoran. These excursions were popular, though they were not often attended by the Protestant members of the community. By 1929 demands were more insistent than ever. With motor cars becoming less of a curiosity, it was becoming evident that, if the Clogher Valley refused to carry Sunday excursionists, the excursionists would make their own arrangements about getting to the nearest Great Northern station. So in some cases grudgingly, the Committee of Management gave in and on 4 June permitted their general manager 'to make any arrangements he considered desirable.'

The economies in permanent way upkeep have been referred to, and it was clear that manual removal of weeds was a luxury that could not be afforded. With agricultural land alongside much of the line, regular weed killing was essential, and chemical methods were the answer. On 4 June McClure was given permission to buy a ton of sodium chlorate, a spray wagon was made, and another step had been taken towards modernisation.

Through the summer of 1929, the Atkinson-Walker tractor remained a useless obstacle at Aughnacloy. By November the builders were in the hands of a liquidator, and to bring matters to a conclusion, McClure was ordered to write to the firm, saying formally that the tractor 'had not fulfilled the requirements of the Committee' and asking them to remove it at an early date. It was further minuted 'that no further dealings be entered into with Messrs Atkinson-Walker Wagons Ltd.'

DIESEL TRACTION

The steam tractor had been a fiasco but at least it had not involved the company in wasted capital outlay. It probably placed steam haulage in an unfavourable light, so far as Clogher Valley experiments were concerned. The Committee had still five Sharp, Stewart engines to contend with, not one of them in first-rate condition, and there was the legacy of the ill-performing *Blessingbourne* which could steam, but could not keep her feet. The only solace that the makers of *Blessingbourne* could offer was to suggest that her slipping might be lessened by a reduction of the steam pressure, which was not a very practical solution, since she suffered from faulty design, which no tinkering could improve. The atmosphere deteriorated when Messrs Beardmore of Glasgow supplied a new boiler and firebox for *Blackwater* at £105 more than the estimate.

Early in 1931 the company approached Messrs Nasmyth, Wilson who were trusted builders of many Great Northern engines; they could offer a suitable steam tractor, but the Committee seem to have been wary, and adjourned decision on the matter again and again.

Meanwhile, Henry Forbes, between attending meetings at Aughnacloy, was gaining experience with petrol and diesel hauled railcars on his County Donegal lines. He arranged a trial run with one of his smaller railcars on the Clogher Valley during May 1932. The trial was a success, Forbes's enthusiasm was infectious, and no time was lost in ordering a diesel railcar. Competitive tenders were examined and it was decided to buy an articulated vehicle from Walker Brothers of Wigan.

Credit for the design must be given to the builders, for neither the Clogher Valley nor the Great Northern played any significant part in its conception. It was built during the latter half of 1932 and went into service in December. It covered 3,950 miles before the year was out and the delighted McClure claimed that its adoption had produced a 26 per cent increase in the number of passengers carried, compared with the same month of 1931. Its success was helped by the fact that it had sufficient power to tow a passenger carriage when traffic demanded it.

As early as 1933, the purchase of a second railcar was considered, but action was postponed because of the state of the bank overdraft. A compromise was eventually reached, and so that the passenger-carrying part of the railcar could remain at work when the power bogie was under repair, a second power bogie with a demountable wagon body was obtained from Walker Brothers. It came in September 1933 and the Clogher men christened it *The Unit*. Like the railcar, it could haul a carriage and, like the railcar, was habitually accompanied by a brake van to supplement the rather in-dequate stopping power. Its principal use was as a tractor on the Fivemiletown—Maguiresbridge section where it was driven by Hugh Murphy. When it deputised for the railcar power bogie, steam working returned temporarily to Maguiresbridge, generally with John Girvan driving and Willie Rea firing.

THE 1933 STRIKE

The new railcar had scarcely been introduced to the Clogher public, when train services were affected by the serious labour dispute which paralysed practically all rail services in Ireland from 31 January to 7 April.

The Clogher Valley men did not come out, but most of the Great Northern men did. The strike had lasted a week when the Committee received a report from McClure: though the Clogher Valley men were generally disinclined to stop work, the fact that the Great Northern was partly paralysed meant that there was much less for them to do. The Committee decided to make what economies were possible in the circumstances and, if the strike was not settled within a week, to close the line from 13 February. As it turned out, the Great Northern were able to maintain a skeleton service and Tynan was never without train connections to Belfast. On the other hand, the limited GN resources did not allow any workings between Clones and Enniskillen, so that Maguiresbridge lacked any broad-gauge traffic.

The position was reviewed on 11 February when it was reluctantly decided that weekly wages staff would have their employment terminated as from 18 February, the normal week's notice, while monthly paid staff would similarly cease to be employed from 11 March. Authority was, however, given to the general manager to continue the 'rail coach' workings 'should the Great Northern connections at Tynan justify it' and 'individuals were to be employed as necessity arose'. As a result, the two railcar drivers, James Kingsbury and Tom Girvan, remained at work.

The slightly defeatist reaction of the Committee was not

echoed by the men, many of whom felt that, if a train service was not maintained, the inconvenience suffered by the public would react against them and the government would be given an excuse to substitute a road service. Such closure, they feared, might mean dismissal of the entire staff without negotiation as to pension rights or compensation for loss of employment. The men were aware that for some time past, many influential ratepayers had been putting pressure on the government to relieve them of the burden of the baronial guarantee.

The Great Northern's emergency timetables in February, March, and April showed Tynan as a temporary broad-gauge terminus. The first arrival was a train that had started from Portadown and arrived at Tynan at 7.45am in February, and 7.40am in March and April. It left promptly at 7.50am and worked through to Belfast. Next appeared a 9.20am ex Belfast, arriving at Tynan at 11.05am and returning to the city at 11.40am. Finally an afternoon working left Belfast at 3.15pm and was into Tynan at 5.08 in February and 4.57pm in March and April. After half an hour it returned to Belfast. To meet these three arrivals, the Clogher Valley sent the railcar; between the two morning arrivals it went to Fivemiletown and back, and to Maguiresbridge in the afternoon. From its base at Fivemiletown, the railcar's daily mileage came to 184, spread across a working day of 13 hours.

Like many other Irish railways, yet through no fault of its own, the Clogher Valley emerged from the strike in worse shape than before. Traffic was still described as 'poor' at the meeting of the Committee on 8 May 1933. The hard fact was becoming evident that the public had learned to do without railway services when forcibly deprived of them. The railway's monopoly had ended, and its public were capable of making alternative arrangements into which sentiment did not enter. Until traffic improved, the Clogher Valley men were employed on a day to day basis.

CASTLEDERG PURCHASE

Through the rest of 1933, the goods and passenger services on the Clogher Valley were operated by steam and diesel haulage, with four of the remaining five ageing Sharp, Stewart engines doing their share. By 1934 No 1 *Caledon* was worn out and was of little use, her firebox patched in several places and her boiler tubes leaking freely. In Aughnacloy yard, *Blessingbourne* lay unused and unloved.

The strike had ended the career of the 3ft gauge Castlederg & Victoria Bridge Tramway, the roadside line in north-west Tyrone that was three years senior to the CVR. When the Castlederg closed, the rolling stock consisted of three engines, five passenger coaches, two brake vans and twenty-nine wagons, and in due course came up for sale.

Henry Forbes had no need for additional steam power on his Donegal lines, but mentioned to the Clogher Valley Committee on 7 May 1934 that the disposal of the Castlederg stock would make a useful locomotive available. Not only might it be bought cheaply, but it would cost little to bring it to the Clogher Valley. The engine was a powerful 2–6–0 side tank type, thirty years old, but nevertheless in a reasonable state of repair following attention in the Great Northern workshops. The Committee charged Forbes and McClure with the task of inspecting it, and of buying it if they thought fit. As it stood, it had two disadvantages: the capacity of the coal bunker was too small for the longer CV workings, and the Westinghouse brake fittings were non-standard. On 15 August the Committee heard McClure say that while he could not recommend purchase of the locomotive, he felt that ten of the twenty covered wagons should be bought, if they could be obtained for £10 apiece.

The Committee dithered for two months. The entire movable stock of the Castlederg Tramway had been sold for £1,361 to a firm of Glasgow scrap merchants, Messrs Arnott, Young & Co of the Fullarton Iron Works, Tollcross.

They in their turn had sold the 2–6–0T engine to Messrs Reid, but it had not been taken away. Already it had been steamed, on 27 July, and had hauled the entire rolling stock to Victoria Bridge, after eighteen months inaction. The Committee had second thoughts and did what they should have tried to do months before. An exchange was arranged, whereby the Clogher Valley received the Castlederg engine in running order, and gave in place of it the worn out *Caledon* and the useless *Blessingbourne*. The minutes refer to No 7 as 'having been withdrawn owing to its unsatisfactory working and the futility of spending any money on its reconstruction,' a reasonable statement of the position. The scrap merchants got two copper fireboxes for the price of one, with a worthwhile tonnage of steel thrown in for good measure.

As is told in Chapter 8, the Great Northern moved the Castlederg engine to Maguiresbridge, where two breakdown cranes unloaded it from the well wagon, and put it on CV track. The Castlederg cattle wagons—there were nineteen of them rather than the ten that McClure had first thought of buying—came by the same train. Already they had been visited at Victoria Bridge by five men from the Aughnacloy workshops, and there had their wheels and fittings removed, and the bodies put on to Great Northern flat wagons. Once on the ground at Maguiresbridge, they were re-erected. When engine and wagons were ready to come to Aughnacloy, John Girvan as driver, Joe Irwin at fireman, and Joe Robinson as chargehand fitter, went to Maguiresbridge to light up and haul the most remarkable train that the valley had ever seen. Things went reasonably well until they encountered the long 1 in 30 climb at Tattynuckle, between Colebrooke and Fivemiletown. There it became very obvious that the engine was steaming exceedingly badly, and had a very poor exhaust beat. The same fault became apparent on every hill, with Tullyvar bank the last and most difficult before home. Similarly disappointing results were found on runs with specials over the next few days. The valve settings were checked, but the reason for the poor steaming remained obscure until reductions were made both in the diameter of the funnel and in the distance of the exhaust blast pipe from the funnel. A sleeve was fitted to the funnel, and a skirting or petticoat below it immediately improved matters.

After trial runs, the Castlederg engine was brought into the shops for the necessary modifications. With a new bunker to be made and fitted, a pair of trailing wheels added, the original braking system replaced, and in the event the original coil springs replaced with laminated, there was much to do. The work went slowly, and at the Committee meeting on 14 August 1935 reference was made to the delay: 'because of the boilermaker's incapacity, his leg had been amputated above the knee, consequent on an injury of many years standing.' Michael Cullinan was the only boilermaker at Aughnacloy.

In its new guise, the Castlederg engine was a decided asset, for it was capable of handling all but the heaviest excursion trains. In complete contrast, the Castlederg wagons, whose purchase McClure had urged so effectively, were never used and they lay in a siding at Aughnacloy yard. As they stood, their couplings and brakes made them incompatible with the Clogher Valley vehicles and, because of that, they never turned a wheel after the early trial runs.

ECONOMIES AND BARGAINS

The great economic depression of the early 1930s had an adverse effect on the earnings of the Irish railways. Of the main line companies in Northern Ireland, the total net income of the LMSNCC between 1930 and 1938 was in credit for only 1931 and 1937; in 1933 a loss of £81,000 was recorded. On the Great Northern, the situation was a little less depressing, but the dividend on ordinary stock had been falling from 5 per cent in 1925 to 1½ per cent in 1930, ½ per cent in 1931, and nil thereafter, while preference stock holders received no dividend after 1932.

The Clogher Valley continued to make a loss, the shareholders continued to receive their guaranteed 5 per cent, but the economic viability of the line was clearly at an end, and it was only a question of how long the situation could be tolerated by the government. Operating costs were pruned where possible, and the locomotives received the minimum of attention. A report by George T. Glover of the Great Northern in June 1930 tells that the fireboxes were in an extremely precarious state, the roof bolts leaking, the crowns and sides cushioned, and the copper tube plates patched.

During April 1930, a saving of £60 a year was accomplished by making the gatekeepers into unpaid 'caretakers', whereby they had free use of the lodges, and still attended to the gates as formerly. Over at Ballygawley, a landmark vanished for the old pw inspector's office lay unused, and Henry Forbes, always glad of a bargain, bought it for £20 and had it brought across to the CDRJC.

Lisdoart level crossing, a mile west of Ballygawley, was perhaps the most difficult one to watch on the whole line: two roads converged on it from the north, and the view of the line towards Ballygawley was restricted by an 8 chain bend. The gatekeeper, a conscientious man named Francis Droogan, looked after the gates, and also cared for the halt just beyond them, a hut and platform neatly set among laurel bushes. It was in January 1935 that the Committee received a memorial from the residents of the Lisdoart district, which drew their attention to Droogan's increased duties at the crossing gates. The relevant minute reads 'Owing to the exceptional nature of this level crossing, and the extra work involved, it was decided, as a special case, to grant the applicant the sum of three shillings per week.' It was another bargain.

SNOWFALL

The Clogher Valley Railway trains were rarely affected by snow, but 1937 brought memorable falls to much of Ireland. After three days of snow in the south of the country, during which some villages in County Wicklow were isolated, the weather deteriorated further and, on 11 and 12 March, the north was swept by a blizzard. On Thursday 11 March, one of the Dublin to Belfast main line trains was delayed for over an hour by drifting snow. Further snowfall came on the following day. There was a fair then at Ballygawley but according to the *Northern Whig* it was 'badly affected' and 'only a small number of cattle were on offer'. They were brave men that went to the fair in that weather. In the afternoon, rising wind caused the dry snow to drift, and the mail train from Aughnacloy to Maguiresbridge, successfully past the Tullyvar summit, charged a wall of whiteness between Dempsey's Crossing and Ballygawley. As a witness described it: 'when it packed under her, she just riz up in the air'. The engine was completely helpless. The train was to have crossed at Ballygawley with one that had come from Fivemiletown, so it was decided to charge the drift from the Ballygawley direction, and plough a way, down which the first train might be released. The second train threshed its way round the bend and up the gradient towards the trapped train, but the resistance of the drift was too much for it as well and both trains were fastened in the deepening snow. During the proceedings, floundering knee-deep and in the gathering winter darkness, someone dropped the train staff, and it plummeted out of sight. The permanent way men dug out the trains the following day, but the staff was not recovered until the complete thaw four weeks later. As the minute book put it 'the service was considerably upset'.

OPERATING METHODS

It has been stated by H. Fayle in his book *Narrow Gauge Railways of Ireland* that the original signals were three-position semaphores, but his statement is in error, and in all probability arose from the illustrations that accompanied Sections 31–33 in the Company's Rule Book. In fact ordinary two-position home and distant signals were used.

Authority for leaving a station was the possession of the Wise pattern staff, or a permit. Staffs were provided for the following sections:

Tynan and Aughnacloy
Aughnacloy and Ballygawley
Ballygawley and Clogher
Clogher and Fivemiletown
Fivemiletown and Maguiresbridge.

Each staff had two locked compartments, one at either end, each of which contained three train permits. These took the place of the more familiar train tickets, and were used when one or more trains were following in the same direction. The permits were replaced in the compartment of the staff after use. A following train was usually a special, and warning to crossing keepers and others was given by an oval red tail-board on the preceding train.

The company had its own earth return telephone system. The working timetable stated that 'in the event of the failure of the telephone, the arrival and departure of all trains proceeding by Permit must be advised by postal telegraph—failing that, by the most expeditious means available.'

As well as the timetable listings, the working books gave very clear instructions about the places where trains were to cross with each other, and also about the use of permits. Thus in the working timetable dated 2 July 1928:

UP TRAINS

No. 1 Up Train on *Aughnacloy Fair Days* must carry Permit Ballygawley to Aughnacloy.

No. 1 Up Special Market Train must carry Permit Fivemiletown to Clogher.

No. 2 Up Train on *Ballygawley Fair Days* must carry Permit Ballygawley to Aughnacloy.

No. 3 Up Train must carry Permit Clogher to Ballygawley, Ballygawley to Aughnacloy.

DOWN TRAINS

No. 1 Down Train must carry permit Ballygawley to Clogher.
No. 1 Down Train on *Aughnacloy Fair Days* must carry Staff Ballygawley to Clogher.
No. 1 Down Train on *Ballygawley Fair Days* must carry Staff Ballygawley to Clogher.
No. 4 Down Train must carry Permit Aughnacloy to Ballygawley.

During the autumn of 1933, with diesel working and steam working, a crossing had to be made between an up railcar and a down mixed steam train at Roughan, between Ballygawley and Augher. The railcar left Augher in charge of the Augher agent, who carried the train staff. At Roughan he put the railcar into the siding, set the points for the main line, walked up the road and round a bend, and flagged the steam train which, meanwhile, was halted at a notice. The notice on a rectangular board set in the hedge, related 'NO. 5 DOWN STEAM TRAIN—STOP—AWAIT FLAG SIGNAL FROM SIDING—BEFORE PROCEEDING'. The steam train had left Ballygawley in charge of the Ballygawley agent, who travelled on the footplate. He returned from Roughan, still without the staff, in the up railcar. The Augher agent returned to Augher with the staff in the steam train.

TRAFFIC THROUGH THE YEARS

To appreciate the pattern of traffic under the Committee of Management, it is perhaps best to retrace one's steps to 1913, the last year before World War I, and the first year in which detailed annual returns were available. In that year there had been 7,861 first class and 107,587 third class passengers. By 1921 the totals were 2,113 and 57,585. Under the Committee, from 1929 to 1932 the figures for the unified class of travel shrank from 58,700 to 33,607, and over the last three years of that period were dropping away at the alarming rate of around 10,000 a year. The nadir was 28,467 passenger journeys in 1933, for which the rail strike, road competition, and the economic depression were together responsible. In that year, however, the diesel railcar went into service, the Unit joined it the next year, and together they were able to give the public an improved service and make a start to regain some of the lost traffic. The year 1934 saw passenger journeys rise to 35,234 and by 1936 they had climbed to 57,072. For the remainder of the life of the railway, five years, they remained around 50,000. The private car and the road bus saw to it that the pre-1913 annual totals of around 100,000 were never approached again. Throughout the entire life of the railway, the average fare per passenger journey was remarkably constant, at around 7d (3p).

In common with other small Irish narrow gauge railways which had a purely agricultural hinterland, the Clogher Valley had a very high proportion of third class passengers, which accounted for between 92 per cent and 95 per cent of the passenger journeys prior to 1913. The first class travellers, averaging around 6 per cent of the total during that period, were offered 15½ per cent of the total number of seats in the carriages. As on the Ballycastle Railway in Co Antim, accommodation in the superior class must have often been greatly under-utilised, and seating in the third class considerably overcrowded.* The recurring problem of finding accommodation for the flood of passengers that descended on the Clogher Valley trains on 12 July and on Fair Days has been referred to. It was fortunate that on such occasions the clientele were sociably inclined, and overcrowding in the carriages, or the need to stand in a wagon, was cheerfully accepted.

The annual tonnage of merchandise in the early years was around 11,000, and had risen to 20,000 immediately prior to World War I. Post-war unrest tumbled this to 3,884 tons in 1921, but it soon recovered and had risen to 11,800 tons by 1929. Under the Committee of Management this traffic was well maintained until 1932. The disaster of the 1933 strike and its aftermath effectively halved the tonnage total, much of

* See the author's comments in *The Ballycastle Railway*, p 58.

which was immediately and permanently lost to road hauliers, so that a new movement pattern was established. Thereafter, merchandise traffic never recovered, the 1934–40 average being just below 6,000 tons per year.

When the Committee assumed control in 1928, coal traffic was around 4,000 tons per year. Since this total included fuel for the company's engines, the introduction of diesel haulage in 1933 caused a marked drop to 1,700 tons. This level of traffic was held for four more years, but by 1937 it had wasted away to 1,000 tons. After that, the annual tonnage of coal moved by the railway became markedly less, and the 1940 figure of 382 tons illustrates how road haulage from distant railheads was effectively competing, for by then the labour costs of repeated manual handling had made transhipment uneconomic.

The annual returns for 'other minerals' was principally stone traffic originating at Tullyvar where there was a steam stone crusher and a siding, and where the county council and later the Hadden family operated a quarry. An annual tonnage of between 3,000 and 4,000 appears to have been representative up to 1929. About then, a mile of road through Lisdoart bog was remade in concrete. Heavy stone filling was called for, and in 1930 the railway hauled 11,407 tons. Over the next seven years the tonnage fluctuated between 1,000 and 3,500 tons, after which it practically vanished, 18 tons being recorded during 1939, when the quarry owner had become lorry-minded.

Livestock totals are in complete contrast to the shrinking tonnage figures of merchandise, coal, and stone. Before World War I, and just after it, around 7,000 head of stock were moved annually from CV stations, the total being made up of horses, cattle, calves, sheep, and pigs. At first cattle preponderated, but later pigs greatly outnumbered them. The early 1930s saw the livestock totals increase to just above 10,000 head per year. Then in 1938 the numbers surged to 12,369, in 1939 to 14,234, and during 1940 to 18,762. In 1939 the number of cattle shipped was 1,965, but in 1940 it was 3,386. For an

CLOGHER VALLEY RAILWAY

(COMMITTEE OF MANAGEMENT) 1928.

AUGUST BANK HOLIDAY.

ANNUAL EXCURSION

— TO —

BANGOR

(DIRECT TRAIN SERVICE)

MONDAY, 2nd AUGUST, 1937.

EIGHT HOURS AT THE SEASIDE.

A SPECIAL TRAIN

WILL RUN TO THE TIMES AND AT FARES AS UNDER:—

		a.m.	Return Fare
Brookeboro'	**dep.**	**7-10**	**5/6**
Fivemiletown	**„**	**7-30**	**5/-**
Clogher	**„**	**7-55**	**4/9**
Augher	**„**	**8- 3**	
Ballygawley	**„**	**8-24**	**4/6**
Aughnacloy	**„**	**8-45**	

The G.N. Train will run through from TYNAN to BANGOR.

Tickets can be purchased from Station Masters at above Stations and an early application is requested as the supply of Tickets will be strictly limited.

Accommodation for organised parties can be reserved on timely notice being given to any of our agents.

RETURN TRAIN is due to leave BANGOR at 7-20 p.m.

Head Offices,
Aughnacloy, July, 1937.

D. N. McCLURE,
General Manager.

explanation, one must look to the south of the railway where, in lonely country, the inter-state border crossed the Slieve Beagh hills. It was here that smuggling of cattle and pigs through the tariff curtain from the Free State to the North was a profitable (and therefore established) way of life for some small men, and a worth-while pastime for others more favourably placed. Police and customs patrols were alike ineffective, and the Ballygawley 'smuggling fairs' were splendidly attended social and business occasions, the steep village street thronged with dealers, farmers and beasts, and the station loading bank an equally busy place for a few hours.

It is related that one member of the Committee of Management, not resident locally, was in the habit of coming early to Aughnacloy to examine the accounts before each meeting. He repeatedly expressed his amazement at the more rapid increase in shipments of black cattle from Fivemiletown than from Ballygawey. What had escaped his notice, and what his fellow committee members never told him, was that it was the result of a geographical accident. Ballygawley was considerably further from the quiet roads across Slieve Beagh than was Fivemiletown, and the traffic was not confined to Fair Days.

TRAIN MILES AND STATISTICS

Up to the outbreak of World War I, the Clogher Valley steam trains covered between 95,000 and 100,000 miles in a year. In 1921 there were economies consequent on the cross-channel coal strike, and the mileage dropped to 83,800.

Under the Committee of Management, reduction in services in 1931 caused a fall in the mileage to 84,034, and in the following year to 69,945. The following year saw the introduction of the railcar and with it, a dramatic reduction in steam locomotive haulage, so that in 1933 steam miles fell to 37,900 while the railcar ran up 33,300 miles. By 1934 steam covered only 29,700 miles, while the combined diesel units clocked 82,000 miles. From 1935 until the end, the relationships of the two forms of motive power remained practically the same, with the mileage of steam fluctuating between 35,700 (in 1935) and 28,700 (in 1940). In round terms, diesel miles were three times those run by steam, a maximum of 102,600 being run in 1935, and a minimum of 95,800 in 1939. It is noteworthy that total train miles between 1935 and 1940 were higher than ever before, amounting to 130,000 miles per year, or practically twice that of the minimal year of 1932.

REPORTS AND REPAIRS

The County Surveyors continued to make their annual inspections and furnish their reports to their respective County Councils. In Tyrone, John Leebody retired in 1934 after 39 years service, and was followed by B. G. L. Glasgow, who stated on 22 September 1935 that the Clogher Valley track was 'quite passable' and that one and a quarter miles of new 55lb rail had been laid during the previous year, and 500 sleepers had been replaced by new ones cut from home grown timber. He concluded 'in my opinion the work of resleepering is getting badly behind, and I strongly recommend that the use of a minimum of 2,000 properly creosoted sleepers yearly for the next few years.' He condemned the use of home grown timber for sleepers, remarking that 'they have not proved satisfactory and can only be used near stations, so that the resleepering programme has been very limited'.

In his report of September 1936, B. G. L. Glasgow noted that the track was 'passable and gradually improving', although 'attention should be given to a short section of line at Annaghilla (about ¼ mile long) which, though quite safe, is very rough and causes uneven riding.' He noted that a furlong of line had been relaid between Augher and Clogher, near 17¾ milepost. During that year, the flying squad had at last started 'programme working', and had used 1,300 sleepers, 400 pairs of reconditioned fishplates and 300 tons of ballast. They had carried out heavy repairs to the track on the Tynan—Glenkeen section, on the Augher bog diversions, and between mileposts 29 and 30½. The whole track had been sprayed twice with weedkiller. He reiterated his plea that resleepering 'be continued at not less than the present rate, in order to overcome the arrears of the past.'

By September 1937, the report was less pleasing, and Glasgow reported that 'the general condition of the track, though still passable, shows signs of deterioration, as expenses have been drastically cut down in view of the possible closing of the line . . . if the railway is to be kept going, it is essential, in my opinion, that a considerable programme of re-sleepering be put in hand next spring—a minimum of 2,500 sleepers would be required for the next few years.'

If the railway was closed, a difficult legal problem would arise because of shareholders' rights. The original scheme of guarantees never envisaged that the railway would be a public liability. It was uncertain whether or not the 5 per cent dividend should continue to be paid, even after the share capital had ceased to exist because of the transfer of the railway to the County Councils. There was a prospect of a long and expensive legal battle.

The government tried to ease matters in 1930. On 22 April the Ministry of Commerce, with the authority of the Ministry of Finance, circulated shareholders and offered to buy up shares at £6 each, which was somewhat in advance of their market value. As a result about 1,400 shares were purchased by the government. To combat the scheme, a Shareholders' Protection Association was formed, which advised its members that the Baronial Guarantee was a perpetual one, and that a Court of Law would provide for lump sum compensation which would yield the same income as before. Another 500 shares were bought by the government by early 1939, by then it was apparent that some form of compulsion would be necessary to end the impasse.

WRITING ON THE WALL

While one may question the wisdom of the parsimony of the Committee of Management during the 1930s, they were attempting to strike a balance between, on the one hand, the provision of an adequate service on track and with steam locomotives and carriages that were wearing out and, on the other hand, avoiding the expenditure of an excessive amount of public money on the renewal of track and vehicles whose foreseeable existence was limited. That the Clogher Valley would never make a profit was hardly in doubt. Over-capitalisation was the primary cause, and the necessary traffic was simply not there and indeed never had been there in spite of the optimistic forecasts of the 1880s. That the creation of such a railway would inevitably create traffic was now known to be a myth.

Road competition in the Clogher Valley requires to be seen, not in its local setting alone, but in the broader context of Ireland as a whole. In the Irish Free State up to 1932, anyone who had a bus, could establish and run a road passenger service. The Road Transport Act of 1932 introduced a system of licensing for such carriers, placed limits on new bus owners, enforced improved operating standards, and gave the railways additional powers to acquire road undertakings. In the following year a further Act placed added restrictions on private bus owners, and went far to reduce uneconomic competition and duplication of services. The railways responded by acquiring road undertakings and by further co-ordinating their road and rail services.

In Northern Ireland there were no parallel moves, and in the six counties competition was allowed to continue, to the detriment of the enormous capital investment represented by the railways. To compete, rail charges were reduced, though wages and material costs were rising, and by 1934 it was estimated that more goods were being carried by road than by rail. In that year, the Government of Northern

Ireland, stung into overdue action, invited advice from Sir Felix Pole, chairman of Associated Electrical Industries Ltd and a former general manager of the Great Western Railway. His remit covered both rail and road, and was tackled with characteristic vigour and urgency. The inquiry opened on 30 April 1934 and a report was published on 23 July. In it were traced the difficulties produced by the geographical peculiarities of the six counties, their almost total lack of mineral wealth, and the problems of railway operation that had resulted from the political partition of the country. Of the nine railway services that served Northern Ireland, six operated in the Free State as well.

After considering various schemes, Pole recommended that in Northern Ireland, the control and ownership of all road services, passenger and freight, be placed in the hands of a Transport Board, which should pool its receipts with those of the railway administrations. Because of the special difficulties involved, he did not recommend the amalgamation of the railways. Since already the railways owned 224 out of the 667 buses licensed to operate, Pole suggested that the railways should be allowed to increase their interest in road transport by investing in the capital of the proposed Road Transport Board.

The Government of Northern Ireland decided to adopt the general principles of the Pole Report, and Sir Dawson Bates, then Minister of Home Affairs, announcing the decision, said that the only practical way of achieving the object which the government had in mind was to bring the rail and road transport systems into partnership with a common financial interest. But a lethargic government did little but postpone the day when statutory integration would have to come about, the numerous omnibus and road haulage firms grouped themselves into the nationalised Northern Ireland Road Transport Board and the services which that mammoth provided were allowed to compete with, rather than to complement, the existing rail services.

The Pole Report recommended that the Clogher Valley should be closed down, and it was under the shadow of that suggestion that the railway management had to operate from the summer of 1934. Though the government took no direct action for some years, it was not an encouraging environment for the Aughnacloy men.

As the Pole Report was being prepared, residents in south Tyrone and East Fermanagh were voicing their serious concern at proposals and rumours of proposals to close down the Clogher Valley Railway, and in the light of the local objections, the County Council unanimously passed a resolution deprecating the proposed closure:

> That this Coucil view with alarm the suggestion contained in Sir Felix Pole's report, viz., to close down the Clogher Valley Railway. We believe it would be detrimental to the best interest of the residents in that whole area, and strongly urge our County Tyrone representatives in the Northern Parliament to oppose any attempt that may be made to close this railway, which is performing a service which could not be replaced by motor transport without a great deal extra expense being involved, which would be payable by the present users of the railway.
>
> We direct that a copy of this resolution be sent to the Members of the Northern Government, also to the Fermanagh County Council.

At a lower level, the subject was similarly considered by the Clogher Rural Council, who resolved to petition the Ministry of Home Affairs. No doubt because of such vigorous objections, the government did not hasten to implement the recommendation of the Pole Report, as it affected the Clogher Valley. Through the energy and imagination of Henry Forbes, the introduction of diesel haulage had been outstandingly successful, and the public were pleased to be presented with a better service of trains than they had ever known before. Meanwhile, the annual failure to show a profit went inexorably on, the losses continuing to run at around £6,000 per year.

A COLLECTION OF CHARACTERS

There can have been few railways that had a guard the age of Tommy Caruth for, when the line closed, he was reputed to be over 80. In spite of his years, he was still physically active, but mentally perhaps a little past his best; he spent the journey restlessly crossing from one carriage end to the next by the gates in the mesh railing, checking, checking, and rechecking the tickets and making certain that everyone and everything was in order. In cold weather, Tommy Caruth wore an overcoat with long tails, and the story is told of a commercial traveller who used to try to catch the waving coat tails by slamming the sliding carriage door shut just as Tommy had passed through it. On one occasion he was successful.

Tommy Caruth had strict views on card playing and this brought him into a certain amount of conflict with the buyers who came up to the grass-seed sales at Aughnacloy on certain Fridays. The buyers were mostly young men from the city, and Tommy decided that these boys from Belfast were having a bad influence on the neighbourhood. They dared to play cards on *his* train. He warned them, he told them that it was against the law, and one day he even reported them to McClure. On the following Friday, the same wicked young men were joining the train at Aughnacloy after the market. The stationmaster had a rick of hay, well saved, by the side of the line. To avoid Tommy's continued harrassment, at the last moment they descended on the hay stack, each grabbed an armful, threw it into an open wagon, jumped in after it, and sat on the mattress of hay as the train moved out towards Tynan. It must have been the only occasion that solo was played en route on an open wagon on the Irish narrow gauge.

The railway owed much to the McFadden family of Aughnacloy. There were four of them in it. The father, Pat senior, was the leading hand in the carriage shop and a very skilled joiner and pattern-maker. Of his sons, Joe and Mick were also joiners, while Pat junior who started as a lad in the fitter's shop, was eventually in charge of carriages and the diesels. Young Pat took a hand at driving the diesels when necessary, for demarcation was not known at Aughnacloy. Joe it was who cut the stencil for the CV monogram that replaced the coloured crest, and had the misfortune to lose his life in a motor-cycle accident on the Monaghan road two miles from home.

For a time, there was a stationmaster at Ballygawley whom everyone knew simply as 'Oul Dickson'. He came from a townland named Tiroony, in the mountainous country not far from Carrickmore. Dickson had a clerk, by name Willie Stinson, who was known to Ballygawley folk as Dickson's Cat, a name that stuck to him well into manhood. 'Oul Dickson' became very stiff as well as a little careless, towards the end of his career. Eventually he retired, and was replaced by Sam Friel. On arrival Sam conducted a spring-clean, and used to relate that he found a small fortune in little silver threepenny pieces when he swept out the ledges and cupboards on the ticket window side of the booking office. Sam got to like the station house at Ballygawley, and continued to live in it in retirement after the line was closed and lifted.

Sam's brother James was carriage fitter-cum-gas fitter-cum-plumber on the Clogher Valley, and looked after the carriages, wagons, windmills, and pumps, being ably assisted in these varied tasks by Harry Irwin. It was James Friel who solved the mystery of the missing brake van. It should have been difficult for a brake van to get itself lost, for there were only five of them, and a limited number of places where one could hide. None the less, one *was* lost, and for two months, though it may have been that nobody bothered to hunt for it. One fine summer day, James Friel had been at Maguiresbridge attending to the windmill. He had a long wait ahead of him and, to pass the time, he took a walk along to the little engine shed, which hadn't had an engine inside it for years. He knew that one of the horse-boxes was inside. So he opened the door, found the horsebox tight up against it, and beyond it hiding in the gloom, the van that nobody had seen for two months.

Colebrooke had the distinction of being the stop for the Colebrooke estate, where the Brooke family lived. It was not every halt that had a Prime Minister living beside it. For many years the crossing gates and the buildings were looked after by Maggie Elliot who was officially there as caretaker. When he was chairman of the Committee, Sir Basil Brooke would not hear of Miss Elliot being put out because of her advancing years. She was allowed to live on at Colebrooke until infirmity forced her to go to the care of friends, not long before the railway closed.

The wife of an early Colebrooke caretaker had the reputation locally of being a witch, and it was said that she boiled quartz stones (presumably with names on them) at the full of the moon. If a stone cracked, the heart of the victim would break.

The boilermaker at Aughnacloy was Mick Cullinan, who had been in Harland and Wolff's shipyard in Belfast and had worked on the *Titanic*. Mick Cullinan's helper was Joe McAdam, who usually deputised for the coalman James Boyle in case of sickness, and looked after the operation of Aughnacloy's unique coaling plant. Joe McAdam was a remarkable man, unable either to read or write, though he could tube a boiler about as well as Mick. He had a few acres of land, kept a cow and dealt in cattle and, in spite of lacking two of the three Rs, he could not be done in money or change. In the evenings, especially during the winter, Joe did all the patching and sewing of the McAdam family clothing and linen, and cobbled the footwear, while his wife sat by and read the paper aloud to him. And so good was his memory, that he could tell it all the next day.

Great railwaymen they were, keeping a little line going that had never been able to pay a dividend out of its own pocket. The engines and the workshops may have been old fashioned and relatively poorly equipped, but they were manned by enthusiasts and craftsmen and not by a variety of tradesmen separated by rigid demarcations. Who but Pat McFadden, to cite but one example, would have come back evening after evening, to work with his general manager on the building of a scale model of a Caledonian Railway 4–4–0?

Taking their rightful place among the characters of the Clogher Valley Railway were three local men, whose names were never recorded in the weekly pay sheet. Yet as schoolboys, and later when their names were becoming household words, they were unofficially recognised as honorary firemen and drivers. They came from Caledon and from Colebrooke, and they took their place in history as Field-Marshal Earl Alexander of Tunis, Field-Marshal Viscount Alanbrooke, and Viscount Brookeborough.

ACCIDENTS

It was the day of the August 1937 fair at Ballygawley. Driver William Brown, a steam man, had brought the 1.15pm train from Fivemiletown to Tynan. There was a fair day special returning from Aughnacloy to Fivemiletown, a small train of a heavy wagon of meal and a carriage, hauled by the Unit, which Pat McFadden was driving. Their work finished for the day, Brown and his fireman, Joe Irwin, were returning to Fivemiletown as passengers in the carriage. At Clogher, a station sheltered by lime trees, the train ran slowly in on the right-hand line, preparatory to making a shunt to the store. Beyond the platforms the level crossing gates were closed, and Brown and Irwin jumped out to assist in opening the gates. There had been a light shower of rain not long before, and the edge of the platform was slippery with drops from the overhanging lime trees. As Brown jumped his boots slid on the greasy surface, and he tumbled and fell between the slowly moving carriage and the platform. His spine was broken and he died almost at once.

Later in the same year, *Erne* was in two collisions with road vehicles at Findermore, though nobody was hurt in either case.

THE TWELFTH IN 1938

Through the years, the Orangemen continued to depend on the Clogher Valley for transport to and from 'the field' at Caledon and elsewhere. Detailed records of the performance of those special trains are not known to have survived, but it is fortunate that in 1938 Dr George Gillespie had time from his rounds that day to photograph the crowded Fivemiletown—Caledon special as it called at Ballygawley. It must have been a fine sight. *Erne* and *Blackwater* were double heading the train, a tremendous caravan consisting of the two bogie wagons, eight coaches, three vans—their doors wide open for air—and five cattle wagons. And, for good measure away at the rear, an unidentified engine to bank the lot over Tullyvar and act as a brake on the descent. What a thunder it must have made as it pulled away on the climb to Dempsey's Crossing and what a pity not a tape recorder was there to immortalise it for us today!

Eddie Bohun was the Ballygawley correspondent of the *Tyrone Courier* then, and wrote one of his characteristic descriptions:

> The Twelfth passed over in a peaceable and orderly manner as was to be expected. The Orangemen went in such numbers to the meeting in Caledon that they had to be conveyed on the Clogher Valley Railway in open wagons. They were well cautioned not to put their heads above the roofs. Some trains had two engines, one in front pulling and one behind pushing. "The Brethren" were accompanied by their friends and many well dressed young gentlemen were seen.

TIMETABLES

Operation under the Committee of Management started with steam power alone, and a timetable practically the same as before. Each terminus had its three departures and its three arrivals each day, while the Fivemiletown—Aughnacloy section had four trains passing through in each direction. There were also certain fair specials, but no Sunday trains.

The more intensive service in railcar days was concentrated on the busier Tynan—Fivemiletown section, which had six workings in each direction. Three of these extended to Maguiresbridge. Thus Tynan sent off diesel-hauled trains (described in the public timetable as 'rail coaches') at 6.15am and 9.40am. A steam train to Fivemiletown followed at 10.50am, and there were three further diesel workings down the line, the 1.40pm to Maguiresbridge and the 4.40pm and 8.35pm to Fivemiletown.

In the up direction, the 7.45am diesel from Fivemiletown to Tynan began the day, crossing with the first down train from Tynan. The 9.50am Maguiresbridge—Tynan diesel followed it. The down steam train, which had arrived at Fivemiletown at 1.00pm, returned up the line fifteen minutes later, to reach Tynan at 3.30pm. Two diesel workings from Maguiresbridge followed, at 1.55pm and 3.55pm, and the 6.55pm Fivemiletown—Tynan ended the day.

Most of the trains had Great Northern connections at Tynan and at Maguiresbridge: Tynan sending five of its six down trains off after Great Northern arrivals, while four of the six up trains afforded connections to Belfast. The north-west was less accessible, and only the two morning railcar arrivals at Maguiresbridge gave connections to Enniskillen and Londonderry.

A Sunday train was introduced between Tynan and Fivemiletown, giving the city dwellers their first chance of a Sunday in the Valley. A Great Northern train left Belfast for Clones at 9.40am and was into Tynan at 11.14am. The railcar left at 11.18am, and was in Fivemiletown at 12.45pm, in time for dinner with the country cousins. In the reverse direction the railcar left Fivemiletown at 5.35pm, and was in Tynan at 7.5pm. A Great Northern train had left Clones at 6.30pm, and was on its way from Tynan at 7.8pm, to arrive in Belfast's Great Victoria Street terminus at 8.37pm.

The four fair day specials were confined to the second Friday in each month, for the Ballygawley Fair.

ONSET OF ANOTHER WAR

No relaying was done during 1939, though 600 tons of ballast was spread, and 1,062 sleepers were replaced. The Tyrone County Surveyor inspected the line during the last month of peace, and wrote his report a few days after the declaration of war on Germany. His final paragraph declared the railway as 'in fairly good order, but if it is to deal with the extra traffic probable in war conditions, two new boilers and one firebox will be required for the locomotives', and repeated his earlier warnings about the need for more thorough re-sleepering.

To the Committee of Management, the general manager stated that, in his opinion, the railway could deal with all traffic, but if the war were to continue for two or three years, some outlay was needed in general maintenance. He asked the Committee for guidance in the matter.

Although the country was otherwise on a war footing, there was no compulsory military service in Northern Ireland, but many men and women joined the forces voluntarily. The Committee encouraged enlistment, and made it clear that men who volunteered would return to their old jobs while, if their forces pay were less than that on the railway, the difference would be met. On 18 September 1939, his own position was discussed by McClure, who brought before the notice of the Committee the possibility of his being called up for military service. He proposed that, in such an event, his work would pass to the secretary and accountant, P. M. Soraghan, with which the Committee agreed. In addition his salary would continue, 'less Army remuneration'. The decision formed Minute No 1493, and was to be of interest within a twelvemonth.

The winter came, with its black-out regulations. Within a few months the minutes recorded that 'quite a number of crossing gates have been damaged by motor vehicles'. As on road vehicles, the light from the engines' headlamps was dimmed and shrouded by tin-plate masks. Some lightening of the gloom was made in February 1940, when a partial restoration was made of the 1928 salary cuts.

HURRIED DEPARTURE

Unexpectedly, it seems, the Clogher Valley found itself without a general manager one day. The day was Friday, and it was the thirteenth of September 1940. In David McClure's absence, control was assumed, as agreed a year before, by Paddy Soraghan.

The next meeting of the Committee of Management convened on Wednesday 16 October. In the absence of Sir Basil Brooke, the chair was taken by Nathaniel Duff, JP, and the other members present were Messrs Darragh, Tavener, and Hadden. Also present was David McClure. After considering the minutes of the previous meeting, held on 8 July, and some routine items of finance, the members turned to a discussion of McClure's withdrawal four weeks before. The matter was opened by Soraghan formally reporting that the general manager had gone to England 'to take up an appointment in connection with the construction of a shell factory'. It had a military ring. McClure then spoke, and referring to Minute 1493 of 18 September 1939, stated that his salary was £400 per year and was paid by the War Office. His salary as general manager of the railway had been £600, and he suggested that the Committee should allow him £250 per year.

Robert Darragh promptly reminded his fellow members of Committee that, in the circumstances and in view of the decision of the Committee embodied in Minute 1493, the amount that could be paid to McClure was limited to £200 per annum, being the difference between his salary from Military sources and his salary from the Committee of Management. Moreover, to satisfy the auditors it would be necessary for McClure to produce either his calling-up notice from the War Office or some section of the Fighting Forces, together with a certificate or other document showing his remuneration 'for Active War Service'. According to Soraghan's minute, McClure's reply to the request was that he would not be allowed to carry such documents on his person at the present time. The Committee must have regarded the reply as not altogether satisfactory, but they agreed to adjourn the matter until the following meeting.

In such circumstances it was difficult to know whether McClure was an employee of the CVR or not. Nevertheless he spoke to another point, presumably as general manager, and told the Committee that since the July meeting he had, in consultation with Sir Basil Brooke, made a special allowance of 10s (50p) a week to certain employees 'consequent on their increased responsibilities'. They were J. Bennett, the chief clerk at Aughnacloy, Joe Robinson and Pat McFadden, chargehands in the loco department, John Conn of the traffic department and J. McCluskey, the permanent way ganger. The Committee of Management gave their approval to the increases.

Darragh over-shadowed McClure's chameleon performance by suggesting that in printing or issuing future timetables or other printed notices 'in meantime Mr. McClure's name should be dropped and *By Order* substituted therefor'. Again the Committee approved.

The next meeting of the Committee of Management was held on Monday, 9 December 1940, under Sir Basil Brooke's chairmanship. Five other members were present, and Soraghan took the minutes. McClure was absent. The chairman explained to those present that he had been in consultation with Mr Darragh since the last meeting of the Committee, and as a result had sent a letter to McClure. The letter was deemed of sufficient importance to be reproduced as an Appendix to the minutes. With little preamble the letter stated 'that the Committee were in doubt about whether your present position is in connection with Military or Civilian work'.

The chairman continued 'It seems to me that you ought to show your calling up papers and a statement of your Army salary, if in fact you were called up for Military duties and you were, therefore, covered by the above mentioned Minute. If the position is a civilian one, you would not be covered by the Minute, and it would, therefore, be necessary for the Committee to come to a further decision.' The letter was dated 11 November.

McClure replied to the chairman on 15 November from an address in Wigan. The letter was similarly appended to the minutes. The job he had taken was 'a civilian one, although, of course, directly connected with Ordnance, in that it involves the construction and starting up of a new shell filling factory'. The contractors for the factory were Walker Bros of Pagefield Iron Works, a name familiar on the Clogher Valley for it was they who had built the two diesel units. They had, it appeared, employed McClure because they 'required someone to make an intensive study of the process and to take charge of the construction and layout'. In view of such a statement, one cannot see why the general manager had thought it necessary or wise to refer on 16 October to his not being allowed to carry call-up papers on his person.

McClure's letter to the chairman went on to say that he had now succeeded in having his salary in England raised to what it had been at Aughnacloy, but that he found himself 'definitely worse off' by having to maintain his house at Aughnacloy and to keep himself in Wigan. He pressed the Committee to allow him 'to continue to act as Engineer', paying monthly or fortnightly visits 'if so required'. He referred the chairman to the fact that Barnhill's visits had only been quarterly 'in the old days', and suggested that the Committee should employ him temporarily and allow him 'say £20–£25 per month . . . for doing the job of Visiting Engineer'. But the railway was not far from closure, and his proposal was not accepted.

The two letters were reviewed by the Committee and the point was made that since McClure had *now* admitted that he was not called up for Military service, but was in Civil employment, his leaving was contrary to the conditions made on 18 September and his case was inadmissible. The Committee then decided that McClure should either return to his position at Aughnacloy, or submit his resignation, before 1 January 1941.

It is related that, during the ensuing months, McClure paid a few visits to Aughnacloy. On 14 July 1941, the Committee considered the case in further depth, and it was minuted that he had 'by his own action, ceased to be in the employment of the Committee'. It was a sorry termination of 18 years service, during which McClure had, as he said in his letter of 15 November 1940 'given his whole thought and best years . . . to the railway's welfare, under very difficult and uncertain conditions.' The company had, in fact, lost a very able engineer.

With the end of the railway to come within months, the matter of compensation to its employees was being formulated, but for McClure 'the possibility of his being eligible for compensation' was regarded officially as 'remote'. The Committee however showed what clemency they could, and as their late general manager had almost twenty years service and was on war work, the Committee asked their secretary to make suitable representations to the Ministry of Home Affairs. Towards that end, on 27 October 1941, it was agreed to record McClure as 'on War Service'.

FINAL SCENE

For a prelude to the finale, one must look back to 1937. The outbreak of war was still far off, but the Pole Report had been on issue for two and a half years, when the next move was taken towards closure of the railway. On 11 January 1937, a three-sided deputation, consisting of representatives of the Tyrone and Fermanagh County Councils, and of the Committee of Management of the railway, waited on the Minister of Home Affairs to discuss the future of the railway.

Rowley Elliott, chairman of the Tyrone County Council, introduced the deputation and explained to the Minister that they wished to raise the question of what was to be done about the continuance or otherwise of the railway. On request, Darragh gave the figures of the net annual loss since 1928, adding that apart from the losses, dividends had to be met. The cost to the county rates was discussed.

The Minister asked Rowley Elliott what course he suggested should be adopted, and was told that, if the ratepayers were relieved of any liability in respect of the dividends, and if the government were to put the road in a proper state to carry heavy traffic after closure, it was thought the case would be met. It was thought that the realisation of the assets of the railway should be left to the local authorities, and that railway employees should either be provided with employment by the NIRTB or should receive compensation.

The Minister regarded Mr Elliott's proposals as reasonable, but thought that if the government took over the liability towards the shareholders, it was only right that proceeds from the sale of the assets should be retained by the government. He would be prepared to recommend the government to accept a proposal on these lines, and he would be willing to make a 72 per cent grant towards road reconstruction. A definite proposal on these lines should be laid before the government. Sympathetic consideration would be given as regards compensation.

Without delay, a seven-point proposal covering the terms of closure was prepared:

(1) The ratepayers were to be relieved of all responsibility as far as the shareholders were concerned.
(2) The government were to forgo claims of excess derating grants.
(3) The government were to be responsible for any loss that might be incurred until the Railway was closed.
(4) The government were to contribute 72 per cent over a period of three years, of the total cost of widening and

reconditioning the roads from Tynan to Maguiresbridge.

(5) The present officials and staff of the railway were to be compensated, a suggested basis being that of the Dublin & Blessingbourne Steam Tramway (Abandonment) Act of 1932.

(6) When disposing of the property, the government were to dedicate to the County Councils concerned any land likely to be required for road purposes.

(7) Subject to these conditions the Committee of Management and the County Councils concerned would be prepared to hand over to the government the total assets of the undertaking, the government to accept full responsibility for all outstanding liabilities.

In February 1938 the Prime Minister, Lord Craigavon, appointed a Committee of Inquiry under Sir William McLintock to investigate and report on the working of the 1935 Road and Rail Transport Act. That Act had followed the Pole Report and, amongst other things, had provided for a pooling of income between road and rail. It had, however, omitted the Clogher Valley from the arrangement. The McLintock Committee had no doubt that such omission was deliberate and had been governed by the view expressed by Sir Felix Pole that the CVR must inevitably be superseded by road transport.

The authors of the McLintock Report commented

> However adequate may have been the reasons for which the undertaking has been maintained in the past by means of subsidy from public moneys, we can find none for its continued existence in present circumstances. The transport needs of the area can be adequately met at less expense by public road transport services, and the payment of Government and rate subsidies to maintain uneconomic competition by the railway is indefensible.

The position received further ventilation in 1939, when a Report was issued by a Joint Select Committee on Road and Rail Transport in Northern Ireland. This report contained as an appendix a memorandum by Mr G. C. Duggan of the

Ministry of Finance which explained the financial situation of the railway in some detail. The Committee noted:

> The continued existence of this Railway is due, in our opinion, not to fear of any lack of transport facilities if it were closed, but to the extremely complicated legal and financial problems which its abandonment would present. Chief of these is that concerned with the question whether the guarantee given at the Railway's inception by the Grand Juries (now the County Councils) of Tyrone and Fermanagh in respect of interest at 5 per cent on the subscribed capital of £123,310 is perpetual or limited in character.

It is in the context of the inevitable closure that one must view the actions of management from 1937 until the end of 1941. There was no future for the railway, no reprieve to be expected, yet while it operated, safe and regular working had to be observed, yet needless expenditure avoided. It says much for the staff that, in such an environment, they maintained their loyalty. It cannot have been easy, for death came slowly to the Clogher Valley Railway.

In early December 1941 the County Councils received from the Ministry of Home Affairs copies of the Order that had been made by the Minister under the Clogher Valley Railway and Roads (N.I.) Act 1941. The railway was to cease operations on the last day of 1941. The County Councils appointed sub-committees to deal with alternative arrangements, and on 29 December, the Committee of Management held their final meeting.

The Castlederg engine hauled the last steam train into the gathering dusk. It went through Ballygawley at 2.55pm towards Maguiresbridge, and came up the line in the black-out at 6.40pm. After Fivemiletown it ran light engine to Aughnacloy, on the way crossing with a special run made by the railcar at Ballygawley. It was then 10.20pm. The railcar was crowded with valley folk making a last sentimental run, and had Hugh Murphy as driver and guard. Though the line was to close in 1941, much to the delight of everyone it failed to do so. The railcar reached Fivemiletown, midnight struck, the railcar was turned, and on New Year's Day 1942 set off up the line on the last journey at ten minutes after midnight. It arrived in Ballygawley at 1.23am to the sound of a fusillade of fog signals—a rather halting fusillade as it turned out, for many of the detonators were too old to explode. Then it growled away into the darkness over Tullyvar and towards Aughnacloy, and with its going the trains of the Clogher Valley passed into memory.

DISPERSAL

The company went into liquidation, and arrangements for the disposal of its assets were made by the liquidator, S. H. Jackson, FCA of Belfast. The disposal of the permanent way was by tender for a single lot: 40 miles of line and sidings, signals, weighbridges at Tynan and Maguiresbridge, and the telephone system. It realised £33,000. Messrs John Ross & Co were instructed to auction the remainder of the movable material. The auction was held at Aughnacloy on 14 April 1942, and buyers found the bones of what had been a railway, broken down into nearly 600 lots, and listed over 19 pages. Intending purchasers were asked to note that:

> Every assistance will be given to facilitate purchasers to remove rolling stock to rail-head before the permanent way is closed.
>
> The Iron Field Gates, Wooden and Corrugated Iron Sheds, Water Tanks and Rams, and Windmill as and where fixed along the permanent way (identified by Auctioneer's lot numbers) will be sold by auction at Aughnacloy.
>
> Transport arrangements have been made for day of sale, as under:
>
> > Bus departs from the Auctioneers' premises, 22 May Street, Belfast, at 8.45 am. Arrives Aughnacloy at 10.45 am.
> > Bus departs from Dungannon at 9.20 am for Aughnacloy.
> > Return Buses to Belfast and Dungannon at close of Sale.

The Donegal Railways Joint Committee spent £4,553 15s

(£4,553·75) that day, and according to their minutes purchased:

1 Diesel Rail Car, complete	£315–0–0
1 Diesel Rail Tractor (minus engine)	£105–0–0
5 small vans	£102–10–0
18 five ton wagons	£249–0–0
1 15 ton bogie wagon	£16–0–0
Quantity of stationery & forms	£3–15–0
Vacuum brake parts, lamps etc.	£12–10–0
10,000 secondhand sleepers, Grade A @ 4/3 each	£3,750–0–0
10,000 secondhand sleepers, Grade B @ 3/3	

The three Sharp, Stewart engines fetched from £115 to £125 each, the Castlederg engine brought in £185. Sixteen Windsor chairs from the board room, used since 1887, were sold for £2 15s each.

On Henry Forbes's Donegal line, the railcar became No 10 of the growing railcar fleet, and did excellent work until that railway ceased to work, at the end of 1959. Its cab was damaged by a collision with a steam locomotive in Strabane yard on 2 March 1946, and was replaced by the cab taken from the motorless Unit, purchased for just such an eventuality. On the Donegal, the railcar ran 348,977 miles, and after being used in demolition work, it finally was taken to Belfast for preservation in the Transport Museum.

Legal matters continued to require meetings of the shareholders and directors until 1944, and the final meeting of the board was held on Wednesday 5 April 1944 in Omagh Court House under the chairmanship of B. G. L. Glasgow, with R. Waterson present, and Alan H. Coote as secretary. Three weeks later, on 25/26 April the final disposals were made, when land, crossing lodges, and station buildings were sold by auction.

CHAPTER 8

The Steam Locomotives

SIX SHARP, STEWARTS

To the best of their ability, the Rolling Stock Committee attended to the ordering of engines during autumn 1885. Eight tenders were received, and advice was taken from J. Tomlinson, a consulting engineer, after which it was decided to order six 0–4–2 side tank engines from Messrs Sharp, Stewart of Atlas Works, Manchester. To meet Board of Trade requirements for roadside tramways, condensers were to be fitted to reduce exhaust steam. Two designs of condenser appear to have been considered: a works drawing dated May 1886 shows the system used on street tramways, a nest of open tubes straddling the boiler between chimney and steam dome. A later drawing, dated April 1887 has the more familiar system of two inverted U-tubes conducting the exhaust steam directly into the side tanks, a method used in Ireland on the Cavan & Leitrim and Tralee & Dingle lines. Sharp, Stewart were fitting this latter system to the Clogher Valley sextet when, in November 1886, the Board of Trade relaxed their requirements regarding condensers. The Clogher Valley management naturally wanted to derive advantage from this change of heart, but found that building was so far advanced that the design could not be altered; probably all the engines came to the Clogher Valley with the condensers, and worked for a time thus.

Other tramway requirements were the cowcatcher, the skirting, and the bell. The cowcatcher was made of sheet iron and was fixed below the leading buffer beam so as to clear the rail by 4 inches. Since the engines ran with the cab leading, the cowcatcher therefore projected below the front sheet of the cab. Skirting was fitted along the full length of the sides, to cover the wheels and motion. At first this had three hinged inspection doors ranged along it, and was of rather light gauge steel. It was found to shake and was replaced by heavier sheet, and at the same time the inspection door below the cab opening was eliminated; this had been provided to give access to a flush valve between the two tanks. The warning bell was sited midway along the top of the boiler, it was later replaced by a deep-tone whistle on the roof of the cab.

The leading dimensions of the engines were:

Driving wheels	3ft 0in diam.
Trailing wheels	2ft 3in diam.
Wheel base	4ft 9in + 5ft 7in
Cylinders	13½in x 18in (inclined 1 in 15), Joy's valve gear
Grate area	10sq ft
Heating surface	48 + 466sq ft
Tank capacity	600 gallons
Bunker capacity	1 ton (as modified)
Length of frames	19ft 1in
Length overall	23ft 3in
Height	11ft 0in
Boiler centre line	5ft 3in above rail
Boiler (2 ring)	3ft 6in/3ft 6¾in i.d., 7ft 9in bet. tube plates
Boiler tubes	127 of 1¾in diameter
Weight	23t 16c

Large rectangular windows were provided in the end sheets of the cab, those in the leading end being deeper to give the crews maximum visibility. The windows, perhaps the leading pair only, appear to have been unglazed for the first couple of years for, at a board meeting on 2 September 1889, instructions were issued to the locomotive superintendent to 'wholly close' the windows in the cab of one engine and to partially close the windows in another 'to protect the drivers and firemen from inclement weather'. They were probably all fitted with glass soon after that and, to protect them from the assaults of fire irons, three metal cross-bars were fixed on the inside.

A very large oil headlamp was fitted between the two windows of the cab, supported by curved iron scroll pieces. Acetylene lamps were used later and were slightly smaller. The original oil lamp was still in use on one of the engines (No 2) as late as 1937. During his inspection prior to the opening of the tramway, General Hutchinson commented: '[The headlamp] will be very useful for enabling impediments to be seen at a long distance, but it may be found to frighten horses in which case it would be desirable to furnish the driver with a means of temporarily screening it'. The suggestion was not followed up, Clogher Valley drivers had enough to do without determining the excitability of approaching horses and staging temporary blackouts for their benefit. For their part, the horses no doubt learned by experience and passed on the lesson to their friends. At first the headlamps were mounted high, so that their tops rose above the cab roof. The lamps were later lowered.

On the steep gradients, and with a wet rail, sanding had often to be resorted to. The makers fitted gravity sanding, delivering by one pipe on each side in front of the leading driving wheel. In December 1889 Akerlind asked his Traffic Committee for permission to change to steam sanding and by the following September he had Gresham's Patent Sanding Apparatus on trial, on one engine. Adoption of steam sanding followed but, while it was effective in minimising slip, it was extravagant in sand and moreover threw a lot of it around the motion generally and caused abrasive wear of the bearing surfaces. Sometime around 1915 Akerlind found the rapid wear intolerable, and reverted to gravity sanding. As a result, sandboxes were placed on top of the water tanks immediately in front of the coal bunker. The sand was kept warm and dry there, and was conveyed by pipes which passed through the water tanks. In turn, the gravity feed had its disadvantages for since the pipes were taken to just above rail level, in damp weather the orifices tended to get blocked with wet sand, promoted by water thrown up by the wheels when they ran through the surface water which accumulated at the numerous road crossings, beside the sunken rails.

Since the exhaust steam, when condensers were in vogue, would be led to the tanks on the roadside sections of the tramway, the water in them would soon have become too warm to be handled by injector. In consequence, although a No 5 injector is shown on the works drawings, the class were designed with eccentric-driven water feed-pumps worked from the leading driving axle. The injector would be operated when the water was cold, and the engine standing. What appears to signify the demise of the condensing apparatus and the associated feed-pumps comes in a rather contradictory minute of the Traffic Committee meeting held on 16 December 1889, when Akerlind was asked to report on the cost of substituting injectors for pumps 'together with the repair and restoration of pumps and condensing apparatus'. Then in January 1890, Akerlind was allowed to replace the pumps by injectors 'but not more than three in one half-year', so that it is reasonable to assume that condensers were removed and the feed-pumps replaced by the end of 1890. While condensing was in use, it is likely that while the train was working on the deviations away from the road it was the practice to put the exhaust up the blast pipe and thereby keep the fire red.

Bunker space in the original design consisted of hoppers in the leading end of each side tank, and was found to be too small. Akerlind proposed to enlarge their capacity and in December 1889 he was allowed to do this on one engine. In due course, all the engines were modified, the original side hopper being enlarged into an open bunker that extended across the boiler and firebox, and which was contained within rather elegantly cut steel sheeting, itself bordered with half-round strip. The bunker stood 15in above the side tanks, its front sheet rose in a curve over the boiler, and thus considerably reduced the backward view from the cab windows.

Reference has been made in Chapter 4 to improvements made by Akerlind to spark arresters, following a spate of lineside fires.

The maker's numbers, running numbers and names of the engines were:

Maker's No	CVR No	Name
3369	1	*Caledon*
3370	2	*Errigal*
3371	3	*Blackwater*
3372	4	*Fury*
3373	5	*Colebrooke*
3374	6	*Erne*

Nos 1 and 5 were named after villages on the route of the tram. No 2 derived its name from Errigal Keerogue, a parish near Ballygawley that is famous for its antiquarian remains. Nos 3 and 4 carried the names of rivers crossed by the line. No 6 took its title from the lough beyond Maguiresbridge.

The board minute books do not often refer to the engines, except for the necessity to order new boilers. The earliest reference to boiler replacement is at the end of 1899, when two boilers were ordered from Sharp, Stewart. Later replacements seem to have been a matter of shopping around, the North British Locomotive Co made one in 1906, while in 1911 it was minuted that Hudswell, Clarke & Co would do boiler work since they were cheaper than the costs in the Aughnacloy shops. Bagnall of Stafford tendered successfully for two boilers in 1918, and Beardmore of Glasgow in 1930.

It is unfortunate that no workshop report books appear to have survived. In 1927 though Robert Killin had free access to records, he had to admit that 'It appears that until the last five years no very clear records were available of the age of the boilers, but it is probable that the boiler now in use on these engines is the third which each of them has had.' This, however, is scarcely credible, for it is unlikely that two

N

replacements would have become necessary in the course of 40 years, for each of the six engines. Killin's report contains specific reference to the boiler and firebox repairs, and includes the following list, which has, however, been supplemented by the probable name of the boiler supplier derived from the minute books:

Engine No	New Boiler	New Firebox	Last Gen. Repair
1	1919 (Bagnall)	1919	1922
2	1923 (uncertain)	1923	1923
3	1914 (H. Clarke)	1914	1925
4	1901 (S. Stewart)	1911	In progress 1927
5	1919 (Bagnall)	1919	1927
6	1914 (H. Clarke)	1914	1924

When Killin made his inspection, none of the engines was in good order as a summary of his remarks shows:

Caledon No 1: Frames, boiler, and firebox in fair order. Cylinders bored out once but in fair condition. Axles recommended for replacement in 1922, but not acted upon. Crank-pins worn.

Errigal No 2: Frames in fair order. Cylinders fair, rebored once. Crank-pins worn and need renewal. Boiler and firebox in good order as far as can be seen. Axles as No 1.

Blackwater No 3: Frames in fair order. Boiler worn. Firebox practically done. Cylinders rebored once, and in fair condition. Axles renewed following failure in 1922, these and the crank-pins in fairly good order.

Fury No 4: Last worked in early 1925, ran 8 miles in that year. Boiler shell pitted, front tubeplate wasted, boiler not worth further repair. Frames in fair order. Axles condemned, crank-pins very badly worn.

Colebrooke No 5: Frames in good order, following re-riveting and stiffening up. Cylinders fair. Boiler and firebox apparently in good order. All axles require renewal. Crank-pins somewhat worn.

Erne No 6: Frames and cylinders in fair order. Firebox worn out. Boiler probably needs renewal. Axles as No 1. Crank-pins somewhat worn.

The 1911 boilers were the last to have Ramsbottom safety valves, which were set in line with the axis of the boiler. The 1918 and later boilers had pop valves, mounted transversely.

As regards livery, a board minute of 19 October 1886 records that the engines were to be painted in the same colours as those of the London & North Western Railway, that is to say, black. Confirmation of this comes from Mr Walter Montgomery of Fivemiletown, whose father and others who remembered the opening of the line, stated that the engines were 'black with gold letters and lining'. Buffer plates were red. Thus, green livery, with which the engines have been credited by some writers, appears to have been derived from the first repainting, though the skirtings and cowcatcher remained black. What is probably this second livery is seen in a photograph of No 3. This shows a pair of lines of contrasting colour, each about ½in wide and set about 2in apart, forming panels on the side tanks, cab, and bunker. The colour of the lining may be conjectured as red outside, and yellow inside, the ground colour appears to be uniform overall. No crest appears on the side tanks, and there is no company name shown.

Other early photographs show various engines without lining, but with everything below the framing in a darker colour which is probably black. This may have been the scheme followed by the workshops at later repainting, and it is noteworthy that the coloured crest is applied, towards the front of the side tanks. Since known examples of the crest are encircled by the legend *Clogher Valley Railway Company Limited* it is probably that it did not come into use until 1894 or later.

The combination of green for cab, side tanks, bunker, and boiler, with black for smokebox, skirting, buffer beams, cowcatcher, and drawbar was continued into the early 1930s. Thereafter the buffer beam below the cab became red, as in the case of the railcar and the skirtings and cowcatcher chocolate. After a shopping in the spring of 1937, *Blackwater* emerged with lake-red replacing the green, and like the others was unlined.

The engine's name was in square-serifed, shaded, gold capital letters disposed along the arc of a circle towards the top of the tank sides. The number as 'No. 1' was placed centrally below the name, and was also exhibited as the digit alone on the front sheet of the cab, midway between the headlamp and buffer beam. The repainting of *Blackwater* in 1937, included the use of sans-serif capitals for the name.

At some date during the 1920s, the attractive coloured crest was omitted, no doubt as an economy measure. It was replaced by a monogram of the interlaced letters 'CV' as on the uniform buttons and later 'CVR' on *Blackwater* alone.

During the thirteen years following Killin's visit, three of the Sharp, Stewart engines were withdrawn. *Fury* never ran again, was cannibalised, and was officially withdrawn in 1929. *Caledon* was scrapped in 1934 and *Colebrooke* followed in 1936. The remaining three existed until the closure of the railway, though latterly *Erne* was in bad repair. The last engine to work was *Blackwater*, distinguished by having a wheel handle in the middle of the smokebox door.

BLESSINGBOURNE

In February 1909 the board decided to invite tenders for a new engine 'in accordance with plan and specification prepared by Mr. Akerlind and approved by Mr. Barton.' Akerlind had designed a 0–4–4 side tank engine; like its forerunners it was to travel with the bunker and cab leading. In January 1910 it was minuted that nine tenders had been received, though the firms were not listed, and it was resolved to accept one of £1,585 from Messrs Hudswell, Clarke. Delivery was to be in ten weeks at Tynan 'subject to thorough investigation by the locomotive superintendent'.

The order was probably placed in late January, for building had not yet begun when, on 5 February 1910, it was minuted that some (unspecified) alterations were being made by the makers to reduce the cost to £1,574, and that Sloan had sent Akerlind 'to inspect the works'. A month later the directors decided to name the engine *Blessingbourne*, after the chairman's house, and in April permission was sought from the Board of Trade and the County Councils to pay for the engine out of the reserve fund. It had the following characteristics:

Maker's number	914
CVR number	7
Driving wheels	3ft 4in diam.
Bogie wheels	2ft 0in diam.
Wheelbase	5ft 3in + 5ft 3in + 4ft 0in
Cylinders	14in x 20in
Grate area	12¼sq ft
Heating Surface	57 + 548sq ft
Tank capacity	700 gallons
Bunker capacity	1¼ tons
Weight in w/o	29 tons 15cwt
Axle loading	9t 0c 0q + 9t 2c 0q + (11t 12c 3q)

At the board meeting on 4 July 1910 it was stated that the new engine had run 1,000 miles, and the directors authorised payment. At the August board the wages of drivers McNeece, Thompson, and McLoughlin were raised to 6s (30p) per day, and Akerlind expressed himself 'completely satisfied' with the performance of *Blessingbourne*. One thing which Akerlind could not have specified properly in his design came to the directors' notice during the next weeks, and as a result in September the tone of *Blessingbourne*'s whistle was altered to sound the same as those of Nos 1 to 6.

In fact, the engine was a dismal failure due to bad adhesion, and it must have been a sad disappointment to Akerlind. The weight distribution was faulty, and on a wet rail it experienced chronic slipping. The steam brake gave much trouble, frequently leaking on, and adding to the load. It rapidly became extremely unpopular with its crews, who christened it 'the ould baste', and one wonders whether the facile rise in the drivers' wages in the summer of its arrival was intended to appease them. Before long, its consumption of coal was found to be higher than the others, which further ensured its disfavour.

According to R. M. Livesey, in his paper to the Belfast meeting of the Institution of Mechanical Engineers in July 1912, the tractive force of the engine at 75 per cent of working pressure was 11,760lb compared to the 9,567lb of the six Sharp, Stewarts. But the proportion of adhesive weight to total weight was 60·8 per cent, compared to the 67·3 per cent of the other six. The two 4–4–2T Kitson engines which plagued the Ballycastle Railway by poor adhesion were listed at 54 per cent by Livesey.

Like the Sharp, Stewarts, *Blessingbourne* was fitted with a skirting over the driving wheels and motion, but it did not extend rearwards to cover the cylinders, nor forwards over the bogie. The leading buffer beam extended downwards into a sheet iron cowcatcher. The front cab sheet had large spectacle glasses, to give good forward vision, and each had four external cross bars to prevent breakage when coaling. A large acetylene headlamp was sited between the windows. The entire coal supply was held in the bunker.

Unlike Nos 1–6, *Blessingbourne* began as a green engine, but even a superficial study of photographs shows detail that has previously gone unrecorded. It is fortunate that the excellent memory of Mr J. R. Robinson, formerly chargehand fitter at Aughnacloy, has enabled existing descriptions to be amplified. A photograph in the possession of Mr Walter Montgomery of Fivemiletown, probably taken when the engine was delivered, is also helpful. The livery was divided into panels, which had green central areas framed by a band of black, the two being separated by a ¼in line of yellow. Panels thus treated were the side tanks, bunker and cab sides, front and rear sheets of the cab, motion cover, wheel skirting, cylinder covers, and boiler rings. The smokebox, funnel, main frames, bogie frames, cowcatcher, cab roof, drawbars, hook and safety chains were black. The dome was green. It appears that at first, the leading cab sheet was black and unlined. At each end the buffer plates were red, edged with black. The cab window frames, inside and out, were of cast brass, with countersunk roundhead screws. The engine name on the tank sides was in gilt, square-serif capitals, arranged in an arc. As delivered, the letters were shaded in relief, a later repaint used unshaded letters. This repaint probably also altered the form of the corners of the black outer lining to the panels on side tanks and bunker, originally with cutaways convex inwards, later with normal radiusing. Below the name was the coloured crest in the original livery, as on the Sharp, Stewart engines this was replaced by the interlaced 'CV' monogram. Lower still was 'No. 7'. As delivered, the leading face of the bunker was plain, later it carried the number alone.

Robert Killin was made aware of the engine's defects in 1927 and reported ' . . . this engine has not been put to work unless absolutely necessary, and then only for a few days at a time, the effect being that in the year 1925 the engine only earned a mileage to the extent of 188 miles run in four days, and in 1926 to the extent of 733 miles run in some 12 days. The engine therefore spends most of its time in the sheds'. Killin was an operating, rather than a mechanical man, and could hardly comment constructively on the reasons for *Blessingbourne*'s inaction, nor suggest a cure for the trouble which both Akerlind and McClure must surely have given thought to. Already the builders had been the target for complaint, but it was not their design and they could do nothing more than to suggest that the boiler pressure of 160lb might be cut by 10lb per square inch to minimise slipping by reducing power. This had been tried, but was ineffective.

As a result of its reduced utilisation and low mileage, the engine was still in good mechanical shape when Killin saw it in 1927. He suggested that it was fit for three more years of full work, but took care not to specify an annual mileage. He reckoned without the opposition of the practical Clogher Valley men, and *Blessingbourne* remained merely a piece of the landscape of the Aughnacloy yard. In September 1926 the directors gave Sloan authority to sell it, but there were no takers. It lay for eight years, unloved and unsung, photographed by occasional visitors, until finally in October 1934 it was exchanged as scrap, along with the toil-worn *Caledon* for the thirty-year-old Hudswell, Clarke engine that the failure of the Castlederg and Victoria Bridge Tramway had released. It fell to pieces in the Aughnacloy yard under the cutting torch and nobody missed it.

THE STEAM TRACTOR

Among the recommendations of the Killin Report was a strong advocacy of the value to the Clogher Valley of an Atkinson-Walker locomotive. Killin, it will be recalled, wanted to see the line reduced to freight carrying, its passengers banished to road buses, and he claimed that the Atkinson-Walker engine would only consume 10lb of coal per mile, compared to the average of 27lb burned by the existing engines. Killin visualised the Atkinson-Walker engine operating a light freight service between Fivemiletown and Maguiresbridge, while the heavier engines kept the line open between Tynan and Fivemiletown. Respective daily mileages were calculated to be 22 and 93, and Killin estimated that the annual fuel bill could be cut from £2,480 to £802.

No less than three times in his report did Killin sing the praises of the Atkinson-Walker locomotive, even to the extent of giving its price as £950 and its depreciation as £50 per year. But he omitted a direct reference to its power, speed or steaming capabilities, and did not state where one might be seen at work. He claimed that ' . . . several types have been considered . . . but the Atkinson-Walker is thought to be the most suitable' and backed this superficial statement by saying that 'Mr. McClure the locomotive superintendent has had an opportunity of seeing one at work and consulting with the makers, and he is also of the opinion that it is the most suitable for the work.'

There is, however, no evidence among the minutes that the Clogher Valley board had asked McClure to formally consult with the Atkinson-Walker company, or with the maker of a similar type of engine. Killin never mentioned the well-tried Clayton or Sentinel engines, though the Abbott committee did. Atkinson-Walker had apparently promised delivery within three months.

As successors to the board of directors, in due course the Committee of Management approached Atkinson-Walker Wagons Ltd of Preston, and in September 1928 that firm offered to send one of their Class A.3 engines on trial. Their offer was accepted, the engine came in January 1929, the builders agreeing to take it back free of cost if it was found to be unsatisfactory. It was finished in unlined grey, and carried no lettering or number. The maker's catalogue illustrates a three-cylinder version for standard gauge lines; that made for the Clogher Valley had a two-cylinder engine, fed from a water-tube boiler. The wheels were not skirted, but at each end the buffer beam was carried down to near rail level, and had a simple cowcatcher of three curved bars. An electric headlamp was provided at each end. The characteristics were:

Maker's number	114
Wheel arrangement	0-4-0
Driving wheels	2ft 6in diameter
Wheelbase	6ft 6in
Cylinders	7in x 10in
Grate area	3·3sq ft
Heating surface	25 + 35sq ft
Tank capacity	500 gallons

Bunker capacity	10cwt
Boiler (vertical)	280 psi working pressure
Weight in working order	12 tons
Tractive effort	5,700lb
Length over cowcatchers	17ft 3in
Length over buffers	15ft 6in
Width	7ft 0in
Height	9ft 9in

From the outset it was obvious that the engine was unable to perform its duties and was deficient both in power and in speed. In February 1929 McClure reported to the Committee that it was thoroughly unsatisfactory, and in the following month Messrs Atkinson-Walker were asked to take it away. Eager to impress, the makers supplied a larger boiler, with a grate area of 5 square feet and a heating surface of 90 square feet, and sent across two fitters to install it. No significant improvement was effected by the change. During November 1929 the makers were again asked to remove the engine, and it was minuted 'that no further dealings be entered into with Messrs. Atkinson-Walker Wagons Ltd.' By the end of 1929 the firm were in liquidation and in the hands of a receiver, who tried without success to find a purchaser. It had cost the makers £1,200. It appears to have been written off by its owners, and it lay out of use in the Aughnacloy c & w shed until 1932.

Henry Forbes, manager of the County Donegal Railways and a member of the Clogher Valley Committee of Management from the outset, was a man of vision and energy. In December 1931 Forbes wrote to J. B. Stephens, general manager of the Great Northern, saying that he had been offered the engine, minus boiler, engine, vacuum brake, and lighting set for £125. He wanted to see it fitted with a 74hp Gardner diesel engine and geared for shunting and goods train working on the CDRJC. He had discussed the conversion scheme with G. T. Glover, the Great Northern's mechanical engineer, and Glover had estimated that the work could be carried out for around £1,000. Forbes was at that time faced with an ageing locomotive fleet, and had been obtaining promising results with petrol and diesel-engined railcars for passenger haulage. He was convinced that the use of the chassis and body of the steam engine, re-powered with the well proved Gardner engine, would enable him to effect economies in one year equal to half of the capital cost of the unit.

So Forbes had his way, and his enthusiasm combined with the sound technical backing he received from H. E. Wilson and G. T. Glover at the GN's Dundalk workshops, produced No 11 of the CDRJC's railcar stock. Fittingly given the name *Phoenix* by Forbes, it was a slow-moving but useful power unit which served the Donegal lines well until their end, and went on to assist in the melancholy matter of track lifting on the Strabane and Letterkenny section of that system. Finally it found a well-merited resting place in the Ulster Museum's transport section in Belfast, where it forms a unique, if unbeautiful exhibit.

THE CASTLEDERG ENGINE

Twenty-five miles north-west of the Clogher Valley, the Castlederg and Victoria Bridge Tramway operated as a roadside line in the north-west of County Tyrone. Its length of 7¼ miles was opened for traffic on 4 July 1884, using a gauge of 3ft, and meeting the Great Northern's Omagh—Londonderry line at Victoria Bridge station.

The early Castlederg engines were 0–4–0 Kitsons, but to get increased power the company obtained a heavier engine in 1904. This was a Hudswell, Clarke 2–6–0 side tank engine (maker's number 698), which cost £1,600. Its dimensions (taken from G. T. Glover's general arrangement book) were:

Driving wheels	3ft 1in diam.
Leading wheels	1ft 8½in diam.
Wheelbase	4ft 0in + 3ft 4in + 3ft 8in = 11ft 0in
Cylinders	13½in x 18in

Grate area	Westinghouse
Heating surface	9·25sq ft
Tank capacity	54·0 + 542·4sq ft
Bunker capacity (inside)	600 gallons
Boiler	15cwt (32cu ft)
Boiler tubes	3ft 3in x 9ft 10in
Boiler pressure	120 of 1¾in diam.
Height	160psi
Maximum width	10ft 3in
Overall length	6ft 6in
Tractive effort	26ft 2in
Weight	12,058lb @ 85%
Brake	21t empty, 25t 10c in working order

R. M. Livesey in 1912 gave the ratio of adhesive to total weight at 80·7 per cent, and the tractive effort at 75 per cent boiler pressure as 10,639lb.

The maker's photograph shows the engine prior to delivery with the name *Victoria* painted on the side tank, but it was not the practice of the C & VBT to name their engines and it did not run bearing a name. At Castlederg and at Victoria Bridge, the engine was not turned and only on the side that was always next to the public road was a skirting fitted, reaching from the framing to the rail level. The skirting partly covered the motion and wheels, but a cut-away portion left access to the driving wheels so that oiling could be attended to easily, and a hinged panel could be lifted to expose the crosshead and slide-bars.

The engine ran on the Castlederg tramway in lined brick red livery, and was numbered 4. It served the company well for, unlike its predecessors, it had sufficient reserve of power to haul the heavy mixed trains that were assembled on Castlederg fair days. The company had its own workshops at Castlederg, but they had their limits and for heavy repair work assistance was sought from the Great Northern. In May 1928 the GN's Dundalk workshops patched the copper firebox and altered the spring gear on the trailing coupled axle from coil to laminated. Further repairs became necessary in 1929 when a crack appeared in the firebox.

The prolonged rail strike which affected the lines in Northern Ireland between 31 January and 7 April 1933 extinguished the life of the Castlederg tramway, for the company was already in debt, and services never restarted. The workshop equipment and rolling stock were bought by Messrs Arnott, Young & Co Ltd of Glasgow for scrapping. Before No 4 could be cut up, the Clogher Valley company saw its potential as a low-cost source of motive power, and made arrangements to exchange *Caledon* and *Blessingbourne* for it.

In October 1934, with assistance from the Great Northern's two breakdown cranes, the engine was moved on a well-wagon from Victoria Bridge to Maguiresbridge. There it was steamed, and taken to Aughnacloy, the journey showing that the valves badly required to be reset. Moreover, the Clogher Valley workings were to take the engine further from the Aughnacloy coaling point than on its accustomed Castlederg runs, and an increase in the limited bunker capacity was necessary. Under McClure's supervision the engine entered the Aughnacloy shops for rebuilding and overhaul.

While in the workshops the frames were lengthened by 2ft 0in at the rear, to accommodate a bunker 2ft 6in in length, and therefore overhanging the frame, and capable of holding 1½ tons of coal. To carry the bunker, a rear radial truck with solid 2ft 6in wheels was grafted on, making the engine into a 2–6–2T, with a weight in working order of 28½ tons. The original Ramsbottom safety valves were replaced by Ross pop valves, and the whistle brought between them and the front sheet of the cab. The Westinghouse brake was replaced by the vacuum gear from *Blessingbourne*, along with the latter's steam brake. The light Castlederg buffers, which were link type with pins, were replaced by the hook type used by the Clogher Valley, their centre line raised to 2ft 2in above rail level, from the 1ft 11in which the Castlederg Tramway used. To improve the running, laminated springs were fitted to all the driving axles. In its rebuilt form the total wheelbase was 16ft 6in. The driving position was on the left-hand side, unlike Nos 1–7. Since *Fury* had been scrapped over five years previously and 4 was therefore a vacant number in the CV list, the Castlederg engine was able to retain its original running number. No name was given to it. Although delivered at Maguiresbridge complete with one-sided skirting, this was removed, for cars, rather than horses, were encountered along the roads by the 1930s.

With an uncluttered boiler top, visibility from the cab over the firebox was adequate and it was general practice to run No 4 smokebox leading. There is, however, photographic evidence that this was not always done, and acetylene head-lamps were fitted fore and aft, one in front of the funnel, the other at the top of the bunker back-plate.

No 4's whistle gave the more usual high pitched sound, quite different from the deep toned 'hoot' delivered by the Sharp, Stewarts. When the engine went into regular service, even the cattle in fields along the lineside noticed the difference in the tone and, being inquisitive beasts, for a time they galloped towards their gates to view the new Thing that was hauling the familiar train.

At least in its latter years on the Castlederg line, a rather widely spaced 'No. 4' was painted on the side tanks, and it was lettered thus on arrival at Maguiresbridge. A photograph taken by McClure in Aughnacloy yard, after rebuilding, shows the engine in steam and still in its bedraggled Castlederg livery, but it only appeared in that state on trial runs. It was re-painted red-brown, with a single yellow line running 2in from the edges of the side tanks, bunker, and cab, and on the cylinder covers, wheel rims, and steps. Two lines encircled the boiler just behind the smokebox. Funnel and smokebox were black. On the tank sides 'C.V.R.' in shaded, sans-serif gold letters 12in in height had 'No. 4' in 9in characters below it. The number as '4' alone, was repeated on the bunker back-plate. The builder's oval works plates remained in their original positions on the side tanks. To commemorate the re-building, McClure obtained a pair of oval brass plates, similar in size to the builder's, inscribed 'REBUILT 1936 AUGHNACLOY WORKS' and had them fixed to the bunker sides, level with the Hudswell, Clarke plates.

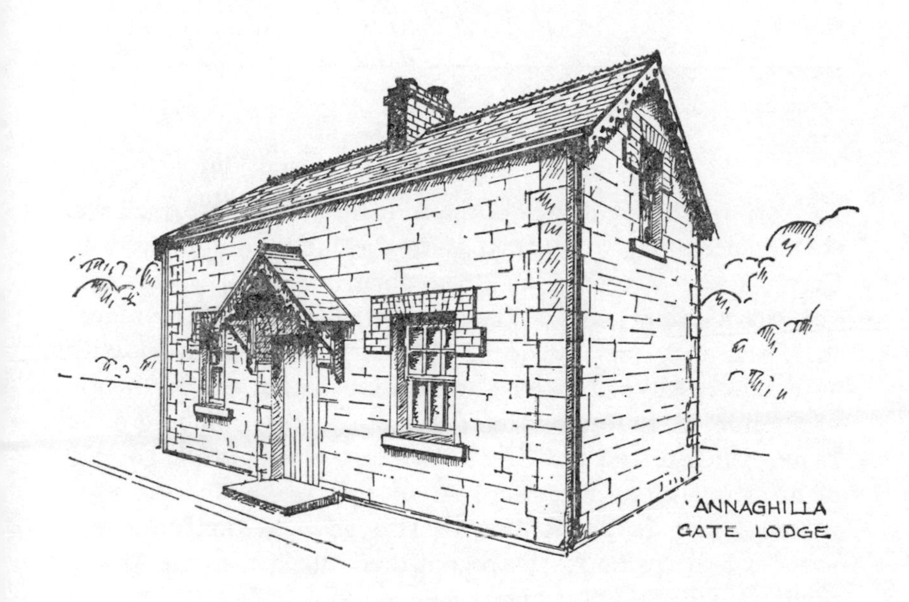

CHAPTER 9

Rolling Stock

COACHING VEHICLES

In April 1886 the directors' half-yearly report informed the shareholders that 'a contract with the Metropolitan Railway Carriage and Wagon Co., Birmingham . . . for 19 carriages and guard's vans and seventy goods wagons' had been entered into, and that the 'whole of the stock shall be fitted with automatic vacuum brake'. The decision to use the automatic vacuum brake is noteworthy, for it was three years before the Armagh disaster on the Great Northern, which led to government compulsion over the use of this brake on passenger vehicles. The Cavan & Leitrim also adopted the automatic vacuum brake when they ordered their stock from the Metropolitan Company in October 1886.

The original order consisted of the following vehicles:

Nos 1–6: 4-wheel, luggage, parcel, and brake vans

Nos 7–9: bogie 1st class passenger coaches

Nos 10 & 11: bogie 1st/3rd composite passenger coaches

Nos 12–19: bogie 3rd class passenger coaches

The thirteen coaches had sliding end doors, which gave access to verandahs, over which the roofs projected. The extremities of the roof were supported at each end by two metal pillars, which also carried a wire mesh grid with a central gate. Communication through the length of the train was possible via these end gates, across metal fall-plates which covered the buffer-couplings. The coach roofs were clerestoried.

The three first class coaches were shorter than the others, and had a length of 24ft 0in over the platforms and 18ft 6in over the bodies. The two composites and the eight third class coaches were 29ft 6in over the platforms, and 24ft 0in over the bodies. Lengths over the buffers were 2ft 10in more than those over the platforms. In both classes the seating was arranged longitudinally, the thirds having perforated wooden seats, while the first were upholstered, with arm rests at the ends and in the middle. All the vehicles had a width of 6ft 6in; the height to the top of the roof was 10ft 0in.

In the shorter first class vehicles there were nine side windows, three of which were droplights, while in the others there were twelve side windows including three or four droplights. The droplights all had three horizontal iron bars, to give inquisitive passengers protection from passing hedges. The seating capacity of the firsts was listed as 18, the composite seated 8 in the first, and 25 in the third class section. The thirds probably had designed accommodation for 40, but the total of 330 seats given in the annual report suggests that five coaches held 42, and three held 40. In the composites, a sliding door separated the two classes, the firsts were similarly separated into smoking and non-smoking compartments.

Buffer centres were 2ft 2in above rail level when unloaded. This measurement matched that of the Cavan & Leitrim stock, but contrasted with 1ft 10½in on the Ballymena & Larne Railway, 1ft 11in on the Castlederg & Victoria Bridge Tramway, 2ft 3in on the West Clare, 2ft 7½in on the Londonderry & Lough Swilly, 2ft 9in on the Cork, Blackrock & Passage and 2ft 10½in on the Donegal. This variety of heights was responsible for later difficulties in the interchange of vehicles between the systems.

Another noteworthy feature of the carriages, and one in which the Clogher Valley were far ahead of their contemporaries, was that carriage heating was done by exhaust steam. At the time, warming pans were the best that most passengers could look forward to in winter time, and indeed were all that ever materialised on the Cavan & Leitrim. The steam heating main was offset to clear the drawbar and buffer, and ran under one side of the coach body. Towards the middle of the coach, two branch pipes were taken across the coach, and connections rose from them to cylinders below the seats. The brake gear and steam main were on the same side of the vehicles, and the additional weight produced a degree of lean that was counteracted by inserting a ½in or ¾in washer between the spring and spring pillar on that side. To connect with the offset steam main, the engines had duplicate pipes below the smokebox, one pipe coming from a T-junction. The unused pipe was blanked off after the engine was turned. The Sharp, Stewart engines had steam connections only at the smokebox end, in conformity with their cab-first method of working. Steam heating was therefore not possible on the rare occasions when the engines were worked with the smokebox leading, though for such occasions a vacuum connection was provided.

For the first twenty years, Silber patent oil lamps provided interior lighting. After a successful trial in 1905, acetylene lighting was gradually introduced. A shortage of calcium carbide during the last year of the 1914–18 war forced a temporary reversion to oil lamps. Under the Committee of Management, electric lighting was fitted to Nos 15 and 17, the current being supplied by the diesel vehicles. Roof ventilators were fitted to the clerestories of the first class from the beginning, but similar accessories did not appear on the thirds or composites until some years later.

First-class travel was abolished after 1 September 1928, and some of the old wooden seats in the third class coaches were upholstered to bring them into line with the comfort of the first class.

Prior to the withdrawal of first-class travel, the carriages were lettered 'THIRD CLASS' or 'FIRST CLASS' twice along each side, the legends flanking a central panel with the company's colourful crest. This crest was a circular device, made up of the arms of the O'Neill and Maguire families, enclosed in a garter which was lettered 'CLOGHER VALLEY

RAILWAY COMPANY LIMITED' in azure sans-serif capitals. It is uncertain when the crest was first used. It may not have been adopted in the Tramway days, and the company cash book contains a record of the payment of £11 8s (£11·40) to Tearne & Sons of Birmingham on 15 June 1903 which may well be the first account for transfers. It is understood that the use of the crest ceased after World War I as an economy measure. As painting became due, it was then replaced by a monogram of 'CVR' in gold, and that in its turn by sans-serif block capitals C.V.R. The number of the vehicle was shown on a lower panel, below the crest, at first as N° 15, and later as the digits alone.

The carriage livery has been stated to have been crimson lake or reddish brown, and while the latter shade might have been a weathered version of crimson lake, it is possible that both were used, but no details have been found in the company records.

The original carriage stock of 13 vehicles lasted until the line was closed, and no additions were made to it after the 1887 purchases. At the board meeting on 4 August 1913, William Coote JP of Lisdoart proposed that additional carriages should be bought to give accommodation for 250 passengers. The scheme was probably the result of the annual overcrowding on the 12 July specials. Though the directors asked the general manager to find the cost, the proposal was not followed up, and was lost sight of during World War I.

The six brake vans had sliding end doors with fixed lights in their upper halves, and had a sliding door in each side. Early photographs show that they were panelled in a similar fashion to the carriages, No 1 was later rebuilt with plain sides and end panels, relieved by a waist moulding. Though a steam pipe ran along them, they had no internal heating. Their length was 14ft, weight 4 tons, and load 6 tons. One of the brake vans disappears from the stock lists about 1900, but its fate is not known. A board minute dated 4 April 1887 contains a tantalising reference. 'The three remaining guard's vans to be widened at a cost of £18 each'. Though the date is only a month before the opening day, it is possible that the instruction applied to work done by Metropolitan just prior to delivery. What was involved is not recorded, nor is it apparent from examination of photographs.

Two four-wheel horseboxes, each holding two horses, were ordered from Metropolitan in August 1887. They were numbered 20 and 21 in the passenger coaching stock list.

MERCHANDISE, MINERAL, AND SERVICE STOCK

The stock returns for September 1887 lists 74 units, made up of 35 covered wagons, 35 open wagons, and 4 timber trucks. By 1888 the total had been increased to 78 by the inclusion of the pair of horseboxes, and by the addition of 2 ballast wagons bought from Messrs McCrea & McFarland.

During 1891 the tramway moved 3,000 tons of timber from Aughnacloy to Tynan, en route to Belfast, and at the June board it was decided to convert 12 of the open wagons to timber wagons. While this may have been done as a temporary expedient, it is not reflected by any change in the stock totals. However, during 1891 the open wagon total fell from 35 to 31, bringing down the total of merchandise units from 78 to 74.

The two McCrea & McFarland ballast wagons were disposed of, following a decision by the Traffic Committee in December 1889. The sale was not finalised until February 1892, when the contractor Thomas Dixon obtained them for £48. He was slow in paying, and by September the directors decided to institute legal proceedings for the recovery of the money.

From 1887, a number of covered goods wagons were employed to convey passengers to the 12 July Celebrations at Caledon. For such a purpose, they were thoroughly washed out and given a hygenic treatment inside by limewashing. From year to year, at the board meeting prior to the Twelfth, the manager asked his directors for permission to use cattle trucks, and assent was invariably given, though care was taken to add 'if necessary' and not to over-publicise the practice, lest the

Board of Trade should have contrary views. In 1911, the minutes contain a reference to 'insufficiency of accommodation' during 12 July traffic working, and the directors had to tell the general manager that in future he was 'to confine traffic of this character within safe limits'. It was highly profitable traffic for the company, and the management were loath to discourage it.

As early as 1893, thought was being given to economic methods of handling the annual surge, and on 6 March the board considered buying a 'gondola wagon', the plan and specification of which had already been submitted by the Tubular Wagon Company. It was to be convertible to a passenger carriage. The directors thought it prudent to approach the Board of Trade, and first obtain formal approval for its use. The minute book then becomes uncommunicative until August 1894, when it was briefly noted that the order for the gondola wagon was cancelled.

Cattle wagons were included in the covered wagon total until 1897, but were separately listed after that. In practice, beasts were put into any covered wagon as and when the need arose, as it did on Fair Days. In December 1894 it was decided to order four cattle wagons at £72 10s each, again from Metropolitan, and these came during the early part of 1895. Thereafter they were listed separately.

The next increase in thc wagon stock came in 1897, after Irwin had asked for 22 more wagons and had been authorised to advertise for 20. The Metropolitan's tender for ten covered wagons at £96 and ten open at £80 was accepted on 6 September 1897. These purchases brought the total of goods vehicles up to 96, made up of 45 covered, 41 open, and 4 cattle wagons, 4 timber trucks, and 2 horse boxes. During 1901, 6 covered wagons were transferred to the cattle wagon list, making the number 10. Later conversions of covered wagons brought the total number of cattle wagons to 30.

The Metropolitan received a further order in December 1903, this time for two 15 ton bogie wagons, priced at £227 10s each. They were delivered in June 1904. Though ostensibly open wagons with four plank sides, their main

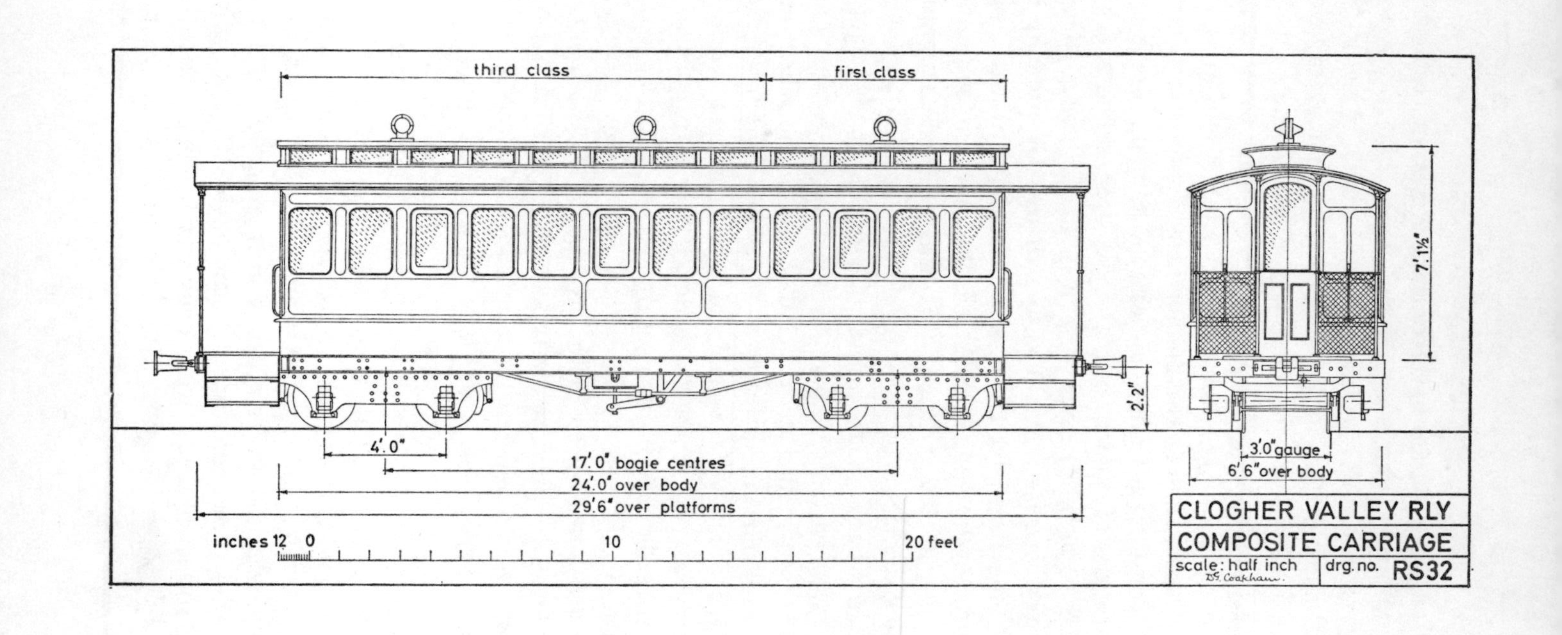
third class
first class
7' 1½"
2' 2"
4' 0"
17' 0" bogie centres
24' 0" over body
29' 6" over platforms
3' 0" gauge
6' 6" over body
inches 12 0
10
20 feet
CLOGHER VALLEY RLY
COMPOSITE CARRIAGE
scale: half inch
drg. no. RS32
D.G. Coakham

claim to fame was the semi-permanent arrangement which was made after their arrival at Aughnacloy, for the safe carriage of Orangemen to the annual demonstrations. To this end, a gable was erected at each end to normal roof height, made of tongued and grooved boards set vertically, and supported by U-section steel girders. When fitted for passenger work, steel bars were run longitudinally on both sides, spaced at 9 inch intervals, and were strutted with light steel verticals. The roof was protected by longitudinal wooden slats, which rested on steel cross-members, and a canvas cover kept the rain off. To complete this pair of astonishing vehicles, two access doors took the place of one of two dropside doors on each side: they were rather like doors on a farm outbuilding, and were hinged and latched. When not in use for conveying passengers, the impedimenta were taken off and were carefully stored in the carriage and wagon workshops until they were again required. These two bogie wagons carried the numbers 96 and 97, apparently No 96 had become vacant through the withdrawal of an older vehicle between 1902 and 1904.

By the time that the line had been over twenty years in operation, increased attention had to be given to the permanent way and, during the second half of 1911, £650 was spent on ten new ballast wagons, the Metropolitan company as usual being the builders.

When Robert Killin came in 1927 to inspect and report, he does not seem to have looked too deeply into the purchase records, and he was content to state that 'there is said to be no definite record about the age of these vehicles, or what was done to them in the way of repairs in the earlier part of their history, though a complete record of the repairs executed in recent years has been kept. In general it may be accepted that this stock is all about 40 years old . . .' He found the brake vans and horse boxes in good order, but thought that in the case of many of the carriages, repairs could 'not be long delayed', for the roofs were particularly weak. By then, however, passenger traffic was falling off, and four years later the situation was eased by the arrival of the railcar.

After 1929, weed killing was done chemically, by spraying the track twice a year with a solution of sodium chlorate. To distribute the weed killer, a spray wagon was built by altering No 62 open wagon. A large cylindrical tank, it had been *Fury*'s boiler, was mounted on the wagon floor, pipes led to spray nozzles, and a pump was driven by an eccentric on one of the axles. By the removal of a bolt on the rocker lever, the pump could be disconnected, and the wagon hauled freely at speed. The spray train was generally worked by a steam locomotive, the usual driver being John Girvan, with Willie Rea firing to him, and Joe Owens on the wagon. Each end of the spray wagon was fitted with a horizontal guard rail.

With the closure of the Castlederg & Victoria Bridge Tramway during 1933, the availability of their wagons was considered as an inexpensive secondhand supplement to the Clogher Valley stock. They had 19 covered wagons, all of Oldbury manufacture and dating for the most part from 1884 though there were two of 1890 and three of 1899 vintage. Fourteen of them had both Westinghouse and hand brakes, five had only hand brakes. McClure recommended to the Committee that ten should be bought at £10 apiece. Eventually the entire 19 were purchased, and transported to Aughnacloy. To run with CV stock they would have needed both replacement of the brake equipment and adjustment of the buffer heights. This was never done, and the rake of wagons lay unused at the side of the yard for eight years, retaining their original lettering and never being numbered into or listed with the Clogher Valley's stock.

Originally the roofs of the covered wagons were of canvas. In March 1894 it was decided to cover three of them with corrugated iron as an experiment. This was successful, and the treatment was extended to all covered wagons 'as the tarpaulin covers became useless'.

There was always a good deal of butter traffic from the creameries at Augher and Fivemiletown. Butter was loaded at first into covered wagons which, it will be recalled, were rather indiscriminately used for cattle on Fair Days. Following complaints, the company agreed in October 1901 to a request from the Department of Agriculture not to carry butter in wagons that were used for the conveyance of livestock. They followed this up by making inquiries about what butter wagons would cost, and then built two in the Aughnacloy workshops, from covered wagons Nos 36 and 37. Apart from cleanliness, insulation was needed to protect the cargo from the sun's heat. The corrugated iron roof was replaced by a heavy double wooden roof, with two torpedo ventilators. Narrow horizontal ventilating slots were cut at the bottom of the doors, and along the top of the sides. During World War II they were also used to carry a considerable traffic in rabbits.

The only mention of wagon livery noticed in the minute books is dated 12 August 1889, when it was stated that all were to be slate grey, with letters in buff. The grey colour remained constant throughout. Lettering was later white, with either CVR or CV RY., and with the vehicle number exhibited both on the sides and ends.

CHAPTER 10

Diesel Traction

THE RAILCAR

Though the first regular timetable workings by a railcar began in 1932, the germ of the idea was there long before that. John Leebody, the Tyrone county surveyor, took his duties towards the CVR seriously, and in September 1904 he recommended to the directors the adoption of 'steam or petrol motors for short distance runs'. Unfortunately the board minute dismisses the proposal in a very few words: the directors formally asked their general manager Irwin to make inquiries and to report his findings, but nothing more came of the scheme. Leebody's vision was ahead of its time, there had been light steam railcars on various railways in 1904, but the Donegal Railways did not acquire their little petrol engined inspection car until 1907.

Under the stimulus of war, a rather similar suggestion came under discussion at the meeting of the board in November 1915, and the directors turned to Sloan, the then general manager, and asked him to consider the question of 'using motors for passenger traffic and other methods of improving the service and at the same time reducing expenses'. Once again nothing constructive emerged, conservatism prevailed, perhaps because experience of the unsatisfactory performance of the *Blessingbourne* engine was remembered.

The pioneer efforts of the County Donegal Railways in railcar development have been chronicled in some detail in another book. Here it is sufficient to state that the Donegal railcars were the product of the enthusiasm of Henry Forbes, who was ably backed in technical matters by H. E. Wilson and other members of the staff of the Dundalk workshops of the Great Northern Railway. Very appropriately, a place had been found for Henry Forbes on the Clogher Valley Committee of Management from the start; he was aware of their problems, they could profit by his experience, and he was eager to collaborate.

On 4 April 1932 Forbes agreed to lend the Clogher Valley one of his railcars on trial. By then the Donegal had eight railcars at work, including two diesel-engined vehicles. Forbes ran his eye over his flock, and No 4 was chosen in May to go visiting. It was a 36hp, four-wheeled, petrol-engined car, weighing 2 tons 12cwt and seating 21. It had been designed around a 30cwt Ford lorry chassis, suitably modified by the Great Northern so that a front pair of wheels formed a pony truck, while a rear pair was driven through a torque shaft and controlled by a screw handbrake. The Strabane coachbuilder, O'Doherty, had built the body. The Great Northern conveyed the railcar to Maguiresbridge, and the Donegal sent over Paddy Lafferty and Robert Parkes from Stranorlar to work it. Forbes watched the proceedings with fatherly pride. The car had fiercer acceleration than anything the Clogher Valley had ever known and, on an unknown, sharply graded and violently curved road, Lafferty is reported to have said he was 'never so glad to have a day finished'. Nevertheless the trial was a success, McClure made a favourable report and the Committee were satisfied that a railcar should be obtained.

Tenders were invited from Harland & Wolff, Edwards Diesel Rail Car Co, Drewry Rail Car Co, and Walker Bros for a vehicle with a nominal capacity of 30 passengers. Walker's design was for a more sophisticated railcar than anything then working on the Donegal: it was articulated, with a four-wheel power bogie forming the driving unit, while passengers were carried in a bus-type body which rode on a fixed rear bogie.

An order was placed on 4 July with Walker Bros (Wigan)

Ltd against a price of £1,950 f.o.r. Belfast. It was probably Forbes's genius for economy that saw to it that the CV supplied an old carriage bogie for the rear bearing unit, and that the CV made the vacuum brake connections.

A saving of around £1,000 per year was estimated by McClure:

1 engine driver	£174
1 fireman	£139
2 guards	£236
1 cleaner	£93
Coal & oil	£496
	£1138
Less fuel for car	£70
	£1068

The Walker railcar went into service in early December 1932. Power came from a Gardner six-cylinder (6LZ) diesel engine, developing 74bhp at 1,300rpm. The drive was taken to the front bogie by a Meadows gearbox. The driving bogie had 1ft 10in wheels, set at 6ft 9¼in centres and had orthodox side-rods. The rear bogie had 2ft 0in wheels, set at 5ft 0in centres. Weight was just under 12 tons, and 28 seats were provided. It hauled one of the brake vans, usually No 5, and had enough reserve of power to take on one of the passenger coaches, or a pair of wagons, if necessary. Heating in winter was to have been from the radiator water, but this was not a success, so that comfort was supplied by the heat from a Valor oil stove. This was set in the aisle between the seats and, since it was not anchored, it hopped along the passageway during the journey.

Once into service, the railcar took on the bulk of passenger train running and was worked hard. It was shedded at Tynan, and left there at 6.15am on the first down train.

In 1933, it was involved in two accidents. It hit a car on the morning of 27 September between Fivemiletown and

Maguiresbridge. The car was struck broadside on, carried 30ft along the track and had its tyres torn and the bodywork much damaged. Neither the driver nor the passenger was severely injured, but it was unfortunate that the driver, Mr Taverner, was a member of the Committee of Management. The police reported driver Kingsbury for negligence. The case went before the Clogher Petty Sessions court on 13 February 1934, and went from there to the Quarter Sessions at Omagh. The verdict was that Kingsbury was not guilty, and he was indemnified by the Committee for any loss. James Kingsbury was also in court following a collision with a lorry at Glencrew crossing.

By January 1935 the railcar had run 90,000 miles and was taken out of service until early March for heavy overhaul. Prior to that, the original trailing bogie had been replaced by one constructed at Aughnacloy, in order to obtain improved running comfort. In January 1939 it was again withdrawn, by which time it had a total mileage of 304,000 to its credit. A report made in June 1941 by the Great Northern indicated that at its current rate of utilisation the railcar would require a heavy repair every 12 to 18 months and that resleeving, piston renewal, and overhaul of the gear box and transmission would be needed 'within the next twelve months'. The railway closed before that.

The railcar was painted brown, with a white roof. 'CLOGHER VALLEY RAILWAY' was lettered between the waist mouldings on each side in shaded, gold, block capitals. Below the title was 'No. 1'.

After running the very last train on the Clogher Valley the railcar was purchased by the County Donegal Railways Joint Committee. On their system, it became No 10 in the railcar series, and served its new masters well until the lines were closed. In Donegal, it ran a total mileage of 348,977. After being used for demolition work, it joined *Phoenix* in the Transport Museum in Belfast.

THE DIESEL TRACTOR

With success attending the railcar workings, no time was lost in acquiring further diesel power, and in May 1933 a diesel rail tractor was supplied by Walker Brothers of Wigan. The vehicle was carried on a four-wheel power bogie, and resembled the front half of the railcar, though behind the cab there was a short open wagon body which was not articulated. The tractor power unit was intended to be interchangeable with that of the railcar. Officially it was 'No. 2 Unit' but it was generally referred to by the men as 'The Unit'. The motor was the same as that in the railcar, the well-tried Gardner 6LZ. Being short in the wheelbase, it could be easily turned, and it was shedded at Maguiresbridge. It worked most of the services west of Fivemiletown.

The Unit was finished in grey livery, with a white roof. The side of the wagon body was plain at first, but later it was lettered 'CLOGHER VALLEY RAILWAY' as on the railcar, with 'No. 2' below it. Many photographs show a cut-away portion at the bottom of the front sheeting of the cab, on the off-side. This was the result of a collision with the Brookeborough crossing gates on a down run one Sunday morning. Joe Murphy was driving, and on the 1 in 33 fall through the townland of Tattendillur the Unit got away. During the racing descent, Joe left his post and got into the wagon, and from that he climbed into the safer confines of a carriage before the impact came. Both gates were destroyed, and the cab sheeting was so badly twisted that it had to be cut out.

Both the Unit and the railcar had vacuum pumps driven off the engine by V-belts. The power units had poor braking on account of their small diameter wheels, and in use the main stopping power came from the carriage bogies and van.

After closure of the line, the Unit went to the CDRJC, but without its engine. The cab was used to replace that on the original railcar, after collision damage sustained in Strabane yard.

THE OLD CLOGHER VALLEY RAILWAY PASSING THROUGH FIVEMILETOWN

Appendices

APPENDIX I

List of Stations and Halts

	Miles	Classification	Crane Power (tons)	Remarks
TYNAN	0	GPLHC	2½	Adjacent to Tynan & Caledon station GNR(I) Waiting room in house
Caledon	1·0	P	—	
Kilsampson	1·6	—	—	
Ramaket	3·0	—	—	Shelter hut
Emyvale Road	4·3	GP	—	Originally Curlagh. Siding, goods store, platform. Closed from 1–8–1922 for goods
Cumber	5·2	—	—	
Glenkeen	6·2	—	—	
Crilly	7·0	—	—	Siding, cattle pen
Glencrew	8·2	—	—	
AUGHNACLOY	9·5	GPLC	2	Station, admin. offices, workshops, 2 platforms
Stormhill	10·5	—	—	1887–? 1889
Tullyvar	11·7	—	—	Hut erected 1909. Stone siding & crusher 1915.
BALLYGAWLEY	13·6	GPLC	3	Goods shed & yard. P. way workshops 1887–1928, 2 platforms
Lisdoart	14·4	—	—	Shelter hut, platform
Annaghilla	15·5	—	—	Shelter hut, platform
Roughan	16·7	—	—	Passing loop, cattle pen, siding

	Miles	Classification	Crane Power (tons)	Remarks
AUGHER	18·4	GPLC	2	Station, siding, platform
Farranetra	19·2	—	—	Originally Summerhill
CLOGHER	20·0	GPLC	—	Station, goods shed, siding, 2 platforms
Carryclogher	20·9	—	—	Platform
Findermore	22·0	—	—	Shelter hut, platform
Ballagh	23·3	—	—	
Kiltermon	25·2	—	—	
Ballyvadden	26·6	—	—	Opened Novr. 1887
FIVEMILETOWN	27·5	GPLC	—	Station, loco. shed, goods shed & yard, pork market siding
Cranbrooke	28·4	—	—	Position uncertain prior to June 1904. Shelter hut
Tattynuckle	28·8	—	—	1887–1897
Corralongford	29·4	—	—	
Killarbran	30·2	—	—	
Claraghy	31·0	—	—	
COLEBROOKE	31·4	GP	—	Station building, platform, siding. Stationmaster in May 1887, thereafter halt
Stonepark	31·6	—	—	
Skeoge	32·8	—	—	Opened Novr. 1887
BROOKEBOROUGH	33·5	GPLC	—	Station, platform, goods siding
Aghavea	34·7	—	—	Shelter hut from 1899
Maguiresbridge Fair Green	36·5	—	—	Originally Maguiresbridge Town
MAGUIRESBRIDGE	37·0	GPLHC	—	Originally Maguiresbridge Station. Adjacent to GNR (I) station, goods yard, loco. shed, sidings

Note: Classification and crane power (where given) is abstracted from *Official Handbook of Railway Stations*, published in 1912 by the Railway Clearing House. Abbreviations used are: G=Goods, P=Passengers and parcels, L=Livestock, H=Horse boxes and prize cattle vans, C=Carriages by passenger train.

Original stations, with permanent brick buildings, are given in capitals. The CVR had no station buildings at Tynan and Maguiresbridge, where accommodation was provided in the Great Northern station buildings.

Halts lacking a shelter hut or platform, possessed merely a name board, situated usually between the line and the hedge.

APPENDIX 2

Officers

Chairmen of the Board of Directors:

1885–98	J. W. Ellison Macartney
1898–1924	Rt Hon Hugh de Fellenberg Montgomery, DL
1924–29	Major-General Hugh M. de F. Montgomery, CB, CMG
1929–44	John Lendrum, JP

Chairmen of the Committee of Management:

1928–29	Major-General Hugh M. de F. Montgomery, CB, CMG
1929–41	Rt Hon Sir Basil S. Brooke, Bart, MP

General Managers:

1884–94	David James Stewart
1894–1907	William Irwin
1907–28	Horace S. Sloan (Adviser 1928–38)
1928–40	David N. McClure

Secretaries to the Board of Directors:

1884–94	David James Stewart
1894–1928	H. S. Sloan
1928–44	P. M. Soraghan

Secretaries to the Committee of Management:

1928–38	H. S. Sloan
1938	G. Sloan
1938–41	P. M. Soraghan

Accountants:

1886–1907	H. S. Sloan
1907–44	P. M. Soraghan

Civil Engineers:

1883–92	Messrs John G. Barton and James Barton

1892–1913 James Barton
1913–28 J. J. S. Barnhill (Consultant 1928–29)

Mechanical Engineers:
1887–89 R. H. Weatherburn
1889–1922 Gustav F. Akerlind
1922–1940 D. N. McClure

APPENDIX 3

Locomotives and Diesel Units

Steam Locomotives:

No	Builder	Builder's No/Date	Name	Type	With-drawn	Remarks
1	Sharp, Stewart	3369/1887	Caledon	0-4-2T	1934	
2	do.	3370/1887	Errigal	do.	1942	
3	do.	3371/1887	Blackwater	do.	1942	
4	do.	3372/1887	Fury	do.	1929	
5	do.	3373/1887	Colebrooke	do.	1936	
6	do.	3374/1887	Erne	do.	1942	
7	Hudswell, Clarke	914/1910	Blessingbourne	0-4-4T	1926	Sold 1934
4	do.	698/1904	—	2-6-2T	1942	ex C & VBT as 2-6-0T
(8)	Atkinson, Walker	114/1928	—	0-4-0T	1928	Sold to CDRJC in 1934

Diesel Units:

(built by Walker Bros (Wigan) Ltd, Pagefield Iron Works, Wigan)

No	Built	Type	Withdrawn	Remarks
1	1932	0-Bo-2 28 seat railcar	1942	Sold to CDRJC, now in Transport Museum.
2	1933	0-Bo-0 rail tractor, wagon body	1942	Sold, less engine, to CDRJC

Relevant dimensions are contained in Chapter 8

APPENDIX 4

Rolling Stock

Coaching Vehicles:

Brake Vans (6 tons)	Nos 1–6	Total 6	No 6 withdrawn c.1900
1st class carriages	Nos 7–9	Total 3	
1st/3rd compo. carriages	Nos 10–11	Total 2	
3rd class carriages	Nos 12–19	Total 8	
Horse Boxes	Nos 20 & 21	Total 2	

Merchandise, Mineral, and Service Vehicles:

Covered Wagons, 13ft 8in x 6ft 8in, 5 tons: Nos 6, 9, 14, 21, 23, 24, 26, 28, 33, 38, 39, 40, 75, 77, 78, 80, 81, 83 *Total 18.*

Cattle Wagons, 14ft 0in x 6ft 8in, 5 tons: Nos 1–5, 7, 8, 10–13, 15–20, 22, 25, 27, 29, 30–32, 34, 35, 76, 79, 82, 84 *Total 30.*
(All these wagons, with the exception of Nos 5, 10, 16, 25, 32, and 34, could be used for goods traffic by the closing of the shutter attached to cross rail over ventilator bars. These six wagons were 8in higher, and were used for carrying horses when necessary)

Butter Wagons, 13ft 8in x 6ft 8in, 5 tons: Nos 36 and 37 *Total 2.*

Open Wagons, 13ft 6in x 6ft 6in, 5 tons: Nos 41, 42, 45, 47–55, 57–71, 73, 74, 85–95 *Total 40.*
(No 56 scrap) (No 62 converted to spray wagon)

Timber trucks, 13ft 0in x 6ft 8in, 6 tons: Nos 43, 44, 106, 107 *Total 4.*
(Nos 44 and 106 have floors in bad order)

Ballast Wagons, 13ft 6in x 6ft 0in, 6 tons: Nos 98–105 *Total 8.*

Bogie open wagons, 28ft 6in x 6ft 8in, 15 tons: Nos 96, 97 *Total 2.*

APPENDIX 5

Railway Inspecting Officer's Report

Railway Department,
Board of Trade,
1, Whitehall,
London, S.W.
13th April, 1887.

Sir,

I have the honour to report, for the information of the Board of Trade, that, in compliance with the instructions contained in your minute of the 29th ultimo, I have inspected the Clogher Valley Tramway. The inspection was attended by the County Surveyors of Armagh Tyrone and Fermanagh through which counties only the tramway runs.

This tramway which was authorised by the Lord Lieutenant's Order of 1884, is the second which has been constructed and completed under the Tramways etc. (Ireland) Act of 1883. It is a single line on the 3 feet gauge, extending from Caledon and Tynan Station on the Portadown and Clones Branch of the Great Northern Railway of Ireland to McGuires Bridge Station on the Dundalk and Enniskillen Branch of the same railway, a total length of 37 miles 3·1 chains, of which about half is on private land and about half on the side (and for a short distance in the village of Five Mile Town, in the centre) of the road.

The steepest gradient whether on private land or on roads has an inclination of 1 in 30, of which gradient and of others between 1 and 30 and 1 in 31 there are in all about 3½ miles, the sharpest curve (in the town of Caledon) has a radius of 100 feet (1½ chains) on private land the sharpest curve has a radius of about 4 chains.

The permanent way consists of flat bottomed steel rails, 27 feet long, weighing 45 lbs. to the yard, secured at the joints by

Ibbotson's patent sheaths and oakside fish plates, the sleepers are rectangular, 6 feet long by 8 inches by 4 inches, 11 to each rail length, those at the joints being at 22 inches central intervals, the rails are secured to the sleepers by dog spikes and clips, the ballast is of stone pitching and gravel, about 1 foot deep below the under surface of the sleepers.

The works on the line are as follows:– one overbridge in rubble masonry of 12 feet span; nine stream and river bridges all built with stone abutments (and in four cases piers) 8 of these (widest span 36 feet) have stone or brick arch tops and one (span 30 feet) has a top composed of wrought iron main girders and corrugated steel crop girders.

Sixty four large masonry culverts.

These works (which are some of them the widening of existing bridges or culverts) appear to have been substantially constructed and to be standing well, with the exception of the pier of the river bridge at 30 miles 62 chains, which shows signs of settlement and should be carefully watched; the girder bridge has sufficient theoretical and practical strength.

There are no tunnels.

There are 19 Level crossings of public roads provided with lodges (where not at stations) and with proper gates.

In cases where the tramway leaves the main road and enters private land (without in doing so crossing the main road) instead of gates, gridirons with a ditch below them, such as are largely used in America and India, have been adopted. These are stated to be efficacious in preventing cattle, etc., from crossing them, but they must be regarded only in the light of an experiment subject to removal if found unsatisfactory and to being replaced by gates and lodges.

The fencing consists of post and wire or post wire and mound. Stations have been provided at Tynan, Aughnacloy, Ballygawley, Augher, Clogher, Five Mile Town, Colebrooke, Brookeborough and Maguires Bridge.

At Tynan and Maguires Bridge the existing station buildings of the Great Northern Railway will be available for passengers on the new line. At the other stations, suitable buildings and accommodation have been provided, the platforms being from 100 to 140 feet long, and the passenger carriages being of the tramway type, 9 inches above rail level.

In addition to these stations, small platforms, 100 feet long and 9 inches high, have been provided at nine other places (chiefly where the tramway is on the side of the road).

The signal arrangements have been made as inexpensive as possible consistent with reasonable attention to safety in consideration of the comparatively low speed at which the line is to be worked and the whole of the rolling stock, engines, carriages, vans and waggons being provided with continuous automatic brakes.

At the principal stations, the facing points are interlocked with home signals and also in some cases, where the sight of the home signals is not good, with distant signals. In other cases the facing points are locked with a key on the train staff applying to the action of the line on which the facing points occur. In two cases, viz in the town of Caledon and the village of Five Mile Town, the tramway has been placed near the centre or in the centre of the street. It was intended originally to provide a guard rail inside each tramway rail where the line was so situated, but in consequence of the width (between the tramway and guard rails) necessary for the flanges of the wheels, which width could not be made less than 1¾ inches, it was considered that the vehicular traffic would be less inconvenienced by the absence of the guard rail than with it, and with the consent of the County Surveyor, the guard rails have not been fixed, great attention will consequently be required in keeping the surface of the macadam as level as possible with that of the top of the rails both inside and outside the tramway.

The following requirements came under my notice:–

1. At 0 m. 50 chains the pitching at the side of the line and the guard rails at the crossing of the road should be extended.
2. At 8 m. 30 chains the disc and lamp of the gate should be placed on the heel post instead of the centre of the gate.
3. At 8 m. 49 chains the fencing at a culvert should be improved.
4. At Aughnacloy station, the up platform requires completion and the up home signal should be shifted to the other side of the line to improve the sight of it.
5. At 12 m. 17 chains a signal is required for the level crossing gates.

6. At 14 m. 32 chains a signal is required for the level crossing gates.
7. At Clogher station the safety points at the Tynan end should be normally open for the siding.
8. At 19 miles 71 chains the level crossing gates should be provided with a high raised disc and lamp.
9. At 35 m. 23 chains, and 36 m. 6 chains, the fencing requires improvement.
10. In several cases the level crossing gates should be prevented from opening outwards; in others the discs and lamps should be slewed so as to be properly seen from a distance.
11. Some of the occupation crossing gates should be prevented from opening inwards.
12. At 31 m. 3 chains, the lodge at the level crossing gates has not been built, and, meantime, a hut must be provided for the gate keeper.
13. Boarded crossings are required at several of the stations.
14. Mile posts and ½ mile posts should be provided.

The rolling stock consists of 6 wheeled engines (made by Sharp, Stewart and Co.) provided with condensing arrangements and speed indicators, arranged to be worked only from the firebox end so as to give the driver the best possible view of the road, of carriages (on bogies) of the tramway type, of open and covered waggons; and of brake vans.

The automatic vacuum continuous brake is supplied to the whole of the rolling stock.

The moving parts of the Engines are properly screened from view, except as regards the pistons, &c. connected with Joys valve gear; these should also be screened.

A kind of fender has been provided in front of the engines to throw obstacles aside. The engines have been supplied with a very powerful head light. This will be very useful for enabling impediments to be seen at a long distance but it may also be found to frighten horses in which case it would be desirable to furnish the driver with the means of temporarily screening it. The opening windows of all the passenger carriages should be provided with bars.

It is intended that the line shall be worked with the train staff and ticket, the telephone being employed (instead of the block telegraph) for preserving proper intervals between trains following each other. The telephone however has not yet been put up, so that the undertaking as to working must for the present confine the working to the train staff without tickets.

The following special rates as to stops and reduction of speed should be observed:–

Absolute Stops.

"Down" means from Tynan; "Up" from McGuires Bridge.

1. Up and down before crossing the road at 0 m. 33 chains–
2. Up „ „ „ „ „ 0 m. 50 chains–
3. Up and down „ „ the High Street in Caledon
4. Up „ „ the road at 1 m. 33 chains–
5. Down „ „ „ „ „ 1 m. 60 chains–
6. Down „ „ „ „ „ 3 m. 0 chain–
7. Up and down „ „ „ „ „ 4 m. 40 chains–
8. Up and down „ „ „ „ „ 7 m. 0 chain–
9. Down „ „ „ „ „ 8 m. 30 chains–
10. Down „ „ „ „ „ 9 m. 42 chains–
11. Down „ „ „ „ „ 11 m. 65 chains–
12. Down „ „ „ „ „ 12 m. 65 chains–
13. Up „ „ „ „ „ 13 m. 55 chains–
14. Up and down „ „ „ „ „ 18 m. 28 chains–
15. Up and down „ „ „ „ „ 32 m. 7 chains–
16. Up and down „ „ „ „ „ 33 m. 45 chains–
17. Up „ „ „ „ „ 36 m. 5 chains–

Speed not to exceed 4 miles an hour.

1. Up and down in crossing the road at 0 m. 50 chains–
2. Up and down „ „ the High Street in Caledon.
3. Up in crossing the road at 1 m. 33 chains–
4. Down „ „ „ „ 1 m. 60 chains–
5. Up in „ „ „ „ 11 m. 40 chains–
6. Up and down „ „ „ 21 m. 23 chains–
7. Up and down „ „ „ 25 m. 20 chains–
8. Up and down in crossing from side to centre of road at both ends of Five Mile Town.
9. Up and down in crossing the road at 29 m. 50 chains–
10. Up and down „ „ „ „ „ 31 m. 45 chains–
11. Up and down „ „ „ „ „ 33 m. 16 chains–
12. Up and down „ „ „ „ „ 33 m. 45 chains–
13. Up „ „ „ „ „ 36 m. 5 chains–

Speed not to exceed 6 miles an hour

1. Down in approaching gate at 12 m. 65 chains–
2. Down on the curve at 13 m. 20 chains–

Speed not to exceed 10 miles an hour.

1. Up and down when running parallel for about 30 m. 7 chains– with the unfenced bog road at 16 miles until this road has been fenced.
2. Up and down, over the bog at 30 m. 70 chains until the bog has become consolidated.
3. In descending all gradients of 1 in 30 and of 1 in 31.

There are several questions connected with the sufficiency of the fences on the side of the road opposite to the Tramway where the latter runs along one side of the road, also with the available width of the road and with the slopes of the sides of the road, next the water tables—to be arranged between the County Surveyors and the Promoters. As by section 30 of the Clogher Valley Tramway Order the County Surveyors are provided with full powers to deal with these questions, I do not think it will be necessary or desirable for me to enter into them.

Subject then to the fulfilment of the requirements before enumerated, and which are to be at once complied with, to the rules as to stops and restricted speed, and to the receipt of a satisfactory undertaking as to working I see no objection to the Board of Trade certifying that the Clogher Valley Tramway is fit for passenger traffic so far as the safety of the public using the tramway is concerned.

I have, etc.,

(Sgd.) C. S. HUTCHINSON,

Major-General, R.E.

APPENDIX 6

Notes on Tickets

by C. R. Gordon Stuart*

When this system was opened in 1887, the tickets were headed Clogher Valley Tramway and later, at about the turn of the century, Clogher Valley Railway. The CVR issued only first- and third-class tickets on its own line, but also issued first-, second-, and third-class through tickets to destinations on the GNR, the seconds presumably being valid as first-class on the CVR, although this was not stated on the tickets. First-class Clogher Valley issues were always white for *singles* and yellow and white for *returns*, excepting for the first-class *privilege* tickets which were green and white. *Excursions* were usually denoted by wavy black lines overprinted on the ticket, or later with an overprinted number, this usually being the validity; *weekend* tickets had usually a white circle on the inward half, and sometimes on the outward half as well. Second-class through issues to the GNR were blue for *singles* and red and blue for *returns*, though some later ones were pink with yellow numeral overprints in the case of *excursions*.

The colour schemes for third-class local *singles*, used originally is quite beyond description here, as at least 23 different arrangements were used; often one finds the same scheme used for two different stations. Early CVR third-class tickets are a galaxy of reds, blues, whites, and yellows, with crosses, stripes, and bands of all descriptions. Through tickets, however, always kept to a more sombre shade and were just plain light buff, a colouring that was eventually adopted for all third-class *singles* somewhere

* This Appendix is reproduced, with minor alterations, from the late H. Fayle's book *The Narrow Gauge Railways of Ireland*, to which it formed an Appendix. The author is indebted to Mr C. R. Gordon Stuart for permission to make use of it.

around 1918. *Returns* were originally green and buff with the usual system of many wavy lines overprinted for *excursions*, etc, but latterly they changed to green only for third-class *full rate returns*, with *excursions* taking all kinds of tints with overprints as well. In addition, towards the final days of the system, it used bus type tickets of many hues, which had the fares overprinted in red skeleton lettering and also marks to show if they were *singles*, *returns*, or *market* tickets. These bus type tickets had no class shown on them, being issued for third-class only; they were issued by the guards on the diesel cars.

APPENDIX 7

List of Workshops and Locomotive Department Staff, June 1941

LOCOMOTIVE REPAIRS DEPT STAFF

		Age	Service (years)	Wages/ week
Joseph R. Robinson	Chargehand fitter	41	23	77/3
Patrick McFadden	do. do., diesel engines, pumping, plants etc.	44	28	77/3
Henry Leaney	Turner & fitter	33	6	65/–
Robert Barrett	Fitter	32	5	65/–
Walter Wright	do.	34	6	65/–
William Rea	Stationary engineman, relief fireman & gas plant attdt.	63	38	48/11
Joseph McAdam	Labourer & coalman	62	42	48/11

CARRIAGE AND WAGON DEPT STAFF

		Age	Service (years)	Wages/ week
R. J. Gillespie	Carpenter	66	29	66/10
James Friel	Carriage & Wagon fitter	61	42	66/10
Joseph McAree	Boy labourer	24	5	30/–
John McKeown	Labourer & gatekeeper	72	26	35/9 + 2/–

LOCOMOTIVE RUNNING DEPARTMENT STAFF

		Age	Service (years)	Wages/ week
John Maguire	Engine driver	56	38	74/11
John Girvan	Fireman passed for driving	59	41	60/11
William Sloan	Fireman	60	2	56/6
Thomas Smith	Cleaner	69	44	37/10
William Brown	Coalman	42	18	38/11

LOCOMOTIVE RUNNING DEPARTMENT STAFF

Joseph Irwin	Rail coach driver	49	28	60/11
Hugh Murphy	do. do. do.	30	14	60/11
James Kingsbury	do. do. do.	48	21	60/11
Thomas Girvan	do. do. do.	48	28	60/11

Note: The above is extracted from a Great Northern Railway report dated 9 June 1941. The following comments are contained in the report:

'With regard to the maintenance staff in both the locomotive, carriage and wagon departments. . . . . . . the different trades required for maintenance work are not represented, no boilermakers, blacksmiths, plumbers or painters being employed, and the work which would normally be done by these trades is carried out by fitters, carpenters or labourers. Further, the wages paid to tradesmen are below those paid to the corresponding grades in our Belfast shops.

The Trades Unions concerned have . . . called attention to this matter, but owing to the position of the railway no action has been taken; but if the Great Northern Railway take over this concern this matter will have to be kept in view, as if we were compelled to take on tradesmen in these grades, or to increase any of the present rates, it would . . . increase the wages bill considerably.'

Q

APPENDIX 8

Some Relevant Verses

'A NEW SONG ON THE CLOGHER VALLEY LINE'

(This was published by an unknown author in 1887, and sold as a broadsheet at the price of one penny; the verses are reproduced verbatim from the original.)

In the 2d of May we must now say in this present year
We opened up the new tramway from what we read and hear,
This lovely rail from hill and dale it cut a glorious shine
From Tynan to Maguire's Bridge on the Clogher Valley Line.

It sends the farmers of Fermanagh and all South Tyrone
To Omagh now or Fintona they have no cause to roam,
From Fivemiletown to Aughnacloy on every market day
They can bring their pork also their flax all by the new tramway.

The old wife in the corner has no cause to complain
She can bring her butter and her eggs all by the morning train,
Unto her house and family she can return in time
For a half-fare we must declare on the Clogher Valley Line.

Through Fermanagh and Tyrone this tramway it does run
We read and find along the line all things are nicely done,
We can lift passengers on the road, and also in the town
By this new tramway from day to day that runs both up and down.

From Maguire's Bridge the tram dost start I wish to explain
There is a grand view as she runs through part of Colebrook Demesne;
You get a sight of Blessingburn and the See of Clogher too,
Round Ballygawley and Carrongal there is a splendid view.

We cannot forget our Irish members that passed this Tramway Bill,
Mr. Montgomery sanctioned it we are sure with free good will,
With Mr. Graham a man of fame and others did combine
To open up our country with the Clogher Valley Line.

Our engines and our carriages they look both grand and neat,
With the buildings all along the line they are finished off complete,
This is the key of Ulster you must all bear in mind,
From Fivemiletown to Caledon on the Clogher Valley Line.

This new tramway three times a day she runs both up and down,
The most mistake I'm sure they make it is at Fivemiletown,
She clears the streets of all she meets it is the whole vexation
Going up and down through the town to and from the station.

'TOMMY THE GUARD'

(A tribute to the veteran Tommy Caruth, written by a Ballygawley resident during 1940)

Its Clogher Fair
  and we're running late
And Tommy the Guard's
  in a terrible state.
For its bad enough
  he's heard to say
To miss the Mail
  on an ordin'ry day.

For people, says he
  if they're left behind
Can look after themselves
  without they're blind
But bastes, says he
  as he peers ahead,
If they're left behind
  has got to be fed
And the Manager'll curse
  to bate the ban'
At fattening bastes
  for a dealin' man.

The carriages dance
  in the August heat
And Tommy sits down
  in the corner seat
His ticket punch
  slides to the floor
And Tommy the guard
  begins to snore.
For its hard enough
  at the best of times
To manage a train
  at seventy nine.

'THE OUL' CLOGHER VALLEY'

(written c.1933 by Arthur Ritchie and W. Trimble, and sung by them in their concert party when it visited south Tyrone).

Reproduced from 'The Impartial Reporter' of 16–2–1963.

Come all ye loyal people and listen to our song,
It's only forty verses and we'll not delay you long,
It's all about the great express that flies along ram-stam,
That noble hearted monster, the Clogher Valley Tram.

It starts out in the morning from the town of Aughnacloy,
And if you happen to be late, just do a sprint me boy,
And if you're good at running, then it's mighty sure I am
It won't be long before you're safe inside the Clogher Valley Tram.

She puffs and snores each day, through the streets of Fivemiletown,
And if you sit between the rails, she wouldn't run you down,
And if you're thirsty for a drink, outside the hotel he'll stand,
It's most obliging the manager is, of the Clogher Valley Tram.

In Clabby there is no picture house, nor yet in Fivemiletown,
But they have an entertainment which is worth half a crown,
I'll tell you what it is, if you'll only all keep calm,
It's Frank McLoughlin shunting on the Clogher Valley Tram.

Some ratepayers say she's costly, and others think she's cheap,
And Willie Graham he says it makes the blood within him leap,
But our express we cannot lose, it's safer than a pram,
It goes ten miles in twenty hours, our Clogher Valley Tram.

It runs along quite joyously, so very bright and gay,
And then it's all hands out, my boys, to shove her up the brae,
And then down hill full speed she goes, and gambols like a lamb,
Sure the divil himself could not houl' back the Clogher Valley Tram.

Bibliography

A. ORIGINAL SOURCES: MANUSCRIPT AND PRINTED MATERIAL

Directors Minute Books CVT & CVR Co 6 vols (PRONI)
Shareholders Minute Book CVT & CVR Co (PRONI)
Half-yearly and annual Reports of CVT & CVR Co (PRONI)
Plans & Sections of the CVT, 1883–4, James and John G. Barton (PRONI)
CVT Contract Drawing No 1 Land Plans, 1885 (PRONI)
CVT Reference Book, 1883–4 (PRONI)
Volume of Arbitrator's Awards & Plans, 1884 (PRONI)
Board of Trade Railway Dept. Inspecting Officer's Report on Clogher Valley Tramway (PRO)
Board of Trade Annual Returns of Railway Companies
Report of Vice-Regal Commission on Irish Railways (1906–10)
Minutes of Evidence & Report &c Railway Commission in Northern Ireland (1922)
Working and public timetables of CVT and CVR
Scheme for the extension of the CVR from Tynan to Newry &c (1897)
Scheme for the extension of the CVR from Maguiresbridge &c (1900)

B. SECONDARY WORKS

—— (1803) *Post Chaise Companion or Traveller's Directory through Ireland*. Dublin.
—— (1815) *The Traveller's New Guide through Ireland*. Dublin.

Lewis, S. (1837) *A Topographical Dictionary of Ireland*. 2 vols. London.

Lewis, W. (1881) Narrow gauge railways, Ireland. *Trans. Inst. Civil Eng. Ireland*, **13**, 122.

Hurst, E. (1900) The Clogher Valley Light Railway. *Rly. Mag.*, **7**, 315.

—— (1904) *General Topographical Index. Census of Ireland 1901*. HMSO.

Livesey, R. M. (1912) Rolling stock on the principal Irish narrow gauge railways. *Proc. Inst. Mech. Eng.*, 599.

Patterson, M. S. (1917) *The Plantation in Counties Tyrone and Londonderry*. Omagh (reprinted from the *Mid-Ulster Mail*)

Marshall, J. J. (1920) *Annals of Aughnacloy & the Parish of Carnteel*. 1st edition. Dungannon (2nd edition, 1925)

—— (1927) CVR: Report of the Committee of Investigation. (HMSO)

Marshall, J. J. (1932) *History of the Parish of Tynan*. Dungannon.

—— (1933) Oil-engined rail car on the CVR. *Loco. Mag.*, **39**, 8.

—— (1934) *Transport Conditions in Northern Ireland*. (Pole Report) Cmd. 160. HMSO.

—— (1936) Rebuilt tank locomotive, CVR. *Loco. Mag.*, **42**, 242.

Coghlan, C. J. (1936) The Clogher Valley Railway. *Stephenson Loco. Soc. Journ.*, **12**, 228.

Kidner, R. W. (1937) *The three-foot Gauge Railways of Northern Ireland*.

—— (1937) The CVR. *Rly. Mag.*, **80**, 351 & 374.

—— (1938) *Public Transport in Northern Ireland*. (McLintock Report) Cmd. 198. HMSO.

'Voyageur' (1941) The Clogher Valley Railway. *Rly Mag.*, **87**, 193.

—— (1942) (Reference to auction) *Rly. Mag.*, **88**, 190.

Fayle, H. (1945) *The narrow gauge railways of Ireland*.

Hutchinson, W. R. (1951) *Tyrone Precinct*. Dundalk.

McNeill, D. B. (1956) The Clogher Valley Railway. *Journ. Irish Rly. Record Soc.*, **4**, 93.

McNeill, D. B. (1956) *Ulster Tramways and Light Railways*, Transport Handbook No 1. Ulster Museum & Art Gallery.

Gillespie, G. (1959) Full Circle, or All Stations and Halts to Belmullet. *Presb. Herald*, No 197, 142.

Livingstone, P. (1969) *The Fermanagh Story*. Monaghan.

McCutcheon, A. (1969) *Railway History in Pictures, Ireland*. vol 1. Newton Abbot.

McCool, B. (1971) Right Royal Welcome at Aughnacloy Station. *Tyrone Constitution* 30.4.71. Omagh.

Note: PRO and PRONI are respectively Public Record Office and Public Record Office, Northern Ireland.

Acknowledgements

The writing of this book has given me much pleasure, not only on account of family associations with the Clogher Valley district, but because of the encouragement and practical help which many people gave me.

It is now over 30 years since the last tram went through the Valley and, though the bones of the story were already known through the work of Dr D. B. McNeill and others, they were brought to life by the personal recollections of a number of ex-Clogher Valley men, Mr Joseph R. Robinson, Mr David Johnston, and the late Mr Patrick McFadden. Their intimate knowledge of the why and when of events has been invaluable.

Living within sight and sound of the line, recording it with notebook and camera, and knowing more of how it operated than the majority of the public, Dr George Gillespie of Ballygawley has inevitably been the target for numberless inquiries. It is difficult to make adequate acknowledgement of his hospitality and help.

My gratitude is due to Col Sir Basil McFarland, Bart for permission to quote from letters exchanged between his father and Basil McCrea during the construction of the tramway.

Consultation of documents was helped by the staffs of the Public Record Offices in Belfast and in London, the House of Lords Record Office, and the County Museum in Armagh.

The surveys of station layouts by Mr D. G. Coakham of

Bangor have formed the basis for the sketches in the book, and his detailed knowledge of rolling stock has been of great assistance. Similar expert guidance by Mr R. N. Clements may be found in the chapter on the steam locomotives. The annual reports of the county surveyors were made available by Messrs Robert Park and J. McCleery, respectively Secretary and Deputy County Surveyor to the Tyrone County Council, and by Mr W. N. Brady, County Engineer for Fermanagh.

Space allows merely the listing of the names of others who have assisted in a variety of ways: W. Adams (Aylesbury), Viscount Brookeborough, S. J. Carse (Dublin), A. G. Ellis (Standish), J. D. Fitzgerald (Armagh), B. G. L. Glasgow (Omagh), H. E. Harper (Chorley), J. Higgins (Ballygawley), R. G. Jarvis (Derby), V. G. Jaycock (London), J. I. D. Johnston (Clogher), I. W. Leebody (Dungannon), D. B. McNeill (Southampton), P. Mallon (Dundalk), G. R. Mahon (Dublin), Capt. Peter Montgomery (Blessingbourne, Fivemiletown), Walter Montgomery (Fivemiletown), Miss L. Murphy (Tynan), K. A. Murray (Dun Laoghaire), H. E. Wilson (ex-GNR Dundalk) and H. E. Wilson (Newtownards).

Index